GET A
FINANCIAL
GRIP

A simple plan for financial freedom

This book is written to provide competent and reliable information on the subject matter covered. However, I do not operate as a licensed financial advisor.

This book is written on the understanding that the author disclaims any liability from the use or application of the contents of this book. The reader should always consult a financial advisor before making any investment decisions.

Big Sky Publishing Pty Ltd
PO Box 303, Newport, NSW 2106, Australia
Phone: 1300 364 611
Fax: (61 2) 9918 2396
Email: info@bigskypublishing.com.au
Web: www.bigskypublishing.com.au

Cover design and typesetting: Think Productions

National Library of Australia Cataloguing-in-Publication entry (pbk)
Author: Wargent, Peter.
Title: Get a financial grip : a simple plan for financial freedom / by Pete Wargent.
ISBN: 978-1-921941-80-1 (pbk.)
Subjects: Finance, Personal--Australia.
        Saving and investment--Australia.
Dewey Number: 332.02401

National Library of Australia Cataloguing-in-Publication entry (ebook)
Author: Wargent, Peter.
Title: Get a financial grip : a simple plan for financial freedom / by Pete Wargent.
ISBN: 978-1-921941-84-9 (ebook.)
Subjects: Finance, Personal--Australia.
        Saving and investment--Australia.
Dewey Number: 332.02401

GET A
FINANCIAL
GRIP

A simple plan for financial freedom

www.bigskypublishing.com.au

Pete Wargent

To my beautiful wife, Heather, without whom I would have achieved very little.

To my friends who have battled tumour or cancer: Amanda, Doug, David ('Arkle'), Frank and Tracey. Your courage is truly inspirational.

To Mum and Dad, for giving me the value of an education
(in spite of what the school reports might have said).

And, to my mate Ridley, for patiently listening to seven years
of me complaining about my job. I owe you one, buddy.

10% of the author's proceeds will be donated to The McGrath Foundation
for breast cancer research and support.

CONTENTS

Pete Wargent offers a simple plan for financial independence at any age.

Chris Gray, Property Expert, Channel Ten's 'The Renovators', TV presenter
of Sky News Business Channel's 'Your Property Empire', author of
Go for Your Life and *The Effortless Empire*.

*I love Wargent's book because he has actually done what he has so brilliantly
written about. It is a must read for anyone wanting to take control of their
financial situation and create wealth for themselves. I love the way he so
simply communicates what can be complex issues. The book has left me
feeling empowered and excited about my own wealth.*

Andrew Jobling, author of best-sellers *Dance Until it Rains*,
Simply Strength and *Eat Chocolate, Drink Alcohol and Be Lean & Healthy*,
Keynote Motivational Speaker, ex-AFL player with St. Kilda.

*This book shows how everyone, irrespective of background or income, can
take control of their finances and live the life they choose.*

Kerrie McCallum, Editor, *InStyle* Magazine

1
THE GAME OF
MONEY

1

Global financial crisis

We are living through a period of great volatility. The world's economies are fragile, and this makes it more important than ever that you have a financial plan to protect yourself. Despite the gloom that seems to be perpetually portrayed in the financial press, the truth is that recessionary economic times offer outstanding opportunities to those who are prepared. Wealth has not simply been lost in the global financial crisis, it has been *transferred*, from the financially uneducated to the sophisticated.

We have had global recessions before, and you can be certain that we will have them again, because economies move in cycles. The facts and the specifics may change, but the patterns are similar. The losers in financial crises will continue to be the same: those who try to save their cash (inflation will quickly eat away at the value of savings), the inflexible, people with extravagant spending habits, those approaching retirement with much of their wealth in a managed accumulation fund and, particularly, many of those with a total dependence on a job for income. Having all your eggs in one basket – a job – is a potentially dangerous approach to personal finance.

So who will the winners be? The winners will be those who have the financial education to spot opportunities, and those with multiple income streams. Winners will also include people with moderate spending requirements and those who are prepared to be flexible. Winners are generally not dependent on highly taxed salaries to increase their wealth. Stock-market meltdowns offer amazing opportunities to those who are able to time the market. Property investors, too, will take advantage of fear to invest counter-cyclically and will capitalise on the low interest rates that often result from a recession.

It is important to be in tune with the financial markets. By the time you read about a hot stock or a flying property market in the media, it is probably too late. Besides, the press print an awful lot of doom and gloom, as it seems to sell newspapers. If you believed everything you read in the press, you would probably never invest at all.

What is not good enough is to blame the government, your fund manager, or your employer for your financial predicament. You must take responsibility for your own financial health and wellbeing. One of the seven Buddhist factors of the path to enlightenment is *mindfulness*, an awareness of reality and clear understanding.

Just as to avoid becoming obese we must be mindful of our diet, to become wealthy and financially free we must apply mindfulness to our finances. The first step is accepting that your financial health is your own responsibility.

Financial freedom

The aim of this book is to introduce a specific financial plan to take you from wherever you are today to financial freedom in only a few years, depending on the somewhat unpredictable timing of economic cycles and your personal circumstances. If your goal is escaping the rat race of reliance on full-time employment, then the principles I will detail can surely be applied by anybody, provided that you have a strong determination to succeed and a reasonable level of discipline.

There are a large number of financial self-help books on the shelves written by acclaimed and self-proclaimed gurus, so many in fact that for many people it seems impossibly difficult to know where to begin. The solution is to identify what your goals actually are, and then to start with the end in mind.

Many financial tomes are written by 50-somethings and 60-somethings who detail how they have made their millions, and decree that younger folk should be following their way. In my experience, a significant percentage of my generation and younger generations don't want financial freedom as a 50-something or a 60-something. In many cases, they are already disillusioned with long hours, ungrateful employers, high tax rates and expensive cities; they desire to be free from the rat race right now, or at least as soon as is realistically possible. You don't need me to tell you this. You already know, because you have seen the queues for Powerball and Lotto tickets.

In order to achieve financial freedom before the traditional retirement age, you will need to engage a different financial plan to those suggested by financial advisors. Taking ten per cent of your net salary and investing in a swathe of managed funds, a diversified portfolio of shares and fixed interest investments may indeed be a sensible thing to do, but it will certainly fail to propel you to financial freedom quickly. Instead, you will need to employ some leverage of other people's time and other people's money, you will need to apply focus rather than wide diversification and you will need to expose yourself to a controlled level of risk.

This book will introduce you to that plan. It is not a 'get rich quick' fad. Financial texts and seminars that promise you instant wealth are often those that are best avoided. Instead, this is a plan that takes time-tested principles of wealth creation and applies them to the Australia of today. It's a plan I have used myself to make myself a millionaire and to quit full-time work at the age of 33. Not having to work for someone else unless you choose to do so is a wonderful place to be, so let's take a look at how you can get there too – *reasonably* quickly.

The Game of Money

In one of his best-selling books, finance author Robert Kiyosaki introduced his concept of the 'Game of Money'[1]. He drew up a table that looks like this:

Figure 1.1 – The 'Game of Money'

Age	Period
0–25	Warm-Up
25–35	1st Quarter
35–45	2nd Quarter
	Half-Time
45–55	3rd Quarter
55–65	4th Quarter
	Overtime
	Out of Time

Source: Who Took My Money?, Robert T. Kiyosaki.

The concept is simple, yet interesting and thought-provoking. For around the first 25 years of our life, most of us are growing up, completing our education and deciding what we will pursue for our career (the 'warm-up'). Thereafter, Kiyosaki divides our working lives into four quarters. Those who have not built a sufficient pension may be forced to continue working after the age of 65 ('overtime'), and still may not achieve financial independence by the time they are physically incapable of work ('out of time').

After many long years of struggle that including a period of homelessness where he lived with his wife in the back of a borrowed car, Robert Kiyosaki 'retired' in the third quarter of the *Game of Money* at the age of 47. The reason I put the word 'retired' in inverted commas is that I am somewhat sceptical when certain financial gurus use this term. They claim to have retired, but then spam you with emails on a daily basis imploring you to attend their expensive seminars, buy their books, CDs and other products, or use their services in some other way. In effect, they have not retired; they have ceased full-time employment to set up a business. There's certainly nothing wrong with that, but they haven't retired, they have simply shifted their focus away from employment.

I want to demonstrate that not only is it possible to 'win' the *Game of Money* in the *first* quarter, it does not have to be an almighty struggle that involves homelessness, turmoil or undue levels of risk. I propose a simple but specific and effective plan to show you how you can escape the rat race far earlier than you may have believed possible.

Why read this book?

I'm in the first quarter of the *Game of Money*, and I quit my full-time job as a millionaire at the age of 33. If you really want to achieve financial freedom, you can too. You will need to follow some simple rules of wealth creation and ally yourself with discipline and patience. It does not necessarily follow that you will leave your job and do nothing when you are able to do so. We can always earn, run businesses, invest and learn – but we can choose to do so on our own terms. It simply means that you will no longer be chained to a full-time job, and you will have access to the most precious asset of all: time.

I know that there is a need for a book like this from personal experience. My background is in finance, but in retrospect, the day I qualified as a Chartered Accountant, I did not know the first thing about investment. I may have tried to sound as though I was clued up about investment (men often do this), but the truth is that I had no idea. Sure, I knew what a *PE ratio* was, and what *net profit margin* or *market capitalisation* meant, but truthfully, I did not have a clue how to profit from investment or build wealth for the long term. The book I have written is the book that I wish somebody had given to me when I was 21.

So many more people could achieve what they consider to be an impossible goal of escaping reliance on their full-time job early with significant wealth. Once I opened my mind and committed to learning everything I could about wealth creation, it became clear to me that building wealth is far more straightforward than most of us realise. I should point out here that if, at any stage of this book, it sounds as though I have breezed through life towards inevitable wealth and success, that is certainly not the case.

In fact, during my late twenties I experienced alcohol and tranquiliser dependence, both cause and effect of the most diabolical panic attacks and generalised anxiety disorder. I also developed a debilitating agoraphobia and endured messy relationship break-ups, and yet I still managed to quit my full-time job young and wealthy. I am therefore convinced that if I can do it, there are many more people who can do the same. We all surely have obstacles in our path, but we can just as surely remove them if our willpower and belief is strong enough.

Property investor and author Jan Somers noted in one of her classic investment books that by the age of 65, out of 100 people, on average, 24 would be dead, 54 would be receiving a pension, 16 would still be working, 5 would be financially independent – and only *one* would be wealthy[2]. Being a mathematician, Somers also presented some terrifying figures on how long a superannuation retirement lump sum might last, demonstrating how quickly inflation and living expenses can eat away at the value of the rapidly diminishing cash pile.

If you want to escape being reliant on the treadmill of full-time paid employment, this is the book for you. Many people genuinely enjoy their jobs, which is a great thing and a wonderful gift. Mark Twain famously advocated that if you could 'make your vocation your vacation' you would never work a day in your life. Mark Twain said a lot of things, and in this case he was absolutely right. However, loving your job does not mean that you should neglect to strive to achieve financial independence. We never know what is around the corner, and when we may not be able to work anymore. Building a solid financial base is important.

The advance of social networking media has confirmed what many of us already knew intuitively – that many employees are bored out of their minds in the workplace, ticking off the hours until the weekend when they can have two days of respite from the drudgery of the office. The common laments are there on the Internet every day for all to see: 'I'm so bored', 'I hate Mondays', 'Thank God it's the weekend!'

Taking control of your finances is critical. There is a significant and growing pension problem in Australia. It is no secret that the average superannuation balances in this country are woefully inadequate. If you were aged 65 in 2010, on average you could expect to live for another 19 years for men or 22 years for women, and you could potentially live for far longer. The average superannuation balances for men and women aged 60 to 64 in 2010 were $245,000 and $170,000, respectively[3]. Those are some terrifying numbers. The system is failing, and the governments of today and the future are very likely to make significant changes (i.e. raising taxes, increasing compulsory super contributions to 12% and increasing the retirement age) to deal with this ticking time bomb.

As noted, there are numerous wealth- and success-creation books available on the market that range greatly in their quality and content. Many are books written in the USA and are therefore not directly relevant to us in Australia. I'll give you just one of a thousand examples: *Money Secrets of the Rich* by John R. Burley. I thought this was a fine book, and I would heartily recommend it as an introduction to the rules of wealth creation. However, the adaptations for the Australian market are not really adequate. For example, we are advised that if we are investing in the Sydney property market, we should counter the prospect of a negative cash flow simply by buying properties at close to half of their market value. If you have ever bought a property in Sydney, you will know that vendors certainly don't give properties away for half of what they are worth.

Other titles are packed full of concepts and ideas on how to improve your mindset, but do not specifically tackle how financial success can or should be obtained. You may know publications that describe how we need to somehow manifest wealth, and it will flow to us. That's not enough. Chanting in the mirror each morning might wake us up a bit and motivate us slightly, but it isn't going to make us financially free. Consistent and decisive action is what counts.

Yet other texts are unrealistic. I remember reading *The 4-Hour Workweek* by Timothy Ferriss. It was highly entertaining, I chuckled a lot and it introduced some useful ideas on the management of a small business. However, I was left to wonder how many people have really told their bosses that henceforth they are working from home full-time (presumably bidding them an upbeat 'Cheerio, then') and disappeared off to backpack across Peru. I'd hazard a guess that the number is somewhere between none and not many. Even if you could pull this off, it doesn't sound like a terribly ethical plan to me.

> 'I will tackle these issues head-on by detailing a simple, specific and effective plan to enable you to achieve your financial freedom.'

Why escape the rat race early?

Why should you escape the rat race early? Only you can truly answer that question. For me, I enjoyed some things about my paid employment, but I did not find it to be at all fulfilling. I probably enjoyed around 80% of my job, but hated the other 20%. The biggest problem of all was that employment took up nearly all of my time.

Even when I wasn't in the office at weekends, which was far from being every weekend, I was constantly fielding an alarming number of phone calls, emails and text messages. However, my real reason for escaping the rat race was to focus on things that were more important to me such as travel and spending time with family. The motivation will differ for each of us.

Since being freed from the shackles of full-time work, I've worked for a short time as a volunteer on the Cyclone Yasi disaster relief, taken an amazing 12 months to complete the 'Big Lap' of Australia, carried out a four-month investigative contract on behalf of the East Timor Government, and booked myself on a 60-day round-the-world cruise on Cunard's *Queen Elizabeth* (taking in 20 countries). I'm eternally grateful that I have been able to do these things. Travel was one major pull factor for me; spending more time with family over in England was another.

Many people will tell you that they dislike their job, but they would be bored without it. Again, this isn't a reason not to strive for financial independence. Of course, you may always choose to continue as an employee even if you are not reliant on the monthly pay cheque. Even some lottery winners do so (but not nearly as many as claim they would before winning).

I was fortunate in that I realised at a young age that the corporate dream we had been sold was unsatisfactory. I looked at the people who were in the roles and positions I was supposed to be aspiring to and considered whether they looked fulfilled, happy and rich. Most of them didn't look to be where I wanted to be 20, 30 or 40 years down the track.

Some of my friends and male colleagues who went on to become accountancy-firm partners bemoaned that they were actually worse off than they had been before they reached their dream roles. They were expected to buy cripplingly expensive houses in Sydney and cars befitting their positions, their wives wanted to give up work and have numerous children, and the government stripped them of half of their pay packets through taxes before they could even think about paying the mortgage. They talked as if they were caught in some kind of a trap. I guess in many ways they were.

If you want to achieve financial freedom and be young and wealthy, an important step in achieving this is to know exactly why you want to reach these goals and to have a detailed plan for what you will do with your wealth. It is a valuable idea to visualise very specifically where you want to be – if you know where you are headed, then you can take specific steps towards your goal. It is sometimes said that if the *why* is strong enough, then the *how* will take care of itself.

The corporate treadmill

When I was 25, I qualified as a Chartered Accountant, a fact of which I was very proud. I still have the certificate somewhere. Not too long afterwards, I was promoted to become a manager at the 'Big Four' accounting firm Deloitte in England, and I was suddenly earning a far bigger pay cheque, more than double the amount of only two years before. However, this only served to put me on that familiar corporate treadmill.

I was soon paying the highest rate of income tax, and I needed a better car, suit and holiday. You probably know the drill. I once stayed in *The Savoy* hotel in London (ouch) and paid £50 for four cocktails. I can't remember why, partly because it was a long time ago, and partly because the cocktails had absinthe in them. It must have seemed like a cool thing to do at the time, I suppose, a reflection of my new status. Anyway, I certainly wasn't any wealthier for my bigger pay cheque.

When I was working in my career job, I would sit in endless meetings and wonder: What are we here for? Why are we actually on this planet? For what purpose? These are far-reaching, existential questions, and I certainly don't know the answers to them. What I do know is this: we are not here to spend 15 hours a day in appraisal reviews, in monthly profitability conferences, in morale or efficiency meetings (that themselves go on for hours with seemingly no purpose), or to try and impress people because they are one pay grade ahead of us. I would look around me and wonder if I was the only person who felt this way. Perhaps I was. I don't know, I never asked anyone. I just pretended to be as enthusiastic as everyone else seemed to be.

I am not saying there is anything bad about full-time employment (actually, I suppose I am), but we should all remember that nobody on their deathbed laments failing to spend more of their time at work.

The role of tax

In this book, I will examine the role of tax and why it is so difficult to become wealthy as an employee in a country with a tax system as punitive as that of Australia. The top rate of income tax in this country in the 2012 financial year is 45% for income earners over $180,000. 45% is a high tax rate, although some countries have it worse than us. In the United Kingdom, the dreaded 50% tax rate has once again reared its ugly head (even as late as 1974, three decades after World War II brought about ridiculous rates of taxation, the top rate for the Poms was still an eye-watering 83% for earned income – and 98% for unearned income[4]).

The unfortunate truth is that, in Australia, once you have paid your compulsory superannuation contributions, the Medicare levy and a huge chunk of PAYG tax to the government, what is left is an unsatisfactory percentage of the package originally advertised to you by your employer.

Where I worked in Sydney, a new Big Four accountancy firm partner might earn around $225,000 per year, a decent enough salary, to be sure. However, that makes for a higher-rate taxpayer in the 2012 financial year, and the government takes from that a whopping $74,800 in income tax and a further $3,375 in Medicare levy[5] – leaving around $14,000 per month after tax (this calculation excludes any superannuation contributions). More senior partners would earn plenty more than this, more than double this amount in some cases, but the spectre of tax is ever present. In 2012, to earn $20,000 per month after tax as an employee, you would need to command a salary of around $400,000.

Let's compare this with prevailing house prices. In my part of the world (Sydney's Eastern Suburbs) the median house price, a figure which includes a great many poky terraces, is more than $1.2 million[6]. The 'home' suburb that I am referring to (it's no longer my place of residence, though I still own property there) is Bondi Junction, which is by no means one of the most exclusive suburbs in Sydney.

A typical 'freestanding property with four bedrooms and parking' – when I was younger we used to simply call this a 'house' – sells for between $2 million and $2.5 million. Take on a principal-and-interest mortgage of $2 million at an interest rate of 7.5% over 25 years and the repayments will be in the region of $15,000 per month, enough to make your ears bleed. And that is before we even dare mention the stamp duty on acquisition. In other words, the numbers don't really work anymore.

The above example is very specific and relates to Sydney, but residents of other cities will recognise the point I'm making. Unless you have substantial equity, the house prices of our desirable suburbs are not affordable from an after-tax salary unless you are a very high-income earner. Migrants to Australia from countries with weaker currencies than the currently stellar Australian dollar must endure a nasty reality check when searching for a property to live in.

> 'Fortunately, there are better ways to build wealth
> without the taxman destroying your gains.'

Study the wealthiest individuals in the world and you will discover that they have built their wealth in a tax-favoured environment. Warren Buffett has built virtually all of his wealth within his Berkshire Hathaway company, and has deferred capital gains taxes by adopting a buy-and-hold approach to investment. Famously, Berkshire Hathaway has only ever paid one dividend (dividend income to shareholders is effectively taxed twice: once in the company and once on the shareholder's income), with Buffett quipping: 'I must have been in the bathroom at the time[7].'

Investing legend George Soros also paid very little in the way of taxes, though his approach was different, incorporating his famous Quantum Fund in a Netherlands Antilles tax haven[8]. Look at the individuals on the *BRW Rich List* and you will find that they did not find their way onto the list through paid employment.

The great media tycoon and billionaire Kerry Packer said it best on tax when addressing the Senate in 1991:

> 'I pay what I'm required to pay, not a penny more,
> not a penny less. If anybody in this country doesn't minimise
> their tax, they want their heads read because,
> as a government, I can tell you you're not spending it
> that well that we should be donating extra[9].'

Couldn't have put it better myself.

Attaining financial freedom

Attaining financial freedom involves a very simple equation: your passive income – income that flows to you without you having to work for it – needs to exceed your expenditure. It sounds so simple, and yet few people manage to achieve it until they are approaching retirement age or beyond. I will examine the reasons why this is the case and then detail the strategies you can use to achieve the goal.

Simply put, you will need to *pay yourself first*. That is, to take a percentage of your salary every month on the day you are paid to invest in and grow a portfolio of assets that provide you with income and continue to grow in value in perpetuity. I will discuss the appropriate asset classes in detail in the following chapters: those that will provide you with rates of return that create wealth, and those that will allow you to use the power of leverage to achieve your goals.

What is 'rich'?

There is no one agreed-upon definition of what being rich actually is, and in an inflationary environment the figure must increase over time. Most often, the figure noted in the USA is a net worth in excess of $1 million. Indeed, President Barack Obama himself quoted this figure. With the current strength of the Australian dollar, I believe it is safe to assume that a similar figure applies to Australians.

Unfortunately, $1 million in present times just isn't that much. I certainly did not feel like James Packer when my net worth passed $1 million. I believe that, depending on where you live and your lifestyle expectations, in order to escape the rat race young and wealthy, you would need a net worth of around $1.5 million and, very importantly, a substantial portfolio of assets that continues to appreciate whether you are working or not.

Perhaps a better measure, therefore, in terms of what you might need in order to switch your focus away from your full-time job, would be *net realisable assets* from your investments. With a net worth of around $1.5 million, this would allow a buffer for any capital gains tax due and slippage (in my experience many people tend to have an inflated opinion of what their assets may be worth, property in particular) and allow realisation of well over $1 million in cash.

Such a figure would allow for a significant investment in a portfolio of income stocks. A stock such as Westfield Group (WDC) has historically paid a strong franked dividend that can be received free of tax in certain circumstances. Some of the banks pay very favourable dividends too. As I write, Telstra's (TLS) dividend yield is up in the stratosphere at close to 10% before franking credits, but then its share price has been well and truly hammered over recent years. Always remember that a tax-free income is comparable to a far higher pre-tax salary. In reality, once you have learned the rules of wealth creation, you are perhaps unlikely to realise your portfolio of assets at this stage to invest in income assets; you are more likely to continue growing your asset base.

Often, it is assumed that the people who are rich are those who earn high salaries, with a big house and two expensive cars, but in fact they may be trapped in employment in order to repay the large debts associated with their lifestyle. Perhaps a better term than *'rich'* would be *'wealthy'*. There is little point in acquiring material success if you do not have good health, happiness and fulfilling relationships. It is certainly the case that the truly important things in life – falling in love, your friends and family, watching the Sydney Roosters – do not cost a great deal in financial terms. Wealth to me also implies sustainability. You can be rich, but if the money passes through your fingers quickly, then you are not wealthy.

To be truly wealthy, you also need the time to appreciate your wealth. Many highly paid executives work more than 60 hours per week, which doesn't leave a lot of time for enjoying one's money. Indeed, in more ways than one, time is our most important asset. Time can assist us to create wealth, and we need time to enjoy it.

Why most people can't quit work young and wealthy

Many people believe that the way in which they will retire will be to build up a lump sum in a superannuation fund that they will withdraw when they are around 65 years of age. Hopefully, the amount they have built up will last longer than they live. Some of those who have the option to do so consider downsizing their place of residence or using a reverse mortgage to free up some capital.

To me, this is a flawed thought process, and a very risky one for obvious reasons. The risk of the cash running out can be mitigated through selecting an appropriate annuity product, whereby actuarial percentages dictate the level of your annual income based upon your life expectancy. This mindset shows why most people are unable to be financially free at a young age. The numbers simply don't stack up.

If you want to retire at 65 the amount you will need as a lump sum is approximately 13 times (see below) your desired retirement income. Therefore, if you want to retire on $100,000 per annum, a lump sum of $1.3 million should be your goal for age 65. But what if you want to finish working full-time younger than that? Well, naturally, your life outside of the full-time workforce will run for a longer course, so the required multiple of your desired annual earnings increases.

Figure 1.2 – Multiples of desired income

Age at retirement	Required multiple of income
65	13
60	15
55	17
40	25

Source: Make your Fortune by 40, Paul Clitheroe

So far, so good, for at least this gives us a target figure. The flaw in this idea, though, soon becomes clear. If you want to quit work entirely at the age of 40 with an annual income of $100,000, you will need a lump sum balance of around $2.5 million. This is fine in theory. The problem as I see it is that if you are a person who has the financial capability to build a balance that runs into the millions by age 40, you are highly unlikely to be satisfied with an annual income of $100,000.

'This is why I believe that what you really need to achieve financial freedom at a young age is a significant balance of net realisable assets – but also a portfolio of assets that continues to grow in perpetuity.'

This book aims to demonstrate that the goal of financial freedom is not nearly as difficult as most people believe. The problem for most of us starts when we are young, as the current school system barely educates us financially at all. When you consider that money and finances affect every single one of us, it is curious that the school curriculum fails to recognise the importance of personal finance.

Never too late

I would like to stress that it is never too late to change your financial habits or to increase your financial education. It is possible to reverse a lifetime of poor financial habits relatively quickly once you begin to believe that you can achieve your goals. I aim to demonstrate that you can make a huge difference to your finances in a relatively short period of time, and therefore this book is relevant to you whatever your age.

SMART plans, SMART goals

I intend to detail a plan with **SMART** goals, that is, goals that are:

S	-	Specific
M	-	Measurable
A	-	Achievable
R	-	Realistic
T	-	Timely

I remember reading this on a motivational poster in my younger backpacking years while working as a data-entry clerk at a multinational insurance company for around $8 an hour. As a general rule, I don't like the insurance industry, and I was convinced I would get nothing from performing mindless data entry for this conglomerate, but as it turned out I learned a zippy acronym *and* developed RSI from all the typing, so in fact I was proven to be incorrect on two counts.

Too many of us are not specific in our goals. We simply say things such as 'I would like more money' or 'I would like a pay rise.' We must set specific goals, because then we can devise a detailed plan to achieve those aims. One strategy is to write down a very specific list of how your ideal life would be: where you would live, what you would own and how your ideal day would pan out. Our brains are powerful machines – if we can picture our goals, we give ourselves visual stimuli, and we will then consciously and subconsciously begin to work towards our target.

The aim of this book is to detail an effective plan to set you on the path to financial independence and beyond. It is specific to Australia and specific to now. I also wanted this book to be reasonably concise. It is not a bible of everything there is to know about wealth creation. If I was to record all of my thoughts on the subjects of personal finance and investment, the book would end up making *War and Peace* look like a pamphlet and few would take the time to read it. Instead, I aim to inspire you on the road to increasing your financial education by giving you a reasonably short but precise plan to escape the rat race.

A short note on terminology

As far as possible, I have tried to keep the language in this book simple and direct, and to avoid using too much meaningless jargon. However, a part of becoming a successful investor is understanding financial terminology and being able to express yourself clearly in financial terms. I have therefore provided a *Glossary of Terms* at the back of the book to assist you with terms you may not be familiar with.

This book is written specifically for the Australian market, and unless otherwise specified, '$' refers to Australian dollars. Some of the numbers may look inflated if you live in different parts of Australia, as I often refer to numbers that pertain to Sydney. Your salary and the value of your property, for example, are likely to be far different if you live in Beaudesert or Broken Hill than if you hail from Bondi Beach or Bellevue Hill. In all cases, the principle of the message is the important thing to grasp.

As I am English by birth, I use English spelling in preference to American spelling (one of my pet hates was a boss who always wanted to change words like 'colour' to 'color' in stock exchange releases I wrote). Although there is an increasing, and frankly quite annoying, tendency for Australian investors to use US terminology, I have tried to stick to traditional Australian terminology where possible. In some instances, the US terminology has now become standardised, so there may be some crossover.

Many times in this book I will use the word 'I' when often I mean 'we' for the simple reason that use of the phrase 'my wife and I' quickly becomes tiresome. My wife is a far shrewder investor than I am, and were it not for her I would not have been able to consider writing this book in the first place. Finally, on gender: on occasion I may use gender-specific terms such as 'he' or 'him' when of course I am referring to either sex. Indeed, as I will note, it has been shown in studies that often it is members of the female sex that are the more rational and superior investors (but that doesn't mean that as men we shouldn't try!).

Take note of people's qualifications

One of the interesting outcomes of the development of the Internet is that it has given a voice to the masses. Read news articles online and you will find dozens of comments attached from armchair critics. In the case of finance and economics articles, the responses are often highly charged, for these are emotive subjects. If you believed everything you read, you would certainly be confused and would probably believe that the sky is falling. It is important to remember, though, that many of these Internet trolls are just bored, underpaid employees with little better to do with their time, and they often demonstrate an IQ that is barely above room temperature.

The quality of finance journalism varies wildly, from excellent to utterly diabolical. Don't take my word for it. Read some copies of some of the widely respected financial magazines from the middle of 2008. I don't need to cite dozens of examples; take a read for yourself and check out some of the shares that were tipped as 'hot stocks', especially those of companies that were no longer in existence a matter of months later as the financial crisis hit. Those TV shows where punters phone in for advice on specific shares from chartists who have often never even heard of the companies they spout forth opinions on are equally bad. The clear lesson is that you must be very careful who you listen to.

Below, I've listed my qualifications, so that you may decide for yourself whether you wish to follow my plan.

Career

I am a Chartered Accountant by profession. My last full-time role was as the Financial Controller of an ASX (Australian Securities Exchange)-listed mining company, and before that I held a number of roles as an auditor and accountant in London and in Sydney. Much of my employment history involved producing annual reports for listed companies, company tax compliance and writing company releases for the ASX. My main area of expertise is in International Financial Reporting Standards (IFRS) but while this is factually true, I wouldn't necessarily mention it as a dinner-party icebreaker.

As much of my past employment involved company secretarial duties, I completed a Diploma in Applied Corporate Governance (again, this wouldn't score too highly on the dinner-party test), and I am an affiliated member of Chartered Secretaries Australia (CSA). In the time since I quit my full-time job, I have periodically worked as a contracting accountant whilst continuing to further my own investment activities.

Shares

Due to my employment experience in writing annual reports and my expertise in IFRS, I have a natural tendency towards a fundamental analysis approach to investing – that is, the detailed analysis of companies in order to find discrepancies between the price their shares trade at and the real or *intrinsic* value of the companies analysed. In recent years, though, I have come to realise that there is also much to be gained from a more technical approach to the trading of shares (the analysis of charts, trading volumes and trends, in order to identify the likely directional movement of share prices).

I have long been an unashamed fan of index funds too, where the investor requires very little skill at all other than the ability to make regular contributions to the fund. My wife began investing in an ethical index fund in 1997 that we have continued to contribute to every single month for the past decade and a half, which is one of the simplest wealth-creation strategies there is.

Property

Property is a strangely unregulated industry, and I suppose because we all have some experience in property, even if it just through renting a place of residence, it is a domain that naturally seems to attract more than its fair share of know-it-alls, opportunists and spruikers. I have read virtually every property book there is to read and attended dozens of seminars on investing in property, but there is always more to learn.

There are some property training courses and qualifications out there too, but in my view not all property investment skills can be learned from a textbook. I am qualified in property through my own investment experience, having built a multi-million-dollar portfolio over the years. Although I own property elsewhere in Australia, together with my wife I mainly buy residential investments in Sydney, and own properties in the Eastern Suburbs, in the inner west and on the Sydney harbourside. We have also owned properties for more than 15 years in the UK.

We invest in property specifically for price appreciation, often referred to as *capital growth*. Of all the properties we own, none is further than 5 km from its respective Central Business District (CBD). However, we never buy in the Sydney CBD itself, for although the demand for property may sometimes be high, the lack of height restrictions on property developments in cities exposes you to a potential risk of over-supply, as has been seen recently in Melbourne and Brisbane.

Depending upon where you live in Australia, building a property portfolio of somewhere between $3 million and $5 million in market value, if backed up by a solid portfolio of dividend-paying shares, equity funds and cash, should give you the confidence to take your focus away from working full-time.

If, using the techniques I will show you in this book, you can attain an average capital growth of somewhere in the region of 7% per annum on your property portfolio, your net worth will then increase by somewhere between $200,000 and $350,000 each year, with you hardly having to lift a finger. Despite what the naysayers may try to tell you, investing in property takes up very little of an investor's time. Better still, if you commit to never selling your properties (selling property foils the plans of so many investors), that figure is 100% capital gains tax deferred.

You will then be able to borrow against your portfolio's value to reinvest in other assets, or simply use (*some* of) the equity to pay for living expenses. One of the beauties of property investing is that once you have mastered the skills, you can repeat the process over and over again to build a massive portfolio.

Personal finance

As I am writing this book, it should be obvious that I have a developed an interest in personal finance, and to that end I have also completed a Diploma in Financial Planning. I should note, however, that while I have obtained this qualification, I do not work as a licensed financial advisor. Lord knows I suffered enough in my seven long years as an auditor.

Not just theory

This book contains intelligent discussion of the theories of investment and finance. However, if this book only supplies you with the theory and you fail to take action, then I will have failed in what I set out to achieve. My goal is for this book to set you on the path to financial freedom, and for this reason I have included a list of practical action points that you can undertake at the end of many of the chapters. Do not wait to take action – remember that procrastination is the killer of opportunity!

Integrity and disclosure

There are an awful lot of charlatans in the world of finance. Authors who write on the subject of property seem to be more full of it than most. Self-publishing US property author John T. Reed has created a useful and entertaining website on which he has detailed what he calls a '*Real Estate BS Checklist*' in which he highlights some of the tactics and ruses used by property spruikers.

It is always the case that you should check out an author's qualifications before determining what value you will place on their opinions. Reed nominates Robert Kiyosaki as the biggest transgressor on his 'BS checklist'[10], and highlights various inconsistencies in his claims[11]. My main criticism of Kiyosaki would be that he makes a lot of generalisations, but, for what it's worth, I genuinely enjoy reading Robert Kiyosaki's books. His books introduce some interesting general ideas and concepts, and I would recommend reading *Rich Dad Poor Dad* for excellent explanations of how you should buy assets and not liabilities.

One of Reed's main gripes is that certain authors try to make themselves out to be far more successful than they really are. It is a simple fact that the best investors *have* made a lot of mistakes, and then gone on to learn from them, usually over a period of decades. Sometimes, property investors don't disclose their portfolios because they aren't as big as they would have you believe, or because they have lost some or all of their portfolios and are trying to rebuild.

I should therefore note that I did not become a millionaire until my early thirties. I am an intelligent but fairly ordinary bloke who started with nothing at all except for my education; I just decided to take a different route from the expected norm of working full-time up to the age of 60 or beyond.

Together, my wife and I have followed a simple financial plan with three key elements to it. We have continued to buy property after property in Australia and the UK over the last 15 years, and have never sold a single house or apartment. Every month since 1997 we have paid money into an index fund and never sold a single unit of that either. We have also built a portfolio of direct holdings in companies (also in Australia and the UK) through investment and trading. While the minutiae of investing may seem complex, it is true that the simplest strategies can be those that create the greatest wealth. By investing for the long term, you can build wealth in a tax-efficient manner and allow the power of compound growth to perform miracles so that you don't have to.

Referencing

It is a matter of wonder to me how many finance authors do not provide any references in their texts, as though they have somehow magically discovered everything about the financial world themselves. It would never be allowed at a university, and would even be frowned upon at high-school level, and yet most of the finance books available provide no reference notes at all.

I have provided references in a section at the end of the book, for there are not many totally new ideas in investment. Trends come and go, but the principles remain the same. I have also added a short list of recommended reading. I can guarantee that if you read all of the books referred to in the references and the recommended reading, you will have taken a significant step towards attaining your financial freedom.

2
MY
STORY

2

My background

It is said that much of your attitude and mindset towards personal finance, wealth creation and success is wired when you are young. I was born in the gritty Yorkshire city of Sheffield in northern England, once famous for steel, later for unemployment and the dark comedy of the movie the *Full Monty* (it is dark in that its comedy masks many painful truths).

My father was from a conservative background and grew up in the Midlands. His father, who was a shopkeeper, fought in the war, and his mother was a successful dentist. By the time my parents had met at the university in Sheffield, my father had developed a different world view to that of his parents. After he scraped through university (with the lowest possible degree, he proudly told me) he took a job with the Probation Service and came to run a hostel for young offenders in the roughest part of Sheffield, where I spent my early years. He wanted to change the world, and voted for the Labour Party at a time when only the coalminers and downtrodden trade unionists voted Labour. He even read *The Guardian*. He was a genuine 'leftie'.

My mother, on the other hand, was left-wing from birth. Her mother was a lifelong socialist, and her father was a hard drinker who had a hardware business until it, and sadly his health, was ruined by the grog. In later life, due to having no money, he had to lie about his age to continue working as a clerk beyond the prescribed retirement age of 65, until he wasn't well enough to do that either. His retirement was a very short one, but one that I definitely enjoyed. I used to love watching the snooker on TV with him as a youngster when he came to live with us the year before he passed away.

Mum was brought up in a Catholic family of nine, or perhaps ten – there were certainly a lot of them anyway – in post-war Liverpool in northern England. As an adult, Mum went to the anti-nuclear marches at Greenham Common and would sooner have committed third-degree murder than vote for Margaret Thatcher, who was busy closing the coal mines and 'un-employing' 3 million Brits with her controversial monetarism policies[1]. My mother read *The Guardian* too, and always thought that the top bracket of income tax should be 'at least 90–95%'. Still does, come to think of it.

My parents' attitude to money was simple, because the world was a simpler place then. My father's job, like many of those in the public sector, offered a *defined benefit pension scheme*. In other words, if you worked until retirement you would be looked after in respect of your pension. For each year of service, he could add one-eightieth of his final salary to be drawn as a pension from retirement until death, and so that is what he did: he worked for 40 straight years in the Probation Service (rising to become the most senior person in the service and being presented with an OBE by the Queen for his commitment), and retired on forty-eightieths – or half – of his final salary. The trip to Buckingham Palace and the Queen's Garden Party were both a huge amount of fun, incidentally.

My mother was a teacher, but quit her career early in order to have us five children, all of us boys. My parents never bought a share or an investment property, as they were fortunate and had my father's defined benefit pension scheme to provide for them in their later years. This was typical of the time. Some people bought shares through the Tory (Conservative Party) privatisations of entities such as British Gas, for example, but most shareholders in those days had portfolios that consisted of shares in one or two privatised companies and nothing else[2].

The defined benefit pension schemes were too good to last as life expectancy increased, and new defined benefit schemes are very rare these days. When the International Accounting Standards finally (and uncharacteristically) began to reflect common sense and forced companies to show the pension liabilities in their accounts (i.e. in the same way as any other liability), many of the big companies were hugely exposed and had vast holes blasted in their balance sheets. By way of an example, in 2003 it transpired that Rolls Royce had a pension deficit of some £2 billion, which was more than the entire company was valued at on the stock market[3].

What was a sound financial plan for my parents 40 years ago is no longer good enough for the young people of today. In Australia now, we predominantly have *defined contribution* or *accumulation* superannuation funds. In layman's terms, this means that the responsibility now lies with *us* as to whether our pension is substantial enough when we retire. If the accumulated fund is inadequate when we finish working, we will be forced to live on the state pension, which for most of us is an unedifying prospect. Job security appears to be something of a bygone era too.

It is difficult to say objectively what I learned from my upbringing. I remember Dad taking me around some of the giant blocks of council flats in Sheffield to see some of the 'characters' who were on probation (in America, they would call them 'jail-swerves') for offences. These flats were monstrous buildings, known as brutalist architecture[4], and some of the grimmest accommodation developments known to the Western world. Did I get some motivation from that? Probably not. I was too young to understand burglaries, drug addiction, prostitution, suicide jumps from the rooftops and urine-soaked lifts. I was mainly just excited at the concept of living in a place with lifts, and with the common areas having the newfangled *Space Invaders* machines.

I do know that the biggest thing that my parents gave me was an appreciation of the value of education. I went to a general comprehensive school in Huddersfield in Yorkshire (also in northern England), and then later to a selective grammar school when we moved south for Dad's job. My oldest brother was a precocious student who scored straight 'A' grades in his Year 11 results and went on to the famous Oxford University. I was never going to outdo such lofty academic achievements, and so devoted a higher percentage of my school years to more fulfilling and worthwhile pursuits, such as playing snooker and smoking.

I suppose that my brothers and I were encouraged to think in terms of a high salary as being important. My oldest brother went on to be a partner in a London law firm, and my second-oldest brother become a broker at Lloyds of London (which seemed from the outside at least to be an excellent job, mainly involving drinking copious amounts of lager and chortling with befuddled clients).

Soon after my oldest brother became a partner though, the firm he worked for was taken over by a US firm and he was made redundant during a recession. After some time, it eventually worked out well for him because he found a better employer outside of professional practice, but it did reinforce a view I had developed on the dangers of relying on your employer for your financial future. The days of a job for life seem to be long gone.

Career

I trained in London to be a Chartered Accountant (CA) with a mid-tier firm. The firm no longer exists, as much later it went under after the 'Sir' Allen Stanford Ponzi scheme debacle ran its gruesome course. On top of a university degree and a series of tough exams, the CA qualification required three years of experience in an accounting practice. As with many accountants, for me this involved auditing.

I wasn't at all suited to auditing, but the end justified the means, and on the day I left, the audit managing partner told me I had been a model trainee. I think by then he must have forgotten about me booking a somewhat over-eager 22 days holiday in my second year instead of the prescribed 20, a transgression that earned me an almighty verbal roasting, and caused the audit department to reconfigure its holiday booking system.

After I qualified I went to work for one of the 'Big Four' accountancy firms, Deloitte, in Cambridge, about an hour from London. It was the original work hard/play hard environment, and at first I thrived on it. It is true that we all like to say that things were harder back in our day, but the hours *were* tough! Cambridge is a famous university city and the bio-tech capital of the

UK, with dozens of small firms bursting with energy and ideas. Many of them eventually listed on the London Stock Exchange, and this created a lot of work for accountants and auditors.

Once a month, a spreadsheet was emailed around the office detailing how many billable hours each employee had accrued. The chart-toppers always had around 300 hours to their name. *Three hundred!* These were chargeable hours to clients, you understand – not hours travelling to work, having lunch or mid-morning breaks reading *The Cricketer* magazine in the bathroom (none of which, I discovered to my disappointment, were chargeable activities).

I was putting in what I thought was a phenomenal amount of time, but as I still lived an hour from the office I could not put in the kinds of hours that some did, and I was never above the bottom of the second quartile in the chargeability charts. The only people below me were generally students who had exam commitments on top of their workload.

The partners had inadvertently created a competition that the managers ached to win. I once worked a 36-hour 'day' – right through the night and through the following day – but this was not unique. People pulled all-nighters fairly often, and some people even indicated a desire to do them, as they gave you a certain kudos in the firm. Employees who were low on the chargeability chart were sometimes derided by their peers. I remember a gentle giant of a South African who calmly turned off his computer at 6 pm every day to head home to his wife and was relentlessly chided. Finishing at 6 pm? *Loser!*

In retrospect, it was a benefit to the firm's partners, who were receiving extra hours from each employee at no additional cost. One wag famously tried to prove that the casual nightshift staff stacking the shelves at the local Tesco supermarket earned a higher hourly rate than the audit managers. I'm not sure it was true, but it certainly made for a good story. It is little wonder there were and are so many divorces and office affairs – if you factor in eight hours per day for sleep and a couple more hours for travelling to and from work and for lunch, that doesn't leave many hours for a whole lot else.

One day, one of the partners called an update meeting that all of the managers were required to attend. He announced that there was amazing news! We had achieved the highest number of chargeable hours per person out of all the offices in the UK. We were Premier League! We were Champions League! In fact, they had stopped making leagues, because *nobody* could beat us in the chargeable hour stakes.

The senior management sat at the front of the room as usual and nodded in agreement. They were not about to express contrarian opinions, or so I thought, but suddenly, one of the senior managers shot her hand up, signalling that she wished to speak. 'Excuse me for asking, but why is that a good thing? Why are we supposed to be enthused that we have worked harder than other employees in the UK, while our home lives are virtually non-existent?'

You could probably have heard a pin drop. Actually, you would probably have heard me snorting coffee through my nostrils. I didn't know her – she was a couple of years older than me and a lot more senior – but I had seen her around, and I knew she was hot; and clearly she was feisty too. I would never have guessed it then, but five years later, we were married on the beach in Kiama, New South Wales.

While I was in Cambridge, I won an unprecedented two Outstanding Contribution Awards in my first year, these being cash bonuses for exceptional project work (fairly small amounts, but a nice gesture). By the time I had completed two years though, my enthusiasm had waned somewhat. This was a pattern that was to repeat itself for me in future jobs before I understood that this is simply the way my brain works when it comes to paid employment. I can operate at high intensity for around a year, or even 18 months at a push, but then it seems that my brain needs a break. I no longer worry about this; I simply accept that we as people are all built differently, and some of us were not designed to work in stressful full-time professional jobs.

I stuck with the long hours for two years, and then handed in my notice to fulfil a long-held dream of returning to Australia. I had lived there while playing grade cricket in Sydney in my early twenties, but this time I would be going for the long term as a permanent resident. After around five more years of living in Australia, I finally became a proud Aussie citizen.

While I had been in Cambridge, I had started to realise the value of building *assets* instead of focussing on *income*. Although I was not in a relationship with her at the time, I could see that my now wife was the clearest example of how this can work. While I had a great salary, I had no assets. In fact, worse than this, I actually had a student loan debt to pay off that I had taken out to pay for my university tuition fees.

By contrast, my wife had bought her first property, a two-bedroom townhouse, when she was 21 for the princely sum of £72,000. It was a mortgage repossession, and friends and colleagues had said she was 'crazy' to pay so much for a terraced property. However, within eight years it had tripled in value and she had paid down an impressive chunk of the mortgage. She also *paid herself first*, by paying the mortgage and by directly paying a percentage of her salary into an ethical FTSE (Financial Times Stock Exchange – pronounced 'Footsie') tracker fund, a cash ISA (a tax-favoured Individual Savings Account) and a Sainsbury's savings account that couldn't be accessed. In comparison, I was absolutely nowhere.

When I arrived in Sydney, I again took up employment as an auditor at Deloitte, in the absence of any other particular plans. I still had not fully realised that earning a high salary is not the way to true wealth. Importantly, I still did not possess the requisite skillset for being a top auditor: detail-focussed, an introverted rather than an extroverted personality and infinite patience. Perhaps a passing interest in auditing might actually have been a small help too! After seven long years in the auditing wilderness, I finally learned the key lesson – work in a role that does not inspire you and for which you are not suited for long enough and eventually you will do it badly. What I lacked was congruence.

We all need to understand that each person is an individual, and we are all different. Not everybody is designed for stressful positions, or for managing large portfolios of clients. It's a simple fact of life that we all have different strengths and weaknesses.

With the benefit of maturity on my side, I can now see that Deloitte is a fine employer and, in my biased opinion, the finest of the accounting firms. The problem was that I was performing a role that did not suit my personality type, any of my interests or my attention span. It is sometimes overlooked that the same person is unlikely to be equally skilled at performing all of the roles from the most junior graduate positions up to partner level. This is why, I suppose, some mediocre performers at graduate and analyst level confound their peers and go on to be the best partners. Ask any partner and I am sure that they will tell you that the required skills at partner level are totally different to those that they needed at other stages of their career. They need to be better salespeople for one thing.

It was around this time that my appalling diet, late-night lifestyle and accumulated stress began to catch up with me. The human body is a remarkable thing, but fail to listen to it for too long and eventually it will go into meltdown. I had been running 'in the red' for a couple of years – I practically survived on full English breakfasts, caffeine and junk food throughout the day and plenty of alcohol in the evening, followed by around five hours sleep before brewing another morning coffee. Throw into the mix a stressful manager position that I was in no way suited to, an ugly relationship break-up (not with my now wife, I should add) and a relocation to the other side of the world, it is little wonder I was destined for some kind of catastrophe.

What had started out as a general nagging anxiety disorder spilled over into the most horrendous panic attacks. If you've ever suffered a panic attack, you will know what I am talking about. If you haven't, suffice to say that it is the single most uncomfortable feeling the human body can produce, and when you don't know what is happening to you, it is very scary. Not understanding that there are therapies and forms of medication that can help, I developed a dependence on alcohol as the only means I knew of to calm me down, before thankfully a mate of mine who had been through a similar experience pointed me in the right direction.

I exercised a lot at this time, and was interested in looking good, but took very little interest in living healthily. I was undoubtedly fit, because I was able to run the Sydney Marathon on a hot day without breaking sweat. However, being fit is not the same thing as being healthy. I can see some parallels here with financial behaviour. Think of a person who drives a Ferrari but has paid for his expensive car using debt. Externally, they may be demonstrating conspicuous signs of wealth, and by driving a Ferrari they probably want you to believe they are wealthy, but behind the veneer they are drowning in debt and expenses. It's the financial equivalent of someone being told they have a wonderful healthy-looking tan only to discover they have a melanoma.

I moved to working in industry, in a role to which I was more suited, and around this time I got married. I worked for an ASX-listed company in the healthcare industry that was taken over two years after I started there, and then I did a further two years as the financial controller of an ASX-listed mining company, a sector I had more experience in from my Deloitte days. These roles involved me producing output rather than auditing, and I discovered that I loved writing, although I accept that company annual reports can sometimes be a little on the dry side! Meanwhile, I read everything I could find on finance, investment and wealth creation and continued to implement the plan that we had come up with – to invest our way to financial freedom. That plan is the one I will detail in this book.

Since, I quit full-time work, I have been back to Deloitte as a short-term contractor (undertaking a review project on behalf of the East Timor Government), and I loved being back there. It is amazing the difference a few years and some maturity can make. What I had forgotten from my younger years was that firms like Deloitte have some incredible benefits: you can immediately slot into a network of like-minded, intelligent individuals of a similar age and outlook to yourself. Industry generally can't offer you that.

It wasn't Deloitte that was the problem when I was in my mid-twenties; it was me. I am simply better suited to contracting and discrete projects of work than to managing a challenging and complex portfolio of clients. Now, I would be delighted to go back to Deloitte on short-term or busy-season contracts if they would have me.

Contracting does not suit everyone, but it works for me. As a Chartered Accountant, it is actually a requirement of my qualification that I continue to gain professional experience and development in order to remain qualified. I explain later in the book how and why I can work as a short-term contractor in a tax-efficient manner and why it fits in with my own strategy for staying out of the rat race. I also trade shares for income and invest in dividend-paying stocks.

There are many ways in which you can continue to generate income without working full-time, such as setting up a part-time business or a home business. I do believe that we should always be looking to improve our skills regardless of whether or not we are working in a full-time job. It does not seem smart to me to sacrifice our peak earning years completely. I discuss these ideas later in the book.

Escaping the rat race

Being an accountant, I felt that I should have a natural affinity towards shares and analysing companies. After all, much of my employment had involved writing annual reports, so I was as well qualified as anyone to understand them. I was not fazed by ratio analysis, discounted cash flow workings or calculating weighted average cost of capital, and so I reasoned that the best investing style for me would be straight fundamental analysis: identifying companies that were trading at a significant discount to their intrinsic value, investing a meaningful amount of my capital in their shares and sitting back to patiently await the inevitable profits.

What I had not yet recognised is that wealth creation is not just about theory. It is about human emotions, how we respond to losses (and indeed profits) and learning to invest in harmony with our personality types. We need to find asset classes and investment strategies that best suit our investing personality. For many years I have attended seminars working on the premise that you should always be able to learn at least one thing from every seminar attended. Even the worst seminars should tell you something about what doesn't work for you. It was in a seminar presented by the obscenely intelligent Chris Howard that I learned what my investment personality type was – I am an *accumulator*.

What this means is that I am not suited to having too large a percentage of my portfolio in volatile assets (i.e. direct share investments); I am more comfortable with acquiring assets for the longer term than timing precisely when to buy and sell them, and I am more comfortable with a 'set and forget' strategy. This realisation allowed me to devise a plan that could work for me.

This is exactly the plan my wife and I followed. We started by cancelling every single one of our standing orders and direct debits (it transpired that my other half subscribed to rather a lot of women's magazines – she tells me that she now buys these second-hand at the market stall, though I'm not 100% convinced) and re-worked our finances from scratch.

'The plan that I eventually settled on was that I should trade shares for income, I should invest for the long term in blue-chip equities both directly and via index funds, and I should invest in residential property for wealth.'

We ditched the luxury apartment with Opera House views and rented a far smaller unit in Pyrmont (which admittedly still had Harbour Bridge views and a pool, but cost $1,000 less per month). We had cheap holidays driving up to Ettalong Beach instead of jaunts in Europe and drastically changed our spending profiles to invest savings in shares, index funds and multiple investment properties.

While at times the subject matter in this book may seem complicated, wealth creation need not be complex. The plan that we followed started with reducing our expenditure and investing the savings in shares and index funds. When a property we owned skyrocketed in value, we refinanced it and continued to add property after property to our portfolio. When some of the newly-acquired properties also soared in value, we were financially free.

Once we had grown a substantial portfolio of equities and a multi-million-dollar property portfolio in Australia and England, we felt we no longer needed to focus on working full-time. We left our full-time jobs to firstly volunteer for a short time for *BlazeAid* on the Cyclone Yasi clean-up and then to travel for a couple of years. We now focus on continuing to grow our investment assets rather than chasing ever-higher salaries.

One of the best things about trading and investing in shares is that it can be done anywhere – in a coffee shop, down by the beach or out on the Harbour on a boat. As I type this I am up by the Great Barrier Reef and can take breaks to indulge in some snorkelling (with stinger suit, of course; I was born a Pom, after all). Investing in property also takes very little, if any, physical presence due to the advent of email, mobile phones and the Internet. I would estimate that I spend less than an hour each month dealing with my investment properties, perhaps a little more at tax time in early August each year. Critics and naysayers will say that this is impossible, but I promise you it is true.

This book will take you through a detailed plan to achieving financial freedom, discussing the best methods and strategies that I believe to be available and that have worked for me.

3
TALE OF
THE TAPE:
Financial Profiles

3

It's not how much you earn...

You may have heard the saying 'It's not how much you earn, it's what you do with the money you earn that counts.' It is true that even if you earn a fairly moderate salary, if you invest in appreciating assets and reinvest your investment returns, you can achieve significant wealth. If you add leverage to your investment portfolio, then even the most modest income earner can build huge wealth over time.

Ian Hosking-Richards is an example of an Australian property investor who never earned a salary higher than $50,000, and yet the last I heard had accumulated a property portfolio approaching $15 million in value. How? By using leverage to invest in property, waiting for his assets to appreciate and then reinvesting his gains to create yet more wealth. This snowball effect is known as the power of compound growth.

As I have lived in Sydney for the last six years and earned a relatively high salary for much of that time, the numbers I have used in this chapter refer to values that may seem high to you if you earn a lesser income or live in less expensive parts of Australia. This need not worry you. As I have noted, it does not necessarily take a high salary to build wealth, only a level of financial education, some discipline and patience. Therefore, it is important to grasp from this chapter the principles of wealth creation. If the numbers look unrealistic or high to you, try to think in terms of percentages rather than absolute values. I will reiterate this several times throughout the book.

Your income statement and balance sheet

> 'The man is richest whose pleasures are the cheapest.'
> – Henry David Thoreau

Every business and every individual has a financial profile that can be summarised in two financial statements: an income statement (this used to be known as a profit and loss account, or simply a *P&L*) and a balance sheet (a summary of assets and liabilities). This is Accountancy 101 and yet, interestingly, even many accountants have financial profiles that look totally disastrous. For some reason, they think financial statements apply to their clients' businesses, but not to themselves personally.

In *Rich Dad Poor Dad*, Robert Kiyosaki summarised this in a straightforward and understandable manner, and via the patronage of the *Oprah Winfrey Show* made himself very famous in the process. What he wisely advises is that people need to focus less on earning an ever-higher income from their salary to instead focus on acquiring assets that bring wealth and income back to you, and steer clear of acquiring liabilities that drain funds away from you.

In his book, there is a detailed discussion whereby Kiyosaki argues that your house is not an asset. In my book, he is wrong – a residential property *is* an asset, but any *mortgage debt* against the property is a liability. We should note here that the tax system with regard to capital gains and deductibility of mortgage interest is completely different in Australia to that of the USA, and it is partly for this reason that the principal place of residence is the most successful investment many Australians ever make. Indeed, for many Australians, it is the *only* significant investment they ever make.

Kiyosaki might argue that his point is more relevant to the USA and less so to Australia, to which I would respond: 'Then don't sell books in Australia that aren't relevant to Australia!' Sadly, there are scores of books on our shelves that are written by American authors with inadequate adaptation (or no adaptation at all) for the Aussie market, making them essentially useless. In fact, worse than this, they can be downright misleading.

The debate on whether your house is an asset is largely one of semantics and terminology, but what Kiyosaki is right to infer is that buying the most expensive house you can afford to live in is not necessarily a smart move. This raises an important idea about whether it is better to rent your place of residence and invest your capital in shares and investment properties instead – if you are directing 40–50% of your highly taxed salary towards your mortgage, how will you ever have funds left over to *invest* your way to financial freedom (and experience the joys of being released from reliance on your paid employment)? This will be discussed in more detail later, but for now let's look at how a financial statement might appear.

The *Rich Dad Poor Dad* concept is simple enough – direct your income from your salary into *assets* that generate *passive income that you don't have to work for*, and when the passive income you earn from your investments is greater than your expenses, you are financially free. Yet the majority of people do not even have sufficient funds to retire at age 65 without the state pension, let alone any younger.

Financial statements

Kiyosaki advocates hiring a bookkeeper to analyse your income and expenses and to produce your personal financial statements every month. That is to say, a detailed budget, an income statement and a balance sheet. Now this is great advice, but I am certain that if this advice was offered to 100 people, very few of those 100 people would take it; perhaps only one person in 100 would decide to have this level of control of their expenses. Interestingly, on average, around one person in 100 retires wealthy too. Coincidence?

When I started out working for a firm of accountants, I worked with a guy who admitted to preparing his own financial statements and bank reconciliations. Naturally, people joked about him being a nerdy accountant (myself included, of course, but that was mainly because a few of the girls in the office liked him and I was jealous), while they obsessively chased their ever-higher salaries and bonuses. Now, the nerdy accountant has assets worth millions, while the other accountants who laughed at him are working harder and harder with each passing year to chase their impossible salary goals.

I prepare a lot of financial information: I have a rolling 12-month cash-flow budget, cash-flow profiles for all of our properties and detailed spreadsheets of all our shareholdings. I always know what our assets, liabilities and forthcoming cash flows are, in detail. Show me a successful and wealthy person, and you'll be showing me a person who knows their finances inside out. You may, of course, think this excessive or even a trifle obsessive, but it seems to me to be absolutely undeniable that success is achieved through careful control of results and measurement of progress.

Perhaps you don't need to go to such extreme lengths, but even a simple summary of where you are spending your money each month is a really good starting point. In any case, you will probably find that when your finances improve, this becomes a far more enjoyable exercise. You might remember from your childhood that it is fun to count your money, but bank statements showing overdrafts are definitely not pleasant reading, and thus often find their way into the bin (or if you are an eco-warrior like my wife, the recycling facility) rather swiftly.

Financial profiles for creating wealth

On the next page is an example of a typical financial profile.

The below financial profile is an example of where someone is focussing too heavily on their salary to make them wealthy. It doesn't work. Salary income in

Australia is taxed very heavily, with a top rate of tax in the 2012 tax year of 45%, plus a 1.5% Medicare levy. Occasionally, governments demand other taxes too, such as the flood levy of 2011. There is little defence for the salaried taxpayer, because the government usually deducts PAYG income tax at source.

Figure 3.1 – Common financial profile

Income Statement		Balance Sheet	
Income	**Expenditure**	**Assets**	**Liabilities**
Salary	PAYG income tax	House	Mortgage
	Mortgage repayments	Super fund	Car loans
	Car repayments	Car	Credit card debt
	Food, other living costs		Other loans
	Credit card/loan repayments		
	Holidays		

The other problem with a financial profile like this is that the balance between assets and liabilities is poor. To create wealth, it is vital to focus on growing the asset column by acquiring assets that will bring passive income back to you. Too many people have a profile like the one above, in that they have a house and their superannuation fund, but no other appreciating assets (the car is a depreciating asset, and will probably eventually be worth $0). Instead, they build up liabilities such as car loans and consumer debt that only serve to increase their expenses column. The money is all flowing out.

With a financial profile like this, the heavily taxed salary income is required to support many forms of expenditure, and there never seems to be anything left over at the end of each month. Each and every pay rise is matched by an equivalent increase in expenditure, and the employee never seems to be able to get ahead. The person with a profile such as this is on a financial treadmill.

Now consider this financial profile of a successful investor who is destined for financial freedom.

Instead of focussing on salary income, this investor is focussed on filling the *asset* column with investments that bring passive income back to the income column. The only liabilities this investor has are mortgages against a portfolio of appreciating investment properties. The interest on the investment loans is tax deductible, so tax payments can be minimised or perhaps totally eliminated if the investor so wishes.

Figure 3.2 – Investor's financial profile

Income Statement		Balance Sheet	
Income	Expenditure	Assets	Liabilities
Business income	Investment mortgages	Multiple investment units	Investment mortgages
Contract pay	Rent	Share portfolio	
Rent	Food, other living costs	Bonds	
Dividends		Index funds	
Interest income		Super fund	

To become financially free, you will need passive income that exceeds your expenditure, and a financial profile such as this also has shares and bonds that bring further income to the investor in the form of dividends and interest.

You might also consider renting your place of residence in order to speed up your charge towards financial freedom. This strategy will be discussed later in the book. It works in part because renting a place of residence is normally considerably cheaper than buying one (rental yields are often lower than mortgage rates, and when you rent, landlords usually retain responsibility for costs such as insurance, strata fees and maintenance).

Renting also frees up the investor to capitalise on the significant tax benefits of owning multiple investment properties. Many professionals today are intent on buying the most expensive house they can afford. This ties them into large mortgage repayments (that do not attract tax deductions in Australia), and too often there is nothing left over at the end of the month to invest in appreciating assets that create wealth.

Case study 1 – Rodney

Below is a hypothetical financial statement of a well-paid executive named Rodney who is not following my financial plan. He is 45 years old with a wife and three children. He earns a salary of $300,000 before tax, of which the tax man takes $115,000. He lives in a four-bedroom house in the outer Hills District of Sydney.

He acquired shares in Telstra many years ago, but these plummeted in value by 50%, and although they pay a handy 10% franked dividend he is considering selling them in disgust. He now only buys shares in an array of speculative mining stocks, as expensive blue-chip shares are not going to catapult him to wealth. Besides, he thinks the blue-chips are 'for light-weights'. He thinks 'investment properties are for light-weights' too. Real men buy mining shares. He will never read an investment book ('I've never learned anything worthwhile from that stuff') and will never seek financial advice from anybody. He believes that he knows best.

Meet this chap at a barbeque and all he wants to talk about is himself, his job and how much he earns. He wants to talk about work mainly because he works for 80 hours a week, though a lot of that time is actually spent in the pub talking about work gossip, and most likely he has no other interests. He is rarely at home and doesn't see a lot of his children.

Figure 3.3 – Rodney's balance sheet aged 45 ($)

Income Statement		Balance Sheet	
Income	**Expenditure**	**Assets**	**Liabilities**
Salary 185,000	Mortgage 50,000	House 500,000	Mortgage 400,000
	Car repayment 25,000	Car 100,000	Car loan 75,000
	Car repayment 15,000	Car 50,000	Car loan 25,000
	School fees 25,000	Boat 50,000	Credit card 25,000
	CC interest 5,000	Shares 100,000	Boat loan 25,000
	Living expenses 50,000	Super 300,000	
	Holiday 20,000	Cash 2,000	
185,000	190,000	1,102,000	550,000

If you knew Rodney, you might think he was the epitome of success, with a good house in the outer suburbs, his children in fee-paying schools, two shiny new cars and even a boat. He must be rich! He would probably tell you that this was the case, but if you could see his financial statements, you would see a different story. He has borrowed a lot of money to purchase *depreciating* assets, such as his two cars and the boat. He is spending more money than he earns. He has built up a reasonable superannuation fund and portfolio of shares, but his chances of early retirement are very low. Worse, if he was unable to work for some reason, he would probably be broke in around two months. This predicament is far from unusual for many salaried employees.

Fast forward 10 years to age 55 and what does Rodney's balance sheet look like? He may have repaid the car and boat loans, together with all of the accrued interest and charges, although the cars are probably worth very little now (indeed, in reality he is fairly likely to have replaced them with newer financed cars). The boat may have held its value reasonably well, but has probably caused a lot of pain over the years in insurance, storage costs and maintenance.

The house in the outer suburbs may have appreciated somewhat, but being in a lower-demand area it is unlikely to have outperformed inflation by much. He did not own enough Telstra shares to make much of a difference to his wealth, and the speculative stocks would most likely have performed haphazardly with some winners and some losers, and none of them paying dividends.

Even at 55, his chances of retiring remain very low. The school fees have been replaced by expensive university fees, the cars need replacing and he is still no nearer to building a substantial portfolio of assets beyond his house and his superannuation fund. Even if he could retire, he probably wouldn't know what to do with himself, as he has become wired to work.

His balance sheet at age 55 may therefore look something like this:

Figure 3.4 – Rodney's balance sheet aged 55 ($)

Balance Sheet	
Assets	**Liabilities**
House 700,000	Mortgage 200,000
Car 20,000	Car loan - nil
Car 10,000	Car loan - nil
Boat 50,000	Credit cards - nil
Shares 150,000	Boat loan - nil
Super 600,000	
1,530,000	200,000

Through thousands of hours of hard graft, Rodney has built a reasonable net worth through his superannuation fund, but he has been unable to contemplate early retirement. Instead, he is likely to be looking at new financed car purchases. In many cases, executives who work the kind of extreme hours that Rodney does jeopardise their marriages, and their relationships with their children too, by spending an ever-increasing percentage of their time at work. This book is about seeking a slicker alternative to this financial plan.

Some of the key lessons to learn from case study 1 are:

- high salaries attract a very high percentage of tax in Australia (a top rate of 46.5% in 2012 including the 1.5% Medicare levy)

- borrowing to acquire *depreciating* assets may give the appearance of success, but ultimately destroys wealth instead of creating it – you will end up paying far *more* than the value of the asset for something that will become worth far *less* than you paid for it (and eventually is likely to be worth $0)

- if compound interest is not working for you, you can be sure it is working against you

- investing in shares without a written plan will virtually guarantee suboptimal performance

- speculating in shares with a controlled percentage of your net worth can be worthwhile as part of a detailed plan, but if the downside is not protected, the results will be haphazard and very likely mediocre

- if you spend more than you earn, you will have no residual funds to invest

Case study 2 – Helen and Phil

Let's look at another hypothetical scenario. These are the combined financial statements of a 27-year-old professional couple named Helen and Phil who live in Sydney. When they were younger, they became interested in investing and learned all they could about the subject.

They have not taken on a mortgage for a principal place of residence, but instead rent a small one-bedroom unit in Surry Hills that allows them both to walk to work at their respective offices in the CBD. They own a rusty Ford Laser runabout that they bought for cash. The time they save on travelling to work they spend together on a variety of other interests, and they devote a couple of hours a week to reading investment books or going to seminars.

Their combined gross income of $200,000 is significantly less than that of the 45-year-old Rodney in the first case study, and equates to an after-tax income of around $150,000 after the tax benefits of their investment properties are taken into account. They have decided to opt out of jumping aboard the corporate treadmill. They do not try to compete with their peers for the best house, plasma screen, holiday, car or wedding. They have no credit card debt. Instead, they quietly but assertively invest in shares and property.

The only debt they have is on investment properties, of which they have bought two each so far, all of them $375,000 units, by carefully saving 10% deposits over the past four years while trading shares to help them grow their capital. They have financed the property purchases with interest-only loans to reduce the negative cash flow, and on average the units have a rental yield of 5% of their market value.

Although they tried to buy in the early growth stages of the property cycle in high-capital-growth areas close to the city, and carefully invested in properties they believe will be in perpetual high demand, the values have only appreciated by around 10% from their original purchase price to a total value of $1,650,000. They added a small amount of this capital growth through cosmetic renovations.

Their residual income has been used to invest in a $20,000 portfolio of shares. They have bought a mixture of mid-cap profit-making and dividend-paying stocks and blue-chip stocks with a good yield. They have committed to continually learning more about investment, and have a written investment plan.

The properties they have bought are *negatively geared* – that is, the properties cost them money at the end of each month, though the taxman pays his share of the loss as I explain in more detail later. They have also counteracted the negative cash-flow in a number of ways by buying at the right price, taking out interest-only loans and buying properties that needed a cosmetic facelift or rejuvenation, enabling them to increase the rents by around 10% while generating a small amount of capital growth.

Figure 3.5 – Helen and Phil's balance sheet aged 27 ($)

Income Statement		Balance Sheet	
Income	**Expenditure**	**Assets**	**Liabilities**
Post-tax salaries 150,000	Property outgoings after tax 30,000	Units 1,650,000	Mortgages 1,350,000
Dividends 1,000	Rent on unit 30,000	Car 1,000	
	Books/Seminars 5,000	Shares 20,000	
	Annual share purchases 20,000	Super 75,000	
	Living expenses 30,000		
	Holidays 5,000		
151,000	120,000	1,746,000	1,350,000

Now, let's look ahead 10 years and imagine what their balance sheet looks like at age 37. It is impossible to know precisely, of course, although we know that their liabilities will be the same, as they have taken out interest-only loans and have no other debts. They might easily have doubled their existing share portfolio and invested an additional $20,000 per annum through continuing to spend less than they earn – and as they have invested in profit-making dividend-paying shares they should be receiving franked dividends (i.e. with tax credits attached) too. The car? Well, the car is probably worth zip, or sitting on a scrap heap somewhere – they have probably acquired another runabout for cash.

Projected growth on property is a hotly debated subject and will be discussed in far more detail later in the book. An often-quoted statistic is that historically the value of residential property in Australia has doubled in value approximately every 7 to 10 years. Of course, this does not mean that this will definitely continue to be the case. Anyone who tells you that it will is, by definition, not telling the truth; there are far too many variables for anyone to know, although it is of course possible that this outcome could eventuate.

However, what we *can* do is note the Reserve Bank's stated target inflation rate (2–3%) and consider the expected supply factors (such as construction approvals) and demand factors (such as population growth and demographic trends). We can then make an assessment of whether we think residential property is the best asset class to invest in *over the long term*. This subject will be discussed fully later in the book, where I will outline the techniques that ensure that you can outperform the quoted median property price growth so beloved of the financial media.

Do Helen and Phil really care what the median value growth of Australian property is? No, not really. They only care what happens to the value of *their* properties. If they were able to achieve an annual capital growth of around 7.2% on their properties using the techniques I will highlight in this book, the power of compound growth would see their properties double in value in only 10 years.

If this were the case, their balance sheet at age 37 would look something like this:

Figure 3.6 – Helen and Phil's balance sheet aged 37 ($)

Balance Sheet	
Assets	**Liabilities**
Units 3,300,000	Mortgages 1,350,000
Shares 400,000	
Super 300,000	
4,000,000	1,350,000

They would have a net worth (assets less liabilities) well in excess of $2.5 million and be in an excellent financial position. I have deliberately chosen a scenario where the couple have still only acquired two properties each by the age of 37. I'm here to tell you that if you so wished, you could definitely acquire many more properties in this time period.

The really exciting thing is that with a pot of equity like this, they have options. They can refinance to buy more properties. They can also take out a *tax-free* line of credit (see the *Glossary of Terms* at the back of the book) that they can use in part to live on, a controversial strategy that will be discussed in more detail later. What they can certainly do is take their focus away from the need to earn ever-higher salaries that attract ever-higher tax demands. They can continue to work if they so wish, but with a net worth of over $2.5 million, they can also afford to rethink their priorities.

Now you might well argue that the property market could be sluggish throughout this period, and you would be right to point this out. Consider this: if the couple don't achieve their 7.2% growth target, and they can only achieve half of their targeted capital growth figure, they will still have a net worth of well over $1 million and they can *still* use the aforementioned strategies of refinancing to buy more properties or taking a line of credit. Property is a superb asset class when you invest in it for the long term.

A number of friends and work colleagues will say that they are lucky. Is that true? They are certainly lucky that they became interested in learning and investing at a young age. However, it is not simply luck that saw them prepared to open their minds to learning, and it is not simply luck that saw them prepared to sacrifice an expensive house, flash new cars and extravagant living expenses to achieve their goals. It is also not simply luck that saw them expose themselves to a calculated level of risk. They made a sound financial plan, and they had the discipline and patience to execute it.

At this stage in your financial development, a curious shift may occur in your peer group. In their early twenties, the high achievers who are paid the big salaries and have the conspicuous signs of 'wealth' (financed new cars, luxury holidays, expensive weddings and the biggest houses) are only too keen to tell you about how big their next bonus will inevitably be. These people may be confused and unsure of how to react when certain peers who appeared to have none of the status symbols of being high-income earners suddenly appear to have a net worth of a couple of million dollars, and are contemplating life away from the corporate earn-and-spend treadmill.

This is one of the key messages of this book, and you will need to be prepared for it. As an investor, you will have people tell you that you are doing the wrong thing every step of the way. Friends, family, work colleagues, newspapers, Internet forums – somebody will always be there to tell you that you are doing the wrong thing. It takes courage to be different and to become wealthy at a young age.

Western society has developed a viewpoint that we need to work hard to be good citizens. I don't dispute that working hard can be a good thing. I work hard myself; at least, some of the time I do. However, being reliant on committing 50 or more hours every week to working for someone else – and having the tax office swipe around half of your income before you even see it – is not necessarily a smart financial plan.

Some of the key lessons to learn from case study 2 are:

- borrowing or leveraging to acquire *appreciating* assets is a time-tested method of wealth creation

- acquiring many properties with a moderately negative cash flow but in high demand and in high-capital-growth areas can over time create phenomenal wealth; note that rental income increases with inflation so that in time the properties will generate a positive cash flow in addition to the capital growth

- blue-chip shares can give excellent growth of up to 20% per annum immediately after a stock-market meltdown and pay very useful dividends too

- there are many smaller and mid-cap shares that are profit-making and dividend-paying if greater capital growth is sought

- short-term sacrifices on lifestyle expenditure can reap enormous rewards over time; remember that humans have a tendency to overestimate what they can achieve in a year, but to hugely *underestimate* what they can achieve in a decade or two

- you should commit to always improving your financial education – you can never know it all, and there is always more to learn.

Once again, I must make the point here that how much you earn from your salary need not dictate your financial health. Even the lowest of income earners can, over time, generate vast wealth if they follow the basic rules of wealth creation: living below your means, investing your spare capital in appreciating assets and reinvesting the profits. The snowballing effect can produce stupendous returns over time.

Four types of income

In his book *Cash Flow Quadrant*, Robert Kiyosaki notes how he believes there to be four types of income[1]. Each of the four types of income has its own characteristics, and importantly, they all have different tax rates and benefits.

Specifically, he notes that the four types of income are:

- Business ownership

- Employment

- Self-employment

- Investment.

Business ownership

The greatest wealth is often derived from business ownership. A successful business attains huge leverage of other people's time (OPT) and other people's money (OPM) to create massive value. The tax laws favour businesses in that a corporation or company pays tax only on its profits (the residual net profit after legitimate expenses are deducted from revenues) rather than on its income. The tax rate is also generally lower than the highest marginal rate of income tax.

I am not an expert on how to build a big and successful business. Building a large business may or may not be a goal I have for myself in the future, but I wouldn't pretend to have the knowledge or experience to write a book on the subject. Besides, there are plenty of books that already explain the topic very well.

One of the problems with setting up your own business is that you will need to devote yourself to it completely. Businesses take up a lot of the founder's time in their early days, and there is no guarantee of success. Business owners also need to be very skilled at dealing with many different types of people – indeed, you require a vast array of different skills that you do not always require or learn as an employee.

Employment

The employee pays tax on his income, which is a principal reason why it is difficult to attain wealth through a job. With a top tax rate of 45% in Australia in 2012 plus the Medicare levy of 1.5%, the government is taking close to half of the top-bracket income of a higher-rate taxpayer before he or she even touches it.

Some people are suited to earning this type of income, despite the high tax rates it attracts. One of my friends has played for the England cricket team for most of the last decade and has gone on to captain his country, and he rightly earns a very high salary. He is what is known in the employment field as a *star* (you could potentially also argue here that a sports star is self-employed). I note, however, that through endorsements, he will also be earning money in the business environment, and although I have never discussed it with him, I expect he also earns a fair amount of money from investments. In other words, smart high-salary earners also earn money from the two quadrants that offer greater tax concessions.

Unfortunately, most of us are not stars. The best most of us can hope for in the professional sphere is to become an executive. Salaries at the executive level in Australia vary significantly, but one thing is certain: the tax brackets ramp up relatively quickly, so that a high earner is generally forced to surrender close to half of his or her income to the tax office, unless he knows how to structure his investments.

Self-employment

Self-employment or small business is perhaps best defined as a situation where if the business owner stops working, the revenues dry up. While the small business owner may sometimes have similar tax advantages to the business owner, he is probably unable to leverage other people's time to the same extent. The person in this quadrant does not earn income passively, as he still has to work each week in order to continue earning.

My wife and I occasionally work in the self-employment sector as contractors in our professional field (accountancy). The problem with being in the self-employment sector is that, just as with being an employee, you are still trading your time for money. Often, a self-employed person does not attain the same tax benefits as a business owner, although as I will detail later in the book, we both (legally) have a tax rate of 0% as self-employed contractors.

Investment

Kiyosaki refers to the investment income sector as the 'playground of the rich'[2]. There are many legal tax breaks available to the investor (such as the tax deductibility of interest on qualifying investment loans or franking credits on certain dividends), and the successful investor will often leverage other people's money and time to create wealth.

Kiyosaki's recommendation is for individuals to start their own businesses and invest the proceeds for investment income. This is certainly a plan that can achieve vast wealth, but starting a business is not for everyone. What this book is about is instead controlling your personal expenditure, taking your income from your employment, and channelling it into the investment sector until you have built enough wealth to escape the rat race completely if you so choose.

If you are successful, you will no longer be reliant on employment at all. If you so wish, you can go on to set up a business, you can go back to work on a part-time or contract basis, or you can just live on the income from your investments and play golf every day. The key thing is, you will be financially free.

Today's professionals and financial profiles

A common progression today is for couples to cohabit in their early twenties, and enjoy a period of two incomes and few commitments, which leads to a feeling of wealth and success. Then, as they move towards their peak earning years, they often get married, have children and buy the best house they can afford to settle into.

It is not unusual at this stage for the two incomes to become one income. The couple need one car for the partner who is working and a second car for taking the children to school. Quite quickly, the couple have moved from two incomes and few commitments, except a small amount of rent, to one income, a big mortgage, two car loans and rapidly mounting school fees.

Many of us are encouraged to take out the biggest mortgage we can afford, and there is certainly an element of 'keeping up with the Joneses' in wanting the best house in the best suburb. This financial profile of taking out a huge mortgage somewhere between the ages of 25 and 40 is a prime cause of why most people have no hope of retiring much before the age of 60. The government takes half of your pay packet before you can even touch it, and the financial commitments just seem to keep on increasing.

I have seen this financial profile time and time again. This book is about an alternative plan, one whereby you start building a portfolio of assets years before the commitments kick in. It goes against the grain of what many people are taught, but I advocate renting your place of residence, reducing commitments on new cars and expensive holidays, and investing in a portfolio of assets that includes shares, funds and property. Take on this role of the quiet achiever and while in the short term your friends might have a better television or the latest toys, they will be staggered when you no longer need to work and you are driving a new Mercedes.

One welcome benefit of obtaining financial freedom is that you are no longer tied to living full-time near your place of work. My wife and I currently have our eyes on buying a place in which to spend a part of the year in the north of England. It is a wonderful, spacious, character property that, if it does come up for sale, would cost around £300,000, which would not even get you a two-bedroom flat around the commuter belts north of London where many of our British friends live.

Decent houses in these 'desirable' areas around London (I suppose they may be desirable if you have a penchant for overcrowding and motorways that take on the appearance of car parks) might cost between £1 million and £2 million – giving you a mortgage that practically guarantees you will be working into your sixties. Provided that work–life balance (incidentally, what a horrible maxim that is – the very term 'work–life balance' assumes that your work is overbearing and unsatisfactory) is maintained and no divorce ensues, what a depressing thought it is that so many of us risk spending the one life we get on this earth dependent on slaving away for someone else, right up until the day we depart.

Another advantage that being free of the rat race can give you is the power of exchange rates. We are presently living in a time of a very strong Australian dollar. When I first came to Australia back in the 1990s, the Poms loved to come to a country where their strong currency could buy them a luxury lifestyle at a fraction of the cost of London life. Those days are here no longer, and for the moment the boot is on the other foot. Of late, the Australian dollar has even been considerably stronger than the US dollar, a remarkable turnaround from the financial crisis in 2008–2009.

Since my wife and I gained the financial freedom and confidence to leave our careers behind we have travelled overseas a lot, and have embarked on a cruise taking in more than 20 countries – in nearly all cases the dollar goes very much further than it would back in Australia. Whatever the state of play with world currencies, we should always aim to use exchange rates in our favour if we are moving funds between countries. While I don't necessarily recommend investing overseas, moving funds between jurisdictions is a strategy that we have used successfully in the past.

Dare to be different

If you want to quit your job at a young age, you will need to think and act differently to the herd. If you adopt the same approach as most people (striving for a high-paying job, two nice cars and the most expensive house you can afford), it stands to reason that you will probably achieve the same results as most people. For our generation, this is likely to mean working until at least 65 – and possibly far beyond, as retirement ages look set to increase to 70 – and taking a substantial cut in earnings upon retirement. You will need to think differently and be prepared to take another course of action.

An interesting statistic is that a high percentage of self-made millionaires in many countries are immigrants. There could be any number of reasons for this. My view is that immigrants are more likely to become self-made millionaires because they are less inclined to be restricted by generally accepted rules. They do not worry what a close circle of friends and family may think of their strategies; they only concern themselves with delivering results. Too many of us do not dare to take the different road for fear of failure, and instead worry about what our peer group will say about us if we fail.

Here's a short anecdote: while travelling in Darwin, we were threatened on a bus by a drunken old lady and her man. The driver made the couple leave the bus, but the old lady returned with a broken brick to smash the window right next to our faces. Nothing much came of it and we were OK. I later recounted this story to a friend in Sydney, and he said, 'You are a millionaire, with all those shares and properties, and you take a *bus*? A bus! I would never, ever travel on a bus out of principle. I always take taxis. Everywhere.'

Although I didn't respond by saying so, a gross oversimplification of the truth is that I'm a millionaire because I am prepared to take a bus. You may not believe that small savings make a difference, but if over time you carefully consider the impact of all your expenditure, seemingly small changes can make a monumental difference to your wealth. This is especially true if you choose to invest the savings in appreciating assets. Even Warren Buffett has been known to pick up a 10 cent coin from the floor of an elevator: '...the start of my next million[3].'

If you are young and the house you want to live in seems forever beyond your reach, think outside the box. Cancel useless subscriptions to magazines you don't read or the gym you don't use. Get a cheaper mobile phone plan and invest the savings in shares or an index fund. If, unlike me, you have wealthy parents, ask them to join you in buying an investment unit, with them supplying some of the deposit, and buy in a cheaper suburb or city that you can afford. Then, you will at least have a foothold in the property market, so that it doesn't seem to increase in value while remaining forever beyond your reach.

The options are too numerous to list here. At some stages of the economic cycle you may be able to find a mortgage broker who can help you find a bank that will lend you 95% or even 100% of an investment property's value, and then, perhaps not too far down the track, that investment property will grow significantly in value so that you can refinance it and buy three more investment properties.

The specifics will differ for each person, but the fundamental concept is the same. If you can begin to appreciate and believe that it is possible to be financially free, then you will automatically begin to reduce the wasting of money on unnecessary items. Start small and grow big. This is the very essence of wealth creation through investment.

Remember, it is all too easy to be a lemming and to follow your peers over the financial cliff – no individual lemming ever received bad press for failing in the conventional way. It takes guts to take the different path.

Controlling personal expenditure

Let me take a guess what you are thinking, even if only subconsciously – you are reading this book because ultimately you want to spend more money, not less? Well, this book is about escaping from dependence on the rat race of full-time employment, and to do this you will need to create passive income that is greater than your expenditure. There are two variables that can be adjusted to help you achieve this: increasing your passive income and reducing your personal expenditure. When you have achieved a net worth that runs into the millions, you will have all the funds you need to fulfil your spending desires.

I am reasonably well qualified to speak on the great modern art of wasting money. In the first half of my twenties, I simply earned money and promptly spent it without a single thought as to building future wealth. I believed that one day I would rise to a great job and would use that income to buy a big house and expensive cars before retiring at 65 years of age to play golf.

Ask anyone who knows me and they will testify to my extravagant attitude to money in my younger years. I was the first and last to the bar, and made most of the trips to the bar in between. In fact, if a genie magically appeared and granted me three wishes, they would be these: world peace, an end to famine and disease, and for all the people in London who never bought their round to give me $20. Actually, at London bar prices, make that $50. Therefore, I would be the last person to preach on this subject…however, let's take a look at some of the big-ticket items that can cause us to become terminally trapped in the rat race.

Huge mortgages

When I was in junior school in Huddersfield (my family moved around a fair bit) back in the 1980s, one of my teachers told us that when we grew up we should buy a house as soon as we could and we should buy the most expensive house we could afford. I didn't give it much thought, and went back to wishing away the minutes until morning break and footy. The teacher's point was related to the proposed Poll Tax that was causing the masses to riot and break shop windows in London at the time. This is not an unusual viewpoint, but let's stop to consider exactly why this is conventional wisdom.

Firstly, it is generally accepted that we want to own a home outright so that when we retire we do not have large monthly mortgage or rental payments to make. Secondly, it is generally and correctly assumed that in the absence of a deflationary economic environment, the long-term trend in property prices is an upwards one. So far, so good.

What often happens in reality is that once an individual attains the highly paid job they aspired to – often in their mid-thirties – they proceed to take out an astronomical mortgage that virtually guarantees that they will not be able to quit their job for at least the duration of the mortgage, by which time they will be approaching normal retirement age or somewhere close to it. If their monthly salary dried up, the mortgage payments would often send them broke after a couple of months.

I am suggesting an alternative financial plan. Firstly, it is about controlling personal expenditure to invest in assets such as funds and shares that build wealth through capital growth and bring yield back to us (instead of spending on depreciating assets such as cars that continually drain funds away from us). Secondly, it is about using the long-term direction of the property market to our advantage. If we agree that over time the market is heading north, then we should increase our exposure by acquiring property whenever we can afford to do so, and getting others – tenants – to pay the mortgages for us.

One of the ways in which we can help ourselves to do this is to rent our own place of residence, which is generally cheaper than buying a place of residence, and invest our capital instead in multiple investment properties. The investment properties will have tax benefits and will grow our asset base. This may be completely at odds with what you have been taught by your parents' generation, and I will explore this idea further later in the book.

Car loans

It is well known that one of the first material items to follow a significant pay rise is often the big lump of metal that sits in your garage, carport or parking space. We should be aware that while a car is often described as an asset, it is a depreciating asset that costs a lot of money to buy, and costs more money in insurance, repairs, fuel, registration and so on. Properties incur insurance and repair costs too, of course, but unlike properties, most cars tend to depreciate over time.

Worse than this, new cars are often paid for through financing. The motor giants General Motors and Ford spent years making more profit from customer financing of cars than they did from actually selling them[4]. In effect, some large car companies became financiers that happened to produce vehicles. A typical car financing deal may have a high rate of interest and could involve paying back an obscene amount over the term of the loan. New cars depreciate very quickly. It is estimated that many cars lose up to 20% of their value the day you drive them off the dealer's forecourt.

I understand the desire for expensive cars because I am a man. In fact, as well as owning an RV, we do have a car that was bought brand-new, a lovely Volvo C70 convertible. My wife had a friend in the auto industry and obtained a 20% trade discount, which made it a deal too good to resist. It was not financed through the vendor, however. Instead, it was purchased using equity from investments and a line of credit that only attracts interest at 1.5% above the cash rate (which in the UK at the time of writing is 0.5%).

Another reason why this car does not create too much pain is that there is no desire to sell it and upgrade, as it has done fewer than 5,000 km per annum since it was purchased. That said, as I've got a bit older I've become more aware of my carbon footprint (and the rising cost of fuel), and I'm starting to think that a car with such a big engine is a little unnecessary.

The biggest trap to avoid is buying a new car on finance, and then a few short years later becoming bored with that car and repeating the process with another new financed vehicle. If you live in one of the capital cities, question whether you even need a car at all, or whether you can rent one as required.

Weddings

One of the biggest expenditures people incur in their lifetimes is often for their wedding day and honeymoon. My two eldest brothers had weddings that cost plenty more than $50,000, each financed by loans. Perhaps I am just a bit tight by nature, but that is a lot of money for one day! I have friends who have spent a lot more than that twice, and have ended up paying off two concurrent wedding loans after the first marriage didn't last until death did them part. Second weddings sometimes have a nasty habit of costing more than first weddings as a means of validation, a kind of matrimonial negative spiral.

On this front, at least, I cannot be accused of extravagance. I was married on the beach in Kiama, NSW, and to the consternation of my mother we didn't invite anyone except the celebrant, a photographer and the photographer's daughter as a witness. The photographer was a lovely old chap who was really a food photographer, and he only charged $200 for the day. He even forgot to bill us until we honourably reminded him three months later. His culinary background didn't impede the photography though, and he produced a lovely CD of pictures for us.

For our honeymoon, we took our RV from Sydney all the way down the Great Ocean Road and back for three fantastic weeks. All up, we spent less than $5,000, which I was of course delighted with, although alas, I didn't escape with being quite so cheap on the engagement ring.

Of course, weddings are a highly personal occasion, and we all quite rightly determine their value to us personally. Just remember, wedding loans can take a heck of a long time to pay back, and the total amount you pay back, depending on the interest rate, is likely to be significantly greater than the loan principal.

Children

Demographic studies show that couples are having children later than they used to. This statistic could be of assistance to young investors, as it potentially presents the couple with more years of earning two incomes before they have children. The key is to capitalise on these years, when you are likely to have far fewer financial commitments, and earnestly invest your dual incomes in wealth-producing assets for the long term. It can be hugely beneficial to start investing before you have a family.

How to be successful at what you do

My first professional role was in the auditing profession. Consider a few of the viewpoints that I held in my younger years.

It would be fair to say that the large audit firms charge a lot in fees. The biggest listed companies on the stock exchange are required to be audited by the 'Big Four' accounting firms, as their financiers and stakeholders insist on it, and naturally enough the auditing firms have no interest in seeing their slice of the economic pie reduced. The value of an audit opinion is regularly questioned in the financial press due to the limited liability of audit firms and the disclaiming nature of many audit opinions. File reviews by monitoring bodies also seem at times to be of questionable value.

If there is a really almighty balls-up on the cards, the auditors – the very people who are supposed to be the honourable watchdogs of the financial system – have been suspected of pushing evidence through shredding machines (cf. Arthur Andersen, a firm that is no longer in existence). The Enron story and the tales of undiversified employees losing their entire net worth were shocking, yet not particularly surprising given the nature of the system. As I write this, Lehman Brothers have filed a lawsuit against its auditors Ernst and Young, alleging that they aided the bank in illegally moving tens of millions of dollars off balance sheet.

These are some of the ways in which I internally represented the profession to myself while I was a part of it. I held a belief system that told me that the auditing mechanism was a waste of time. So was there any chance of me being a star performer in this role? Absolutely not, because I didn't believe I was providing any value. If I was instructed by a superior to raise my client's audit fees and cite a 'change in auditing standards', or to invoice my clients more quickly because the firm was having a billing blitz, my instinctive reaction was defensive.

Some of my peers held totally different representations of the audit profession and went on to become very successful auditors. They may have been motivated by a different representation of the value they provided, the remuneration, or the kudos of being the best manager or the top technical accountant in their field. Auditing requires a certain skillset, one that I don't possess. There is an obvious and clear lesson to this: we need to be passionate, and believe in what we do.

We should always aim to add value in what we do. The path to success involves *finding ways to add more and more value to as many people as we can*. I recently read about Geoff Jowett, an ambitious personal trainer who read Napoleon Hill's *Think and Grow Rich*, which inspired him to think of ways in which he could reach more people with his message of health and fitness. He understood that to reach more people, he needed to use the power of television and newspapers, and went on to successfully launch the ubiquitous *Bodytrim* brand.

My first passion was cricket, indeed it was playing cricket for the Eastern Suburbs club in Sydney that first brought me to Australia in the 1990s. So if you asked me who the greatest ever Australian was, would I say Sir Donald Bradman? Definitely not. In my view, the greatest ever Australian was Steve Irwin. If you drive down Steve Irwin Way near Beerwah to the amazing Australia Zoo and watch the videos of Steve talking excitedly on the big screens, the *congruence* of his message is enough to make your spine tingle. This is what he says:

'Come with me. Share it with me. Share my wildlife with me, because humans want to save things they love. My passion, my mission, the reason I was put on this planet is to save wildlife... I thank you for coming with me. Yeah, let's get 'em!'

Source: Australia Zoo

With a passion as intense as that, do you think there was any way Steve Irwin could not have been a success? Highly unlikely. If you think about it, it would actually have been impossible for Steve Irwin not to have been successful because he was doing what he believed he was put on the planet to do. One of the most prevalent myths today is that success takes the form of a mountain to be scaled. In fact, by doing what you believe you are here for and behaving accordingly, you can start to be successful right this moment: today. If you do what you are passionate about, then the money will follow.

When Steve made his TV series *The Crocodile Hunter* (if you view the books of condolence at Beerwah, every single entry addresses him as 'Steve' or 'mate', showing how successfully he connected with his audience), more than 600 million people around the globe tuned in to watch, and his message genuinely changed the world. To be successful at what you do, do something you are passionate about.

Once I quit my full-time job, I realised that what I love to do is write. When I was at work, the best part of my day (apart from knocking off to head home) was composing witty and insightful emails. Some of them were even work-related. After I finished working full-time, I still spent a lot of time indulging in my love of language by writing emails, updating my blog, penning letters to my family back in England and sending postcards to friends overseas. Writing seems to be my strength, and it's also what I love doing.

One of the things I noticed while travelling around Australia was that some of the most truly successful people in our amazing country are those who have discovered their calling, people like the flying doctors who commit their lives to improving the lives of others, or the ophthalmologist Fred Hollows who devoted his life to preventing blindness in deprived children and has given the gift of eyesight to an estimated one million people[5]. Hollows was a Kiwi who became an Aussie in 1989 and was made Australian of the Year just one year later[6]! There are many ordinary yet brilliant Australians I could list here. These are the truly successful people.

Generational attitudes

The wartime generation had things tough. They believed that debt was bad and being frugal was good. In one sense, they didn't have a lot of choice. In Britain, it is often forgotten that even after World War II ended in 1945, rationing of food continued for more than half a decade[7].

The so-called baby boomer generation were a little more inclined towards taking on debt for a place of residence and working hard to pay down their mortgages by the time they reached retirement age. Early retirement was not something that was widely sought, and perhaps it was even a little frowned upon. Many people had a defined benefit pension scheme, so a normal retirement plan would be to work until the retirement age and then live on the pension benefit, which would be paid for as long as you lived.

There has been a huge shift in the pension system for my generation (christened Generation X). Defined benefit pension schemes have largely been replaced with defined contribution pension schemes. This is a monumental change in emphasis as, despite what many people seem to believe, we are now responsible for our own asset management. The generation that is younger still, known as Generation Y, is becoming known as the generation that wants it all now. People are increasingly inclined to change jobs and even careers far more quickly than ever before.

The problem appears to be that the younger generations have not yet appreciated what the change in the pension scheme system means for them. If your accumulated pension fund is meagre, inadequate or has been mismanaged by a fund manager, then that is your problem, and your only alternative will be the meagre age pension provided by the government. Many people do not invest at all outside of their compulsory superannuation contributions, and this could prove to be a huge mistake. A significant number of people don't buy their own property as a place of residence either. This may prove to be a disastrous financial plan.

A cursory glance at the superannuation statistics for Australia makes for terrifying reading. Many superannuation balances are so inadequate for retirement needs as to be almost farcical.

How to save a deposit or start investing

It is often said that it is 'impossible' for young people today to get on to the property ladder. Not true. It is unquestionably difficult, but it is not impossible. We should be wary of the language that we feed to our brains, for if we tell ourselves that a goal is impossible, we will subconsciously not even attempt to achieve the goal, and we will surely fail. Firstly, it needs to be accepted that we do not buy our dream home as our first property. That has never happened for any generation, and it certainly won't happen today. My parents' first house, for example, cost £4,250. Two years before they bought it, they looked at one in a far superior location for £2,500 but they felt it was far too expensive (and then, of course, over the following two years values boomed). There was nothing much wrong with the house they bought, but it certainly wasn't their dream house.

At the age of 21, my now wife bought a two-bedroom house for the princely sum of £72,000 (which at the time equated to around $200,000) that had been repossessed and looked like an opium den inside, with wiring hanging from the ceiling and mould in the bath. She then suffered a string of itinerant lodgers for years, and for half a decade it was decorated with borrowed or second-hand furniture and rugs. A perception that things were far easier for previous generations is misguided and unhelpful. I was a fair few years older when I bought my first property, and although it was very spacious and cost a lot more ($500,000), I can tell you, it most certainly was not my dream property.

Property in Australia is unquestionably expensive, but it seems that often, my generation (Generation X) and the younger generations are totally unrealistic in their expectations of life. It appears that because someone was perhaps the clever kid in school or did well at university, they expect to walk into executive roles without doing the hard yards to get there. Often, people want to believe that because they have the title Manager or Director, which makes Mummy and Daddy proud, they have some kind of divine right to live like James Packer.

Quite simply, this is not the way of the modern world, and it was not the way of the old world either. The wealthy are those who own successful value-creating businesses, big share portfolios and multiple properties. Often, the wealth has been passed down and inherited from previous generations. Average middle managers and single-income executives on highly taxed salaries are destined for the average suburbs. They may not like it, but that is the reality: only those people who add the most value get to own the finest houses in the best suburbs.

If you want to live like a multi-millionaire, you have to somehow add millions in value. It is very, very difficult to add millions in value as an employee, because your own time is limited, and each day you have to go back to work afresh. Your income is linear.

I have lost count of the times I have had conversations over the last 15 years with migrating Poms and South Africans that go like this:

THEM: *Property in Australia is so expensive! The world has gone mad. It's unsustainable. It has to crash soon, so I'll think about buying then.*

ME: *Where have you looked?*

THEM: *Sydney.*

ME: *Well, Sydney is the most expensive city at the moment.*

THEM: *Well, we want to live in Sydney. And we want a four-bedroom house.*

ME: *Fair enough. Where have you looked?*

THEM: *Heaps of places. Bronte, Clovelly, Coogee. Heaps of places.*

ME: *Those are the expensive suburbs, I agree.*

THEM: *Well, we want to live by the best beaches and close to the city. And we want a pool. And ideally a view of Bronte beach and the ocean…you know, back home, we could buy a four-bedroom….*

It is noteworthy that I have not once met an Aussie in London who planned to buy a luxury pad in Mayfair or South Kensington as their first step on to the property ladder. Not once. No, mostly they head to Earl's Court, perhaps later relocating a step or two up the property ladder from there. The world has moved on, and Australia is no longer a poor relation to the mother country. Australia is ideally located in the Asia-Pacific region to capitalise on the growth of China and the shift in power from West to East. With the mineral wealth located on this continent, there is no reason why Australia cannot become a major economic powerhouse over the next few decades. The term 'The Lucky Country' was once partly used ironically; now, Australia may well truly be the lucky country.

Due to the low yields of these types of higher-end properties in Australia, it is perfectly possible to rent them for far less than it would cost you in monthly mortgage payments if you bought them. It is also possible to buy perfectly good investment properties in parts of the country for less than $100,000 with a deposit of $5,000–$10,000. We do not have to invest in the suburb, or even the state, we live in. Here is yet another idea: club together with a friend and invest in a property together.

Others will say that they cannot afford to invest at all, but we can start investing in shares with as little as a couple of thousand dollars. Indeed, we can begin investing with even less than that. We can take an evening job to earn some extra dollars. I used to wash dishes, and then when I was old enough I worked as a barman, and then I worked for 12 months in a timber yard, before returning in my university holidays to push timber through a machine on and off for a further three years. Warren Buffett was once a paper boy who ran multiple rounds and began investing the proceeds.

If you are not prepared to entertain the idea of a couple of extra shifts, then this may be an indication that this is not the book or the plan for you. Every investor started somewhere. Success involves some sacrifice, and nothing that is worth having comes easily. The key is to associate pleasure with the achievement of saving towards your goal, and pain with frivolous spending on unnecessary items.

How about gym membership and personal trainers? This is a cost we can easily save on if we want to. During my travels, I discovered that by buying a resistance band and a kettlebell for $100 and using the power of focus in my exercise and nutrition, I can achieve just as good a physique in just fifteen minutes of exercise per day as I ever obtained from spending many hundreds of hours in the gym.

For cardiovascular exercise, if you live in the outer suburbs or the regions, you are lucky – you have the great outdoors as your gym. A brisk walk is the most wonderful exercise you can do, better still if you have a mate or partner to walk with; you can have meaningful conversations that rarely seem to happen in front of a television. If you live in the inner suburbs of a city, try drawing a 10 km radius around your unit or house on a map and power-walk to some suburbs you might like to invest in. My wife and I have done this for the last seven years. If at first your friends laugh at you or think you have lost the plot, I can guarantee you they will have a different reaction when you tell them you have just bought your tenth investment property.

Then, you may hear people start to say things like:

The property market is overvalued and is going to crash

I like my job anyway – I'd be bored without it

You were very lucky

I'd be scared to have that much debt.

Another thing I hear people say is that they do not have time to invest, but we all have 24 hours in a day and seven days in a week, Richard Branson, Bill Gates and George Soros included, so by definition that cannot be true. What this statement really means is that they are prioritising other activities over investing. If that is the case, then that is fine, but it is definitely not the same thing as not having the time to invest.

Set yourself a decent period of time for saving investment capital. People often underestimate what they can achieve because they want results instantly and do not allow themselves time to succeed. If you can save $500 in a month, then over three years you will have saved $18,000 in capital, and if it has been invested wisely, this will have increased in value to significantly more. The government has introduced a savings account scheme for first home buyers whereby the government will add contributions to your account and tax income at a low rate. Check out the rules on the ATO's website[8].

I don't need to insult your intelligence by writing a long list of items, from cosmetics to coffee to Chinese food, on which you can cut down expenditure. Using common sense and identifying where your extravagant expenditure lies should be enough. I'm going to mention one major bugbear of mine, though – iPhones.

I often hear people complain that it is impossible to save for a home deposit, but when I ask them what kind of iPhone bill they receive, it is invariably more than $300 a month. That is $3,600 a year coming straight out of their after-tax salary. When I suggest that they use a $29 cap with a basic phone (as I still do), they insist that is not a possibility. At this point, sympathy evaporates. What we are then discussing is not an inability to save towards a home deposit, but a prioritising of mobile phone status over taking responsibility for your financial future. That's a different discussion. Not interested, sorry.

Practical Action Points

- Prepare a personal balance sheet: a summary of your assets and liabilities. Note whether the assets column has many depreciating assets, such as cars, and consider how you can fill it with appreciating assets that bring growth and funds back to you. Do you have debt for depreciating items or credit card debts? How can you devise a plan to reduce these as quickly as possible?

- Prepare a simple personal monthly income statement summarising your typical income and expenditure. Is your income linear and all from one source, namely a highly taxed salary? What are the major expenditure items? Do have significant expenditure on luxuries that can be reduced? Does much of your income get spent on debt repayment? Consider how you can have funds left over at the end of the month that you can invest in *appreciating assets* that will create wealth for you.

- Consider whether you can stop all direct debits and standing order payments. Get rid of those you don't need, and replace the required payments with cheque payments. The simple act of writing a cheque can make the payment feel more 'real' and help you to form a new attitude towards expenses.

- Resolve to never purchase consumer goods or luxuries on finance again.

- Devise a repayment plan to clear your bad debts. Start by paying off the debts with the highest interest rates, such as consumer debt and credit cards, and work down towards those with the lowest rates of interest. Once you have cleared all of your bad debts, you are ready to start investing.

- With your bad debts cleared, divert excess funds into a new bank account to build yourself a buffer. Two months of salary might be a good starting point.

- Start living below your means *today*!

- Recondition your thinking – wealth is created through investing in appreciating assets and *reinvesting* the returns.

4
WIRING FOR
SUCCESS:
The Power of Mindset

4

Open your mind

'The most expensive thing you can have is a closed mind[1].'

In my view, mindset is the most important factor in becoming financially successful. An investor with the right mindset will always achieve wealth. Too many people believe deep down that they will not achieve their goals, and therefore their actions do not allow them to succeed.

Back in the days when Poms were still rather good at stuff, a man called Roger Bannister ran the first ever sub-four-minute mile. He had trained his brain to visualise himself running a 3:59 time over and over again until he simply *knew* he could do it[2]. The curious thing about this story is that before the feat was achieved, it was widely believed that this was an impossible goal for a human body, that perhaps the body would somehow expire or even explode[3]. Within one year of Bannister's record-breaking run, 30 people had run a sub-four-minute mile, and within two years no fewer than 300 had done so[4]. It was not that people could not physically break the barrier; it was that until Bannister, nobody *believed* it could be done.

To succeed in achieving the goal of becoming wealthy and financially free, you first need to *believe* that you can achieve the goal. In life, it is nearly always more important how we respond to events than what actually happens to us. Having an unshakeable belief that you can reach your goal will mean that, whatever happens, you will always pick yourself up and continue on your course to financial freedom. The second key is the 'why'. The 'why' for me was twofold: I wanted to split my time between living in two countries and I wanted not to have to work for someone else. I realised when I was in my mid-twenties that working for someone else and relying on an employer to make you wealthy is a dangerous strategy.

Challenging preconceptions

Here is a preconception I once held: I unquestioningly ate meat for the first 30 years of my life. Why? Because my parents did and so did everyone else I knew, I suppose. Vegetarians and vegans were both chided and misguided. For years, it didn't occur to me that the fact that I would never knowingly kill a living creature myself was a value that was not congruent with being a meat eater.

Eventually, I opened my mind and researched nutrition for myself (if you are interested, take a look for yourself; what you will discover is enlightening, riveting and rather revolting), and have not eaten meat or fish since. Open your mind. Challenging preconceptions is not only a good exercise, it is a key for success in any field. Life and success therein is a continual learning process.

Many people at least subconsciously believe that they will always be reliant upon a job. As a result, they do not try to save and invest or take actions that would allow them to become financially free. Their subconscious belief becomes self-fulfilling. In order to achieve financial freedom, it is vital that you challenge any preconceptions you may have that this cannot be achieved.

The ugliest word in the English language

Remember that Henry Ford quote? 'Whether you believe you can or believe you can't, you're right.' It is so true. Have you ever had or heard a conversation that echoes the one below? Of course, the details may change, but the underlying message is often the same.

- I hate my job. It makes me morose and I've never got any money left over at the end of the month.
- Why don't you quit then?
- I *can't*. I have to work there!
- Well, you don't *have* to work anywhere. Nobody is forcing you to. We live in a free country after all.
- I have bills to pay, and my car loans. And you know about that holiday I put on my credit card. I told you about that.
- Couldn't you get a job somewhere else?
- No, I *can't*. It's impossible. I mean, where would I work?
- I don't know…what would you most like to do? If you could do anything?
- Well, you know I love sport. I'd probably be a sports teacher. Or a swim coach.
- Why not do that?
- *What?* Have you gone *mad?* I *can't*. My wife would never let me do that. I would earn less.
- Have you discussed it with her?

- No. No point. She would never allow it.

o Why don't you think about a business? Or invest in some shares or an index fund perhaps?

- Not a chance. There is a double-dip recession on the way. It's all doom and gloom. My mate John over in London told me. He knows about this stuff.

o I see. How about property then? You could save a deposit for an investment property.

- No way. I was talking to this Irish guy down at the pub and he is convinced the government will release thousands of acres of land soon.

o In Sydney? Really? Where exactly?

- Just around Sydney. House prices can't stay this high, they are definitely unsustainable. They are going to collapse by 50% any day now…

The conversation could go on for weeks (and has taken place somewhere every year for decades), but the outcome would be the same. The saddest thing about this is that this person will quite possibly die doing that same miserable job he hates. All because of that one word – can't. That is why *can't* is the ugliest word in the English language. Consider for a moment this question: have you ever met or heard of a rich pessimist?

The doomsayers will always be there, in every newspaper, in every online discussion and in every pub. The best thing you can do is ignore them. Every day in every market you care to name – property, gold, silver, shares, bonds, pork bellies, coffee futures, currencies – someone with a high level of financial education is making a very handsome profit. The doomsayers will maintain their views to the end, and in the end there is nothing surer than that they will have achieved precisely nothing. Even if the world order does collapse and new fortunes are made, it will not be by them.

The doomsayers

'Keep away from people who belittle your ambitions, little people always do that..but the really great make you believe that you too can be great.' – Mark Twain

Ah, the doomsayers. They are always there. Every step of the way to your financial freedom there will be those who try to hold you back, who caution, chide, sneer, laugh or tell you that you are doing the wrong thing. Sometimes in investment books these people are referred to as 'dream stealers'. If you are ever going to achieve financial freedom, you must be able to overcome these people and their negative comments. In his book *Accidental Millionaire*, property investor Steve Fagan identified how you can instantly recognise a person that he would term a 'dream stealer'[5]:

> 'When you share your goals or dreams with these people,
> you will feel bad about the conversation afterwards,
> and you may begin to doubt yourself[6].'

This is an insightful definition, and in my experience an absolutely correct one. Fagan goes on to note that this category of people can be broken down into two types. Firstly, there are those who are well-meaning in their advice[7]: they are genuinely concerned for you and are worried that by getting into areas that they themselves do not understand (i.e. investment), you are exposing yourself to a grave risk. This group of people can include your closest friends and family, and very often, your spouse. Different attitudes to money and financial risk profiles are known to be a huge cause of tension in personal relationships. Fears can be allayed through education and open discussion, but the process can be an undeniably difficult one.

The second group of people is rather more sinister; those who simply want you to fail[8]. They may not actually say those words, but nevertheless, that is the case. It is a curious phenomenon that many people simply cannot bear the thought of others having more than they do; the prospect makes them uneasy.

I'm no psychoanalyst (although my mother is; perhaps I should ask her) but my understanding is that this is a result of feelings of inadequacy and jealousy. It is quite likely that this attitude is also caused by a mindset of scarcity rather than one of abundance – if someone else has more, there must be less for me. Either way, it is a mean-spirited and deeply unpleasant personality trait, and the suggested remedy is simply to avoid discussing your finances or goals with any such people.

How to believe the impossible is possible

If you don't believe you can achieve something then you will not attempt it with full enthusiasm, and you will likely not achieve it. It is crucial that you believe you can escape the rat race if you want to achieve that particular goal. Here is a powerful three-step technique to enable you to believe that the impossible is possible. Firstly, write down a list of your three biggest phobias, be they public speaking, heights, confined spaces or whatever. Secondly, rationalise the fears by learning about them and getting to understand them better. Thirdly and finally, devise and carry out a plan to confront your fears.

Anthony Robbins uses this technique in his live seminars by having the attendees complete a fire walk across a bed of hot coals[9]. Does Robbins care whether people can walk on smouldering charcoal or not? No, not really. He cares whether they can achieve something that they previously thought to be impossible, and the avenues that this will open for them in the future[10].

I had three phobias in particular. I was terrified of flying, I had avoided the dentist for nearly 15 years and – the biggest of all of my phobias – I had a pathological fear of snakes. Most Poms who migrate to Australia have a fear of snakes of course, but my fear was beyond rational; I was totally and utterly terrified of them. What I did first was to learn how to understand animal behaviour patterns. Then I travelled to Queensland to seek out a photo opportunity with the biggest snake I could find, and now I have a treasured picture of myself with a gigantic five-metre python draped around my neck. These days, I love snakes, and am always the first to volunteer for photos at the zoo.

So, I am no longer afraid of snakes, but, far more important than having been half-throttled by a reptile weighing as much as myself is that I now believe I can tackle any problem that I am dealt. Incidentally, my fear of the dentist was solved for me when I needed a double root canal (and couldn't endure the pain any longer) and the fear of flying simply receded, as I often flew to mine sites for work and eventually rationalised the risks. One closing word on this subject: this is only a useful technique if you actually go out and take action. Reading about it on this page is not enough!

The roadmap to wealth

Believe it or not, there is a proven pathway to achieving wealth. This topic has been covered many times by many authors, from Wallace D. Wattles to John R. Burley, Robert Kiyosaki, Napoleon Hill and many, many more. For that reason, I want to keep this section brief. With due regards to the authors listed above and many others who have covered this subject, here are some of the key rules of wealth and how they relate to this book in particular.

Add more value

We have probably all heard the saying that if you give then you shall receive. Like many such sayings, there is a heck of a lot of truth in it. If friends ask me to do some accounting work for them, I would not dream of charging them for it, and it is true that they have always given back to me without fail. What comes back is not necessarily received in kind, but receive you will. The first thing my wife and I did when we quit our jobs was go to Queensland to work on the Cyclone Yasi disaster relief for a short time. It was unpaid work, but so much more satisfying than working for oneself.

In your employment field, whatever that may be, you should also strive to add as much value as you can. You should add more value than you receive and aim to make yourself priceless. In some jobs, it may seem impossible to add more value, but it is important to think laterally in order to add as much value to your employer as possible. Perhaps you can simply become more efficient. People often think in terms of entitlement – that they should get paid more each year regardless of whether they have added more value. This is a dangerous strategy, and one that could eventually see you looking for a new job.

Napoleon Hill advocated that in order to achieve wealth, we should aim to add to as much value as we can to as many people as we can. Think about the service we provide, and brainstorm ideas about how we can reach more people. If we can't think of any ways we can do this, think harder, he said[11].

These same principles can be extended to your investing. I have read of property investors who will not spend on furnishings for their tenants, and invest in cheap, run-down properties that they would not live in themselves with a goal of grinding out a positive cash flow of $50 or less a week.

I have certain rules in property that I abide by. I will not rent out any property that I would not be prepared to live in myself (indeed, I have lived in several of my own properties at various times), and I always say 'yes' to any sensible requests for repairs. Could I have saved a few dollars over the years? In the short term, yes I could have. However, most of my tenants sign up for repeat leases and I have never had an extended vacancy in any of my properties, so in the longer term it's a win-win situation for landlord and tenant. If you want to create more value for yourself, first create value for others.

Think big – and see the big picture

Property investor, businessman and author Michael Yardney says that the rich see the big picture while the poor only see problems in the detail[12]. Before Donald Trump started telling people that they were fired, the catchphrase he was known for was 'Think big!' It is important to have a big goal and to write it down. I have a goal of taking my portfolio of assets past $10 million in value before I am 40. I may or may not achieve the goal, but the results will surely be better than they would be if I had no goal at all. As they say, aim for the stars and you may hit the moon.

An example of someone not seeing the big picture would be a person who says, 'Investing in shares is a lottery; whether they go up or down is a 50/50 guess. There is so much insider trading it is impossible to know.' They are focussing only on the short term, and have closed off their mind to the idea of investing. As a result, they will never succeed financially in shares. If they took the time to look at historical charts of stock exchange performance from around the world, they would see that the odds of making money in shares are not just as simple as the chances of tossing a head or a tail.

The uptrend in stock markets has been running for decades. This is in part driven by inflation, and can sometimes be impacted by survivorship bias in the data, but the uptrend is a definite one. The lesson to learn here is that the longer your time horizon for an investment, the lower the risk can be.

Alternatively, you may hear a property investor who focuses on cash flow say, 'If the cash flow is even $5 a week negative, we must move on.' They could miss out on some of the finest property investments they will ever find for the sake of a measly few dollars a year. They have totally missed the big picture.

Pay yourself first and invest in appreciating assets

We cannot save our way to wealth, as taxes and inflation eat away at the value of our savings. Although cash in the bank does provide an income in the form of interest, this income is at a low rate due to the low-risk nature of a bank account, and it is taxable. Cash also provides no capital growth, and therefore in an inflationary environment, each year your cash is worth less. Inflation may not seem to be too damaging over a year, but over time the effect on the purchasing power of your cash is crippling. Think back to when you first saved what seemed like a decent sum of money (I remember as a child saving one English pound). Are you glad you spent it, or do you wish you had held on to it in the bank?

It is also very difficult to invest with what is left over at the end of the month. Take at least 10 to 20% (or more if you can) of your net pay and immediately invest it in assets that provide a high average rate of return. Do so before you spend money on anything else. This is known as *paying yourself first*. I will discuss the best asset classes in which to invest later in the book. Adhere to this rule, invest in the right assets and, eventually, you will become wealthy.

Focus on assets, not income

Why do most people focus so much on chasing an ever-higher salary? It is probably because they have been conditioned to believe that this is their only available path to wealth. Unfortunately, the government takes away a huge slice of your salaried income before you even see it, and the rest is quickly spent. Take a look at the *BRW Rich List* and see how many of the 100 richest people in Australia made it to the top from their salary. Answer: zero. The key to attaining wealth is to build a portfolio of appreciating assets and hold on to them for the long term. Wealth will follow.

Don't follow the crowd

There is an old saying that if you do what everyone else does, you will get the same results as everyone else. Warren Buffett famously advocated being fearful when others were greedy...and vice versa. You have probably heard that quotation. Another way of saying this is that we should invest *counter-cyclically*, i.e. don't follow the crowd. In respect, of the stock market, we should be cognisant of Dow Theory and the cycles of the market, and be looking to buy when most investors are totally despondent. Likewise, in property we should aim to buy at the bottom of the property cycle when buyers (and sellers) are fearful and bargains abound.

Become a specialist

Modern portfolio theory advocates that we should diversify in order to mitigate risk. On the face of it, this is sensible advice. However, diversifying too broadly leads to a lack of specialist knowledge and necessarily average results. I am going to suggest that while we should aim to have a portfolio that encompasses a range of asset classes, we will need to specialise in one of them in order to outperform. Just as a specialist doctor or physician gets paid more than a general practitioner, the investor who learns to specialise can command higher returns on his capital.

Reinvest your profits

Anthony Robbins says that your ability to grow wealth quickly is directly related to the rate at which you reinvest your profits[13]. He is absolutely right. The reason is because this approach allows you to capitalise on the miraculous power of compound growth[14] (essentially, a snowballing effect of your wealth), a phenomenon that will be considered in more detail in later chapters.

The effect of compounding growth when you start out in investing may seem to be insignificant, but as your assets grow over time, the effects can be truly staggering. That is why Albert Einstein said that the most powerful force in the universe is compound interest.

You will need to adjust your mindset. One of the main reasons why the majority of people never achieve wealth is that they have a mindset dictating to them that if they come into money it must be spent, usually on items that they don't need and will be of no value in the long term. Have you ever seen or heard of someone receiving a significant inheritance only for them to have spent it within a year or two? This happens where the recipient has no context for investing the funds.

Protect your wealth

The final part of the wealth-creation mindset is to protect your wealth. There are several key steps to wealth protection:

- Holding on to the assets we build and **not selling** them

- Holding assets in an appropriate **structure**

- **Insuring** our assets and income

- Having an appropriate **plan** for changes in circumstances.

One of the reasons why so few people become wealthy is that they feel that in order to realise wealth from investment they need to sell their assets. This is not necessarily the case, and I will demonstrate in this book how holding on to your assets can still allow you to improve your cash flow and your lifestyle.

I do not provide specific or direct advice to individuals on structures, such as whether to hold assets in your own name, jointly with your spouse, in companies or in trusts, because this subject is beyond the scope of this book. However, be aware that there are structures that you can use to protect your assets from lawsuits and similar threats. This is a subject best discussed with your accountant or financial advisor. Just be wary that your accountant doesn't try to sell you a complicated trust structure that you don't necessarily need, and then charge you handsomely for setting it up.

Do note that while a company may be the ideal set-up for running a business due to the limitation of liability and tax benefits, it may not be ideal for some forms of investment (for example, a company doesn't qualify for the 50% capital gains tax discount).

There are many, many types of insurance that can be taken out to protect your assets and to protect your income. You probably already have some of them, such as home insurance, health insurance, life insurance and auto cover to name a few. As an investor you may require further types of insurance, such as landlord insurance for a property investor. You may also have other forms of insurance as a share investor, such as the use of sell stops or put options to insure your portfolio against dramatic adverse movements.

This is a huge topic, and space does not permit a full discussion of every type of insurance you may wish to consider. Speak to a financial planner if you are unsure, and they will be able to help you ensure that you have all the cover you need.

Finally, as we will all die sometime, we should consider estate planning. I haven't found any firm statistics for Australia, but if America is a useful guideline, then fewer than 50% of people die with a will in place. Here are some of the reasons why people do not have a will:

- Haven't got around to it yet
- Have not considered it
- Unwilling to face important issues
- Think they are too young
- Believe they have insufficient assets to make it worthwhile.

Guess what? We're all going to die, so we should have a will. If you don't, then your assets may not end up being passed on in the manner you intended. If you are cohabiting or married, it is also important to consider what might happen if your relationship circumstances change. They can and do.

Obstacles to attaining goals

Every one of us has obstacles that are stopping us from achieving everything we want. There is a very simple three-step plan that the most successful people consciously or intuitively use to overcome obstacles to success:

1. Identify and accept the obstacles
2. Devise a plan to overcome them
3. Implement the plan.

My main obstacle to success was alcohol. Intoxicants, apart from costing an extortionate amount of money and giving one an unfortunate tendency to talk gibberish to strangers, are a big impediment to success. There are few more lethal killers of motivation than a binge drinker's hangover.

I was never going to succeed at anything (other than perhaps being a complete numbat) unless I overcame my hedonistic lifestyle. Observe the most successful people. Do they regularly snort cocaine, binge drink or smoke 40 cigarettes a day in order to change the way they feel? Rarely. What is more likely is that they associate pleasure with success and application to their chosen field and pain with wasting time and health through the use of narcotics.

Everyone will have different obstacles. It might be your spouse or friends and family that hold you back, your own lack of self-belief or any number of other factors. It has been suggested that some people are uncomfortable with success, and therefore subconsciously sabotage it. It does seem to be the case that for most people, they reach a level of net worth that they are comfortable with and then they appear to plateau or fall. *Raising* your self-esteem is vital.

Certainly, it is well documented that most people who receive a monetary windfall manage to rid themselves of it in a remarkably short space of time. This is because they do not have a mechanism in place for investing or holding on to the funds. Anthony Robbins refers to this as 'holes in their financial foundations'[15]. Sometimes, lottery winners panic after buying two new cars and a luxury holiday, and then spend a huge percentage of their dwindling winnings on a house because they fear they will have spent the lot within a year. The windfall often creates as much or more pain than it does joy.

One common obstacle to property investing is a fear of debt. You may hear people say that they would not be comfortable with having debt related to investment property. The same people often have mortgages on their own homes (and often car loans and credit card debt too), so the argument lacks logic. So long as the mortgage value is less than the value of the property, and the property is appreciating in value, I'll accept any money that the banks give to me.

Have you ever heard it said that successful people have ideas that are opposite to those of the crowd? This is an example – successful investors and businessmen love debt, because it affords them ever greater opportunities to create wealth.

Modelling and mentors

Anthony Robbins has written some outstanding works that are an excellent read for those seeking success in their lives. His books are user manuals for your brain and for your life. One of the key concepts he advocates is *modelling*. This involves the seemingly simple strategy of finding a mentor who has achieved what you want to achieve and following their plans and actions. Obviously, this idea has some limitations, for you can't know what your chosen mentor is thinking at all times. However, you should be able to learn a lot from what has and has not worked for them, and save yourself from having to reinvent the wheel.

One very important caveat to this is to choose your mentors wisely. There are many investing books and prospective mentors out there. One of the key things I look for, whether I am reading advice on shares, property or wealth creation, is the author's *track record*. You want to know that the author has successfully followed the advice that he or she is advocating.

I recently read a share-investment book that ended with a note from the author promising that he is soon planning to begin using the techniques he had advocated to make himself wealthy. Even Robbins himself, who frequently dispenses sage-like relationship advice, neglects to note that he has been married twice and had a baby with a third woman. I'm not 100% convinced by the suspiciously rotund Dr Phil's never-ending dieting advice either, but perhaps we are getting off subject here!

There are a huge number of books available on investing in shares in Australia, and I have read nearly all of them. Actually, this is not quite true, as I don't always read books that refer to the most famous ever investor 'Warren Buffet'. There are a fair few of these around, but I take the view that if the author cannot be bothered to learn how to spell Buffett's name correctly, then it is unlikely that they will have many earth-shattering viewpoints on finance either. A strange rule, perhaps, but one I usually adhere to.

The property market has many different kinds of spruikers promising almost instant wealth through various schemes. Avoid these. Good books to avoid often include those that are touting a recently discovered fad or angle, as the best investors are almost invariably those who have honed their skills over decades of experience. Remember that often, authors of property investment books have businesses in the industry, and are therefore often extremely bullish and refer to few or none of the risks of property investing. There is little to be gained from reading marketing documents targeted at sucking ever-more people into property investment regardless of the price.

The Internet can be a useful source of information, including forums. However, be wary of sponsored links that continually preach doom and gloom, and those that promise you almost instant wealth. Wealth is something that is built over time. Sponsored links have often been paid for by authors who are serving their own agendas. Try to steer clear of websites upon which an innocent or inadvertent click anywhere on the screen sentences you to at least an email per day until the end of time (replete with prerequisite poor spelling – 'Hi Peter do u want 2 invest like Warren Buffet' (*sic*)).

Finally, remember to be healthily sceptical. Be particularly wary of seminars that invite you to part with thousands of dollars for the privilege of attendance. If you are spending a significant sum, you need to be certain you are getting value for your money, and not just advice that you could find in your local bookstore. The only way to be sure is to check with independent people who have completed the course as to whether they believed it offered value. It goes almost without saying that the testimonials section on the promoter's website is not the best place to check.

Market gurus and the search for the 'Holy Grail'

As investors, many of us have a psychological need to latch on to a market guru or find an investment system that we can turn to in order to absolve ourselves from making difficult decisions. We all need to acknowledge that there is no one fail-safe system that we can rely upon to succeed all of the time. It does not exist.

In respect of market gurus, there are many intelligent commentators that we can learn from. However, what we should be wary of are those who try to make market or economic environment predictions. Humans love to make predictions, and yet we are notoriously very poor at them. There is nothing wrong with making a prediction, but we should not have an investment approach that relies upon a specific market prediction being correct.

A peculiar arena is that of the market commentators who make predictions and then later subtly amend their views when they prove to be incorrect. If by chance they get a prediction right, they will dine out on their correct 'calling' of market conditions until the next prediction, which they then call incorrectly. As new generations of investors arrive on the scene, the cycle repeats itself endlessly. The bottom line is that there is no point placing any reliance upon market predictions, because they are so often wrong.

In the property market in 2009, we were apparently due for 'the mother of all property booms', by 2010 this had turned into a 'mid-cycle slowdown' and by 2011 it had become 'a new market phase, a definite downturn' – all of these viewpoints from the same commentators.

In relation to the share market, in the middle of 2011 I received a number of phone calls and emails from stockbrokers telling me that now was *definitely* the time to invest in shares and *definitely not* the time to invest in property. Of course, they picked the top of the market almost to the exact day, preempting a 20% plummet in stock valuations. Naturally enough, there was then further mail imploring me that now bargains were abounding in the market, it was an excellent time to buy in. The specifics change; the dynamics repeat themselves.

In respect of the economy in general, we had self-congratulatory market commentators and inflation hawks as late as August 2011 calling that 2–3 interest rate rises by the end of the year were a 'near certainty', and yet within a fortnight, the markets were pricing in no fewer than six rate cuts for the following 18 months. Cue rapid changing of tune. Confusing? If you spend too much time listening to predictions, very.

In summary, there is no problem with listening to market predictions, but if you have an investment strategy that relies upon these predictions being accurate, you may eventually end up with a financial disaster on your hands. Instead, what we should aim for is an investment plan for the long term that will withstand short-term market gyrations.

Procrastination

Why do people procrastinate when it comes to investing? Intellectually, I suspect that most people know they should invest, but most people make very poor plans for their financial futures, if they even plan at all.

Here are a few of the reasons why people delay investing:

- Fear of failure
- They are impossibly disorganised
- They are 'doing fine' without investing
- Marital disagreements
- People may feel too incompetent to invest
- An inability to face serious issues
- They 'can't afford to invest'.

Fear of failure

It is human nature to have a fear of the unknown, and for many people, investment is an unknown quantity. Many people are afraid of investing for fear of losing substantial amounts of money, or worse, being conned out of it. This is natural, as none of us wants to lose what we have worked hard for, or appear foolish. The fear comes from a lack of clear understanding of the risks of investing. Fortunately, there are easy ways to begin investing in a low-risk manner with little or no risk of loss of capital. Then, as you learn more, you may begin to feel comfortable taking on more risk.

Impossibly disorganised

We probably all know people who are totally disorganised, seem incapable of arranging their affairs and never look at their bank statements. They often appear to be busy or scatterbrained people with a short attention span and no appetite for detail. There can be any number of causes, such as stressful jobs, addictions or relationship problems, but these are habits that can potentially be 'un-learned' relatively quickly.

Generally, people are not keen to look at bills, credit card statements and bank statements because they fear that they will bring only bad news. However, not looking at them will not improve the news they bring. The good news is that once you begin to take your finances more seriously, looking at bank statements and investment accounts automatically begins to bring you pleasure rather than pain.

'Doing fine'

This is perhaps the most common thing I see in young professionals of today: an attitude that they don't really need to invest because they are earning a good salary and intend to earn a higher salary in the future. I believe that this attitude partly comes from a misunderstanding of how wealth is created. Many of us have been taught to work as hard as we can and earn the highest salary we can get, but the taxation system is loaded against us achieving wealth in this manner.

How many people do you know who spend every dollar they earn, and sometimes more? A fair few, I expect. There is a dangerous tendency towards consumerism in the modern world. Too many of us believe that money should be earned and then spent on depreciating assets such as cars, big televisions and other toys. While these items give the impression of wealth, they do not create wealth. Instead, they destroy it. Sometimes, it seems that people feel rich if they have a large amount of cash in their pocket. The problem with this is that cash in the pocket tends to get spent unwisely.

Marital disagreements

Money and finances cause a huge amount of tension in some marriages, particularly where spouses have different attitudes, risk profiles and priorities in life. When it comes to investing, it is certain that you and your spouse will have a different attitude to risk, because every person is different. This can be problematic where one party has a very strong aversion to risk and the other is naturally a gambler or drawn to high-risk investments. The solution to this situation is to be open, discuss an agreed plan of action and stick to the agreed plan.

Feel too incompetent

This is related to the fear of failing, and the remedy is education. Generally, in life, people feel afraid or nervous when they do not know what they are doing. Therefore, by educating yourself, the fear and feelings of incompetence will diminish.

Inability to face serious issues

As we have noted, many people do not have a written will, and this is indicative of an unwillingness to confront serious issues such as financial welfare, retirement and death. Many people, therefore, adopt an attitude of living for the day and relieving stress through impulsive spending, known as *retail therapy*. While there is a tendency for peers to admire such a carefree attitude, it is not smart to fail to plan for your future.

'Can't afford it'

There is sometimes a misconception that it takes a lot of money to start investing, but it definitely does not. We can begin to make a difference to our finances *today* through cutting down on expenditure and saving a small pool of cash, perhaps in a separate bank account. This is a good way to start – simply by reducing consumer debt, and saving a small pool of funds. It really does not take much capital per month to begin an investment plan, so please do not be misled into believing that it does.

Preconceptions about wealthy people

Most of us have some preconceptions about the nature of wealthy people, even if it is on a subconscious level. I know that in my family whilst I was growing up, there was an unspoken feeling that wealthy people or wealthy family members were somehow to be mistrusted, they were likely to be greedy and that there was something vaguely unethical about having wealth. In fact, my mother still believes this ('Well, they get hold of money and then keep hold of it!'). You should understand that you are unlikely to move towards a wealthy life, and certainly less likely to become wealthy, if this is reflective of your mindset.

Here is a list of some of the things I used to care about when I was working in my full-time job: my bonus, my friends' bonuses, my pay review, my friends' pay reviews, my promotion prospects, 'coffee-pot seminars[16]' (who is sleeping with whom), social media networking, having the best holiday, having the best car…the list could go on and on, but you get the picture. These are interests that characterise and reflect a self-centred and narrow-minded view of life. If I was being brutally honest, there was a part of me that found a modicum of comfort in the failure of others too, which is a sure sign of a person who views the world with a mindset of scarcity rather than one of abundance.

Here are some things I *now* care about that while I was on the corporate treadmill saw little or none of my attention: wildlife conservation, climate change, travelling the world, experiencing something new every day, renewable energy, health and nutrition, reading as widely as I can, charitable giving, voluntary work, my nieces, history…the full list would now include dozens of varied and interesting subjects. And I'm a far more rounded, more generous and more interesting person for it.

The underlying point is that while we may have a subconscious belief that the wealthy are greedy and uncaring people, the reality is that the reverse is often true. Mixed subconscious beliefs lead to mixed results. In order to attain the results we desire, we need to rid ourselves of limiting preconceptions and replace them with beliefs that are congruent with the success we are aiming for.

Don't pretend to be wealthy, BE wealthy

In *The Millionaire Next Door*, Thomas J. Stanley and William D. Danko revealed some surprising details concerning the profiles of US millionaires in the 1990s[17]. What they discovered was that the majority of millionaire households did not have the extravagant lifestyles people tend to associate with millionaires. They found that most millionaires rarely spend large sums of money on expensive cars, consumer goods, depreciating assets and luxury items. Instead, crucially, most millionaires live below their means.

Too many people today are preoccupied with the appearance of wealth and not sufficiently concerned with building a sound financial plan. The classic scenario is where an expensive sports car is bought using debt for the purpose of impressing peers with a conspicuous sign of wealth. Beneath the surface, though, the finances are taking a battering. The opportunity cost of this choice – the potential great investments that are not made – could be huge.

Again, the challenge is to dare to take the different path. Instead of 'spending tomorrow's cash today'[18] and being a slave to your possessions, why not live frugally today and invest sensibly in appreciating assets? Tomorrow, you will have an abundance of cash instead of a poor retirement and a reliance on the age pension.

Practical Action Points

- Review your attitudes to money and any preconceptions you may hold towards wealthy people. Do you have any patterns of financial behaviour that you wish you could change?

- Consider your circle of friends and your family – are they encouraging you or do they hold you back? Be mindful of negative people and doomsayers. You do not need to ditch them as friends, but you must not allow them to unduly cloud your judgement.

- Consider joining an investment club. Remember to do your due diligence before deciding to join a club, and do not be pressured into buying any investment you are not totally comfortable with.

- Read online financial blogs (mine is quite good – and free!) and magazines, and resolve to read the financial press as often as you can. You will begin to learn the language of investment relatively quickly.

- Consider your 'why'. Why do you want to achieve financial freedom? What would your ideal day be like? Spend some time designing your ideal day and be as specific as possible (where will you be, who will you be with, what will you be doing?). If you give your brain specific goals, you can then devise a specific plan to reach these goals. The human brain is very powerful; visualising your target is an invaluable exercise.

- Read any books you can find by Anthony Robbins. You will not find everything he says useful to you, but his books are packed with information and ideas, and can only serve to improve your mindset and outlook on life.

5
CHOOSE YOUR WEAPONS:
Asset Classes

5

Asset classes

So, you have decided you are going to invest (if you haven't, I ask you to consider how long your current superannuation balance would last in retirement before you'd be broke: five years? Two years?). But what to invest in? Below is a brief summary of my thoughts on the main asset classes and their characteristics.

Cash

Have you ever been envious of friends or colleagues who could save their money? I have. I remember school friends who could save their pocket money for months on end. When I was in my teens and early twenties, you could have given me virtually any sum of money and I would have found a way to spend it. I observed with some jealousy people who could receive money and diligently put it away for a rainy day, carefully adding to their growing stockpile.

In all such cases, I look back and can draw two conclusions. Firstly, in every case the amounts of money involved seem, in today's terms, to be almost comically small. Secondly, at some point, something changed, and the savers spent their money: they needed a new car, a partner came along to help them spend it, or an emergency occurred that required funding.

There are three reasons why we cannot save our way to becoming rich. Firstly, if we attempt to save money in a bank account, it is generally the case that sooner or later it is likely that a situation will arise that results in the savings being spent. Secondly, even if we are directing the funds to an account that pays a good rate of interest, the government taxes the interest that we earn. Thirdly, and crucially, should we somehow manage to grow a savings account to, say, a $1 million balance, by the time we have done so, inflation will ensure that the funds will be worth far less than the $1 million we had in mind when we started in our quest. Compare this route to being able to, for example, borrow $1 million and invest in an asset that doubles in value.

What we need are growth asset classes that provide excellent rates of return, outperform inflation and allow compounding growth to work in our favour rather than against us. There are three principal growth asset classes that are used for the accumulation of significant wealth. These are: businesses, shares (sometimes known as *stocks or equities*) and property. Most people have a natural preference or inclination towards one of these asset classes.

Business

The richest people will always be those who own businesses. While Warren Buffett is known as a share investor, his wealth is held in the business of Berkshire Hathaway. Owning a business offers the potentially wonderful leverage of using other people's time and often other people's money to make the business owners wealthy. Businesses operate in a tax-favoured environment, as company tax is levied on the net profit of the business after legitimate deductible expenses. This is not how the tax on an employee's salary is levied. You have probably noticed that the government usually takes its cut before you see any of your pay.

It is certainly true that the richest people I know own businesses. If you aspire to be a billionaire, business is the only route to take. One of my housemates from my university days (who actually had the fine distinction of being the only student I knew who was lazier than myself) has gone on to make his millions from owning a series of successful Internet businesses and now only works a handful of hours each week. As Anthony Robbins often points out, people are not inherently lazy (or for that matter, industrious) – they may simply have impotent goals[1]. A business is a fantastic way to build wealth that can outperform inflation and benefit from compounding growth.

Ask any business owner and they will tell you that owning a business can be tough, and sometimes all-consuming. This is a book about creating more free time rather than less. Not everyone has the skills for running a business. Indeed, if you do have the natural aptitude, drive, desire and skillset to be a business owner, it is quite likely that you have already realised this and you are in business already. Note here that Robert Kiyosaki draws a distinction between those who are self-employed and those who own businesses – essentially he argues that if you are self-employed, then the money stops rolling in when you stop working.

This is not a book about setting up a limited company or corporation, leasing premises, hiring staff, firing staff and calculating workers' compensation insurance. If that is your calling and your passion, then that is truly excellent, and there are other books written by entrepreneurs that are right for you. However, this is a book about creating the precious assets of wealth and time. I am therefore going to suggest that you make property and shares your business.

Property or shares? Or both?

I will discuss both of these asset classes in detail over the forthcoming chapters. My proposed route to wealth, and the one that I have followed, is to invest directly in shares and index funds for the long term, and trade shares over the short-to-medium term to generate capital, which is then invested directly in residential properties. A further option is investing in certain types of Exchange Traded Funds (ETFs) or Listed Investment Companies (LICs) for long-term diversified exposure to equities (and, if you wish, commodities and other fixed income investments).

Whether property or shares is the better asset class is frequently debated, but it is not a debate that can be conclusively won. Each asset class has differing rates of return, volatility, liquidity and risks to be managed. Most people have a preference for or inclination towards either property or shares. What is certainly the case is that either asset class can be used to attain massive wealth – there is no 'better' asset class, only the best asset class for you. Below is a very brief comparison of these two asset classes.

Returns

The long-term returns from shares on the Australian Securities Exchange (ASX) is said to be somewhere in the region of 10–15% per annum, depending upon which source and which time period you take this information from. This is generally derived from approximately 4–5% received in dividends and the remainder in capital growth.

The long-term returns from property are probably similar, although I will mention several times throughout this book that there is not really one 'property market' in Australia, or indeed any other country. Different types of property in different areas behave markedly differently both in terms of yield and growth. The capital growth of residential property has historically been somewhere between 7% and 10% depending on the location, the property type and a host of other factors.

Property yields also vary depending on the location and type of the property. A rental unit in an inner suburb of a capital city might achieve a 5% gross rental yield (meaning 5% of the property's value per annum) before expenses, while a house in the same area may achieve a lower percentage. A property in an outer suburb or regional centre may achieve a yield of up to 7% or even higher, though this is sometimes at the expense of some capital growth. There is a long-running debate as to the benefits of investing for cash flow or capital growth, and the assumed inverse relationship between yield and growth in Australia. This is discussed in more detail later in the book.

Volatility

Shares are a volatile asset, partly because of their liquidity (see below). As shares can be bought and sold very easily, the price at which a share trades can move very sharply on a daily or even an hourly basis. The emotions of investors are ruled by fear and greed, and the ability to buy and sell quickly results in a volatile market.

Property values are far less volatile for a number of reasons. Firstly, it takes a lot longer to sell a property than it does to sell a parcel of shares. Secondly, around 70% of properties in Australia are held by owner-occupiers, who are less likely to sell their property in the face of a market meltdown; they are far more inclined to ride out a downturn in property values. The historical lack of a quoted daily market for property values (incidentally, a a daily quoted market has recently gone live) has had some effect, and the headlines trumpeting how shares have 'crashed' or 'plummeted' by 3% probably has some impact on share investor (and trader) psychology too.

Liquidity

Shares that are listed on a stock exchange are generally a liquid asset in that should you wish to sell a parcel of shares, there is generally a buyer available to take the other side of the trade. Share investors should note, however, that shares in larger companies are generally more liquid than those in smaller companies. If an investor is forced to sell a parcel of shares in an illiquid stock, they may have to accept a price that is lower than the prevailing market price (i.e. the price at which the last trade took place), and in some cases they may not find a buyer at all.

Property is generally seen to be a less liquid asset, because buying and selling properties takes far longer. There are stamp duty and legal fees associated with the purchase of property (share purchases in Australia do not incur stamp duty at the time of writing), which tends to discourage a high frequency of turnover of stock. However, it should be noted that property can be a liquid asset for the property investor in the form of a line of credit, which is effectively the option to borrow against the increased value of the property. I will discuss this in detail later.

Leverage (also known as gearing)

A significant reason for advocating property for the average investor is the leverage that it offers. Depending on the property purchased, the stage of the economic cycle, the purchaser's economic situation and the confidence of the lender, a property may be purchased with a deposit of between 0% and 25%. Generally, when you start out investing in property, 5–10% may be enough, although at present banks in the UK, for example, are so twitchy about the market that they are often insisting on deposits of 20% or more.

Leverage is available for share trading and share investing too. As investing in shares is perceived to be somewhat riskier than property, margin loans for share investing (refer to the *Glossary of Terms*) may charge higher interest rates than an equivalent mortgage on a residential property. The property versus shares debate is usually vastly oversimplified with regard to leverage. It is definitely possible *if you know what you are doing* to use significant leverage when dealing with shares. Firstly, margin loans can be ramped up by borrowing against the value of newly acquired shares, but there are other forms of leverage too (options, for example). The argument is not quite as straightforward as property allowing 80% leverage and shares 50%, as is sometimes cited.

What I will say is this:

'Using significant leverage in ANY asset class if you do not know what you are doing is extremely dangerous.'

The problem with the extensive use of margin loans in share investing as I see it is that in the event of a sharp downturn in the value of your holdings, the lender is likely to issue you with a margin call, requiring you to put up more cash as security or sell some of your shareholdings at what is potentially the most inopportune moment. In my experience, the best share investors are those with the clearest thought processes and investment plans. Leveraging through margin lending can cloud the thinking process.

The implications of leverage for the property investor who acquires properties that are in high demand are huge. It can take some time for an investor to build a pool of capital to begin meaningful investing in property, but when an investor is able to get the bank to lend 80%, 90% or even 100% of the value of the property to him or her, they have huge leverage to begin creating wealth. Banks do not generally issue margin calls in the event of a residential property market downturn, because it is simply impractical for them to do so. Instead, they take comfort in the fact that over time, the property market has always increased in value. As investors, we should take heed of this fact too.

The best asset class for you

Most people have a tendency to favour either property or shares. In the absence of a preference, I recommend that residential property is the best asset class for most average investors. That is to say, property is the *asset class that affords the greater likelihood of being able to achieve financial freedom at a young age.*

One distinct advantage of property is that you can add value to a property through a renovation. As a shareholder, unless we have bought a sizeable stake in the company, we are stuck with the decisions of management. We may have a vote at the Annual General Meeting (AGM), and can cast a non-binding vote on the remuneration of the key management personnel and directors, but we are effectively at the mercy of management (whose own interests are not necessarily well aligned with those of the shareholders). At times, it can be incredibly frustrating, and all we can do as shareholders is post our frustrations on Internet chat rooms (such as www.hotcopper.com) in the vain hope that somebody, somewhere takes heed of our comments.

Some property investors try to argue that it is possible to pick up incredible bargains in the property market by buying at a huge discount to 'true' or 'intrinsic' market value. In my experience, while bargains always exist, it is not quite as simple as that. Dramatically undervalued properties are usually priced that way for a reason.

The stock market, on the other hand, periodically throws up some outrageous bargains, and this is why I cannot accept the black-and-white argument that property is always a better asset class than shares. This is simply not true for the educated share investor. Perhaps even more importantly than this, in a capitalist economy, an investor who can successfully pick an outstanding company can see his investment increase twofold, tenfold or even a hundredfold over a relatively short period of time. Property investment can't offer you that. There really is no better asset class; there is only the best asset class for you.

In my experience, many amateur share investors don't do particularly well or particularly badly over time; they just do not achieve very much at all. The outspoken share investor will often be quick to tell you about a killing he has made on a particular share, but fail to mention those he has lost money on and held on to. Indeed, this is what most amateur share portfolios I have seen look like – they have a couple of outstanding performers, a number of shares that are small gains or losses, and one or two shares that have performed so badly that they wipe out most or all of the other gains.

The key to successful share trading or investing is minimising losses. If you can achieve a 12.5% return every year, you can turn $100,000 into well over $1 million in 20 years thanks to the power of compounding growth. If you can ramp up the returns to 15% per annum, the time period required to reach $1 million is slashed to just under 17 years.

While there are scores of books available on the subject of share investing, very few authors disclose their investment returns in any detail. One author and share investor who is generous enough to disclose his returns is Colin Nicholson. Nicholson has been investing in the Australian stock market for more than four decades. He discloses in his books and on his website (www.bwts.com.au) that he increased his pool of trading capital from a notional starting point of $100,000 (his real capital is significantly higher than this) to more than $400,000 between 2000 and 2010[2].

Nicholson has effectively doubled his capital more than twice in the 10-year period between 2000 and 2010, a period that included a dramatic stock-market crash. Make no mistake, over the period covered, these are phenomenal returns that were achieved with a very small risk of loss of capital. Nicholson had some huge winning years, such as 45% growth in the 2006/7 financial year and more than 33% in 2005/6[3], but the real key to his success is not the big winning years; it is the lack of big losing years. In the 2007/8 financial year, a rough period for the markets, he sustained a loss of only 5%, not enough to significantly impact his capital[4].

Could I potentially achieve the same result, doubling my capital twice in a decade? Of course I could. I could do it in two hours by laying Melbourne Storm to lose their next home game. Unfortunately for this strategy, the *Betfair* fraternity believes that I am several times more likely to lose all of my capital than to achieve my stated goal.

So the real question is: can I achieve the same returns in shares while exposing myself to the same level of risk? The answer is definitely not. Nicholson is probably as close as you will meet to an investing automaton. He risks no more than 0.5% of his trading capital on each parcel of shares purchased and has honed his investing skills over more than 40 years to treat gains and losses with an equal lack of emotion. To him, the process is almost as important as the result. A blackjack player who twists on 20 and is dealt an ace has still made a bad play; he just got lucky.

I can compete, however, by investing in residential property. This will still entail taking some risk, as I will need to employ leverage, but if I can achieve the Holy Grail of around 7% capital growth per annum, I am able to compete. If I use starting capital of, say, $100,000 to invest in a $500,000 property (not forgetting to pay my stamp duty, of course) that doubles in value over a decade (which will happen given 7.2% annual growth), I will have outperformed the return achieved on shares, achieving equity of well over half a million dollars.

Importantly from my perspective, I will not have to actively manage a portfolio of shares. The hidden embedded value in this approach is that I could also refinance the property when it has grown by, say, 50% and reinvest in further properties. Indeed, that is exactly what we have done over the past 15 years.

This is an age-old (and, at times, tedious) debate between share and property investors, and by the time it is played out in full we will have discussed stamp duty, negative cash flow and negative gearing rules, dividend yields, leverage, margin loans, margin calls and so on. In my opinion, the best chance the average investor stands of not being average is to use the power of leverage that investing in property offers and hold on to properties for the long term.

Nicholson discloses that by 2005 he had increased his trading capital (in a tax-favoured environment, his self-managed super fund) to over $1 million and by 2011 he had increased this figure to almost $2 million[5]. This means that he does not need to worry unduly about his later years because he has his own place of residence, a significant portfolio of capital and, crucially, the financial education to increase that capital in perpetuity.

The stock market is undoubtedly the best arena for Nicholson to invest in, as he has the skills and experience to achieve outstanding returns. I do believe, though, that as educated property investors, if we invest in the right properties in the right suburbs we can become millionaires in a far shorter period of time (due to leverage) than the vast majority of share investors – while not forgetting, of course, that a million dollars in the future will almost certainly be worth significantly less than a million dollars today. I was a millionaire when I quit my full-time job at the age of 33, and I simply would not have achieved this without employing leverage. It's far easier to create wealth quickly using millions of the bank's dollars than a few of your own.

The leverage that we can achieve through property and the powerful effect of compound growth are the twin forces that make millionaires out of many ordinary Australians.

Asset allocation

Ask a financial advisor how to allocate your assets and he may advocate a balanced allocation of assets across property, Australian equities, international equities, fixed interest investments, diversified funds, commodities, superannuation, cash…and so on. The advisor will suggest this because it is his or her job to do so, and, at the time of writing at least, they will probably earn commission from the products they push. A financial planner's job is not to advocate placing a large percentage of your portfolio into any one asset class.

If I was to suggest an efficient (i.e. balancing risk and return) portfolio allocation to enable you to retire wealthy at 65, it could look something like the one presented below. Don't worry if you don't understand all the terminology; it is merely an example, and the terms are included in the *Glossary of Terms* at the back of the book. In order for a portfolio like this to work, you only need two things. One is the *discipline* to be careful with your spending to ensure that you can pay a good amount into your investment portfolio each month. The second thing you need is *time* to allow the portfolio to compound and grow.

Figure 5.1 – A diversified portfolio: the slow but sure route to wealth

Asset Class	Target %
ASX 200 Large Cap Index Fund	10
Small Ordinaries Index Fund	10
Vanguard Emerging Markets Shares Index	10
FTSE SET Large Cap Index (UK's largest 30 companies)	10
High-Yield Corporate Bonds	10
Investment Grade Corporate Bonds	10
Capital Indexed Bonds (inflation hedged)	10
A-REIT Index (property trusts)	10
ASX All Ordinaries Gold Index Fund	10
Cash	10
Total	**100**

If this looks like double Dutch to you, don't worry; I simply use it as an example. Financial jargon has a tendency to make investing sound a lot more complicated than it actually is. In essence, there are only two types of investments, ownership and lending[6]:

Figure 5.2 – Investment types

Ownership investments e.g.	Lending investments e.g.
Shares	Bonds
Property	Notes, bills
Commodities	CDs (a type of bond)
Businesses	Your bank savings account

As a general observation, in a capitalist environment such as exists in Australia and the rest of the Western world, lending investments tend to have a lower risk, while ownership investments tend to create greater wealth when held for the long term due to compounding growth (refer to the section on compounding in Chapter 6, and to Figure 6.3). Ownership investments are therefore ideally suited to younger investors.

Based upon historical averages, it is reasonable to expect a portfolio like the one in Figure 5.1 to achieve average returns of 10% per year or higher[7]. It is diversified through funds, but also diversified in that the individual components of the portfolio do not act in a correlated manner. In other words, when stocks, for example, are not performing well, other assets, such as bonds, may well be. The portfolio includes assets that are traditionally used to hedge against deflation (gold mining companies and bonds) and also those that thrive in more inflationary economies, such as equities and A-REITS (what used to be called Listed Property Trusts – they invest mainly in commercial properties that may be beyond the reach of the individual investor).

Stocks are commonly acknowledged to be the best-performing growth asset in terms of percentage capital growth measured over time. Bonds are often considered to be lower risk than shares (in the event of a company being wound up and assets liquidated, debt holders and secured creditors rank higher than equity investors) and therefore tend to command a lower return. Therefore, a portfolio of this nature is efficient, as a fair percentage of the investor's portfolio is exposed to equities, with the remainder a mixture of bonds, property and cash.

Why not invest 100% of your capital in stocks then? Well, plenty of people do, and when they hold for the long term, they are often very successful. The only reason why this may be better avoided is that if your whole portfolio is in shares, it can be very nerve-wracking during a stock-market crash, which can result in investors abandoning the strategy at precisely the wrong moment. Diversifying into assets that do not act in a correlated manner with stocks can help you to sleep soundly at night.

Once a portfolio like this is created, it requires virtually no active management at all. That said, it would make sense to rebalance the portfolio once per year, as advised in *The Gone Fishin' Portfolio* by Alexander Green[8]. This means that if, for example, the emerging markets fund is steaming ahead, the investor might choose to sell a portion of it in order to rebalance the portfolio (i.e. to ensure that no one investment represents a significantly higher percentage of the portfolio than the rest).

Better still, the investor may choose to add more dollars to the lagging assets, a strategy that will avoid an unnecessary capital gains tax bill through selling. While it may feel counter-intuitive to put more dollars into the lower performing assets, it needs to be remembered that assets tend to perform in a cyclical manner, and the asset class that has forged ahead is likely to subsequently have a period of low returns (and vice versa).

Problems with this approach

Diversification is one of the fundamental conclusions of 'modern portfolio theory'. Spreading your capital across a broad range of investments has the benefit of reducing the risk of the loss of a large percentage of your capital. The problem with diversification is that it almost guarantees that your results will be average, which has led sceptics to instead term the practice 'de-worsification' – protecting the returns from being 'less worse'. If you want to become wealthy more quickly, you will need to seek returns that significantly outperform, and the way to do this is to specialise.

Incidentally, diversification is far easier to attain than people generally believe. The availability and accessibility of Exchange Traded Funds (ETFs) and Listed Investment Companies (LICs) now means that, in exchange for paying a fund management fee, it is possible to choose a fund that mirrors the asset allocation and risk profile we desire. Better still, by choosing an index fund, we can minimise the fees too. Index funds are cheaper to hold because they do not actively trade stocks, but simply hold them for the long term.

If you have ever played poker or bridge, you will instinctively know that diversification is not the way to win the game outright. To win the game, you do not divide up your capital into 10 equal parts and bet 10% of your capital on each hand, regardless of the strength of the cards you hold. The winner will be the player who places big bets on higher-probability hands. This is a concept that can be successfully applied to asset allocation in your investment portfolio if you want to quit your job earlier than the traditional retirement age.

The other problem with the diversification approach is that it lacks leverage. A carefully balanced portfolio, such as the one detailed in Figure 5.1 above, may be perfect if you were starting with investment capital of a few million dollars, however, most people (including myself) start out with very little or nothing, and therefore it can take a long time to start seeing any meaningful results. This is where leverage is so important for the average investor.

The Kelly Optimization Model[9]

When I was in maths class at school, my ears pricked up when the teacher mentioned a mathematical equation that could turn us into better gamblers. Although I was only 15 and not (ahem) legally allowed to gamble, I was very interested to hear of an algebraic model that could give us an edge over the casino when playing blackjack.

The idea was that by mentally noting how many high cards have been dealt (9s, 10s and the colours) and how many low cards have been dealt (2s through to 7s) we can ascertain our own probabilities of being dealt a high or low card. Based on our calculations of the probability of a good hand of cards, we then determine the size of our bet. I used this theory with very limited success…in later years, of course. Sadly for the maths lesson, the teacher then reverted to Pythagoras' Theorem, and I tuned out again as usual.

The Kelly Optimization Model was borne of this idea, and works on the same premise, that high probability events should attract a high proportion of your capital. This is a theory based on sound logic. If you are 100% sure that an outcome will occur – say, the odds of Sydney being seen as a more interesting place to live than Canberra – then it would make sense to place 100% of your capital into a bet on that outcome. In the real world of investment, however, we are rarely 100% sure of an outcome occurring, so this is where the model can help. Here is the simple equation of the model:

$$2p - 1 = x$$

Here, 'p' represents the probability of the event occurring and 'x' represents the percentage of your capital that should be staked on the event occurring. Don't worry if algebra scares you; the maths is done for you in Figure 5.3 below.

Figure 5.3 – Kelly Optimization Model applied to capital allocation

% likelihood of outcome	% of capital to allocate
100	100
90	80
80	60
70	40
60	20
50	–

Therefore, if we are 100% certain of an outcome, we place 100% of our capital on that outcome occurring. If we are only 50% (or less) certain of an outcome occurring, then our chances are no better than winning a game of two-up on Anzac Day, and we should not risk any of our capital at all.

This is relevant to the choice of asset classes. We need to consider what the best asset classes are for us – those assets that are most likely to create financial freedom for us. I will argue in this book that I believe the asset class most likely to help the investor achieve financial freedom is residential investment property. The Kelly Optimization Model dictates that, when the odds are in our favour, we should place a big bet.

The asset class that gives you the leverage to power ahead

The asset class that allows you achieve more with less is property, particularly residential property. Banks will generally lend a high loan-to-value ratio (LVR) on property, and this allows investors to significantly increase the value of their assets, which can then grow for them to create wealth.

Personally, I am bullish on Australian residential property, and believe that due to population growth and our inflationary economic environment, the best long-term bet for the average investor lies in exposure to this asset class. I will discuss the reasons for this in detail in the next chapter. However, unlike other books on property, which religiously chant only the positives, I believe it is wise for us to first consider what the risks of property are and the severity of the outcome should the risks occur.

Some property investors openly declare that they are 100% in property and 0% in shares, and plenty only invest in specific areas of one city. There are benefits to this strategy. For example, they will instinctively know a bargain when they see one, and they will develop a sound team of contacts and professionals in their chosen area. They will be able to control their assets closely too.

However, being 100% invested in Australian property exposes you to certain risks, and authors and investment clubs who disregard them with comments such as 'property goes up by 10% per annum' or 'property obviously always doubles every 7 to 10 years' are either deliberately misleading or have not considered the risks. Perhaps they may have businesses in the property sphere, and are therefore bound to promote the idea that property is a risk-free investment. Property does have risks, just like any other growth asset class. Remember that all growth assets have periods where their value remains flat or falling, but this can be countered by investing for a longer time horizon.

While I will discuss the asset classes in far more detail in subsequent chapters, I want to briefly discuss the risks of property and my beliefs surrounding the risk of a price crash. Some economic commentators have been saying for years now that the Australian property market will crash by 40, 50 or even 60%, but that obviously has not happened yet (at least, not in any major cities). A crash, for the purposes of this discussion, is defined as a dramatic fall in economic value. There is no numerical definition of what constitutes a dramatic fall in value, but you may argue that this could mean a 30–60% fall in value. My own belief is that this will not happen any time soon to the types of property I advocate investing in.

Property price risks

Risk 1 – Deflation

Firstly, there is a risk that Australia enters a prolonged period of having a deflationary economy. I believe the risk to be relatively low, but not without precedent in the Western world, and the doomsayers will all too frequently point to events in Japan as evidence. In my view, it is the very severity of the impact of deflation in Japan that reduces the likelihood of prolonged deflation occurring in Australia.

The Australian government is unlikely to allow deflation to continue unabated for years, as the Japanese government did without intervention, due to the potentially disastrous impact this would have on a leveraged economy such as ours. The implications of deflation for property investors would be that they are exposed to leveraged assets that could slip downwards in value. There are also significant differences between the respective industries, geography, population growth and cultures of Japan and Australia that make the validity of a direct comparison dubious.

You have to make your own call on this. From reading the rhetoric of the Reserve Bank's press releases (and from observing the composition of the Bank's board members and their respective backgrounds), I have a long-term inflation bias.

Risk 2 – Policy change

Secondly, there is a risk that prices could collapse from an unforeseen event such as a change in government policy or a significant change in lending criteria. There could be a change in economic policy if a future government believes that property prices have become undesirably high, although they would face stiff opposition from the banking industry.

Perhaps future corporate collapses could see a drive towards restrictions on lending practices so that banks are no longer inclined to lend more than, say, 80% of the value of a property. Negative gearing tax concessions could also be scrapped, as they were in the USA (and in Australia too, albeit briefly). This is quite possible over a long-term time horizon, but I believe the property market would overcome the setback, as it has all others to date.

Risk 3 – High interest rates

Interest rates in Australia have been very high at certain points in time, and could again rise to levels that cause everyday homeowners to default on their mortgage repayments. The Reserve Bank (RBA) should be able to avoid this happening any time in the near future, as rates are not currently particularly high, but history shows us that interest rates can become very high indeed (well into double digits in recent decades). The compensating good news for property investors already in the market is that when interest rates become very high, this may reflect of a period of high capital growth.

Again, I do not believe that the risk of prices collapsing as a result of high interest rates is particularly high, but I would advocate investing in median-priced property in inner and middle-ring suburbs of capital cities. If I were to foresee a risk of prices collapsing, then it would be areas of low demand, low household incomes and with a reliance on a few industries – such as undesirable outer suburbs and regional or tourist areas – that are at risk. In these areas, high interest rates can cause severe financial distress. When property books claim that property prices 'obviously' double every 7 to 10 years, I believe that they are failing to consider the expansion in lending practices and higher rates of inflation that allowed this to occur in decades past.

Risk 4 – Severe recession and high unemployment

Australia could experience severe recession or depression with high unemployment. Of the factors identified here, this is the most likely to actually occur. Economies are cyclical in nature, and it is not unusual for an economy to go into recession. Property can be robust through a recession, and indeed sometimes the resultant lower interest rates and plunging stock markets can make property seem more attractive than ever. Renters can become abundant, resulting in very low vacancy rates. However, a severe recession with unemployment can impact confidence and see prices fall sharply.

With the current strength of the mining sector supported by strong commodity prices, we may not see a severe long-term recession soon (although by the time this book goes to print, we may know more about the European debt crisis outcome that alters this view). However, over the longer term, it is a distinct possibility. This is one of the reasons I cannot advocate putting all of your net worth and focus into just one asset class: some flexibility to adapt to the prevailing economic circumstances could be vital. Remember the old adage: 'Don't put all of your eggs in one basket.'

Abnormally high unemployment levels that cause a significant proportion of people to become unable to meet mortgage repayments appear unlikely in the near future with unemployment levels being as low as they are in Australia. In the longer term, we are fortunate in Australia to have more control over our migration policies than many other countries, in contrast with the more volatile inflows and outflows experienced in many European countries for example.

Risk 5 – Oversupply of properties

A huge oversupply of properties can occur in areas where developers have built too many units or in areas with a declining industry. The clearest example in Australia is on the Gold Coast, where supply has easily outweighed demand in recent years: prices have reportedly fallen by as much as 40% or more in some areas. This can happen in areas where prices are driven by speculative 'investment' rather than being driven by fundamentals.

We can sidestep this risk by investing in areas with continual high demand and low potential for new land release. Also, we should avoid CBDs where approvals can be given for huge new tower blocks that can flood the market with new units. Where there are no height restrictions on new developments, the sky is, quite literally, the limit.

Risk 6 – Super-catastrophe

There is the risk of a super-catastrophe such as a tsunami or earthquake. While we have a tendency to believe that such devastating things cannot happen on the eastern seaboard, some believe that there is evidence to suggest that massive tsunamis have occurred in Australia the past. Recent flooding and cyclones have shown that Mother Nature is unpredictable and very powerful.

This is an argument against investing only in one city. It is another diversification versus specialisation debate: investing in multiple cities diversifies risk and allows one to take advantage of property cycles more easily, but we may know less about the market in a distant state. We do not need to become climate change experts, but we do need to acknowledge these risks and recognise that, for example, a nuclear meltdown in China could result in a property meltdown in Australia. Other areas to consider the risk of investing in are those prone to fires or floods. Remember, it is not just the risk but also the severity of the potential outcome that we need to consider.

Assess the risks

This is where we need to make an assessment of what we believe the risks of these outcomes to be, and the potential severity of the outcome. As I am in the first quarter of the *Game of Money*, I invest in property with a 30-year time horizon in mind, and so should consider what the risks are of me aged 65 wishing I had directed my portfolio away from Australian property. I would say I have a significantly lower than 20% chance of this being the case, and history is in my favour, as property prices have risen relentlessly over time since records in this country began.

The arguments against a property crash

I don't believe we will have a major property crash any time soon. Look, a 500-page thesis could be written on this topic, which would be an interesting exercise for me, but nobody would read it. Briefly then, here is my reasoning for my belief that prices will not crash.

Reason 1 – Lack of supply (in certain urban areas)

There is an acute shortage of property in Australia. I will not cite reams of numbers here because every set of figures that is produced on this topic is subsequently disputed (how does one define a 'shortage'?), though a shortage of 200,000 dwellings is a number sometimes put forward by banks and other institutions.

What is not disputed is that there is a shortage of dwellings, and that in certain areas (Sydney's inner and middle-ring suburbs, where vacancy rates are very low, represent one such example) the rate of building new properties is nowhere near enough to keep pace with the rate of population growth and property demand. Shortages of properties drive up rents and drive up prices.

Developers are also finding real difficulty in obtaining finance for new developments post-GFC – combined with rising construction costs, this ensures that new developments are very expensive and thus underpins the value of established dwellings.

I will add a caveat to this, however, and say that this is not a reason to invest in any area without due consideration. Invest in an area without height restrictions on buildings (such as CBDs or the Gold Coast) and you could find that one day in the not too distant future there may be an oversupply of properties in that area. Instead, it is important to invest in areas with a continuing high demand where the supply of new properties is constrained. You should also avoid investing in areas where there is vacant land potentially available for release.

Reason 2: Growing demand

The population of Australia is growing rapidly. While some developed countries have falling population growth rates (Japan, Germany) and many have population growth rates of around 1% per annum, Australia has headed the charts with growth rates of more than 2% per annum in recent years.

Recent figures quoted by the Australian Bureau of Statistics have suggested a fall from the higher growth rates seen in recent years, but Australia's population is still expected to grow by at least 1.5% per annum on average. This may not sound like very much, but this level of growth for the next three decades would result in a huge Australian population surge to somewhere between 30 and 35 million.

We must also consider that on average, people are having fewer children and having them later (this offsets the impact of immigration to some extent), but the point is this: the Australian population is growing rapidly. This is not only a trend that will impact us sometime in the distant future; it is already doing so now. Invest in the cities and suburbs that the new migrants are heading to and this could significantly improve your capital growth returns.

Figure 5.4– Projected population growth of Australia

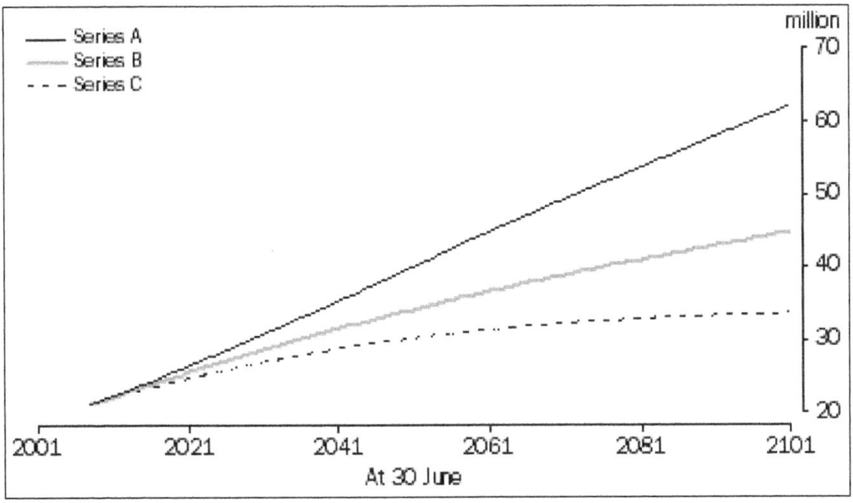

Source: Australian Bureau of Statistics, www.abs.gov.au

This graph shows the Australian Bureau of Statistics' high, low and median projections for the future population of Australia. As governments and policies come and go, it is uncertain exactly which path we will take, but we can be sure that Australia's population will increase very significantly over time.

Population growth is the only way in which the country will be able to support the vast numbers of baby boomers heading into retirement with greater life expectancy rates than ever before. The government needs a steady supply of new taxpayers to support its pension and Medicare liabilities. Another thing that the pension problem suggests to me is that we can expect tax rates to head higher rather than lower, which is yet another reason to move away from a reliance on a high salary.

Reason 3 – Inflation reigns

The RBA has told us that its target rate of inflation is 2–3%. The graph below shows the rate of inflation in Australia over the last half century or so.

Figure 5.5 – Long-term inflation in Australia

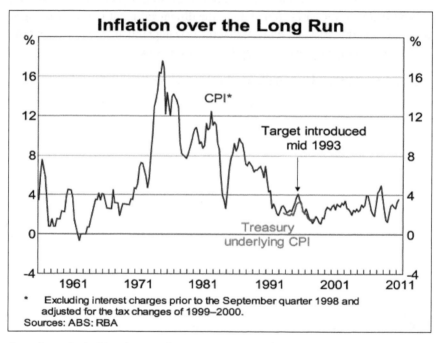

Source: Reserve Bank of Australia, www.rba.gov.au

While there is not a direct correlation between property prices and inflation or consumer price index (CPI) rates, it is the case that in an inflationary economy the prices of goods and commodities generally increase. It is unsurprising that property prices have increased significantly in the past when you consider this graph. The CPI rates spiralling way over 15% may have been an anomaly, but we had a period of nearly two full decades where CPI rates were between 5 and 10%.

You will note from the graph that in recent years, the levels of inflation have been lower than those in, for example, the 1970s and 1980s. The RBA will be pleased with this, as their stated goal is now to maintain an inflation rate of 2–3%. Since the introduction of the target range of inflation in 1993, the CPI rate has mostly hovered somewhere close to the stated target range. This might indicate that the RBA understands and can control the drivers of inflation, and that we might expect inflation rates to be considerably lower in the future than they have been in the past.

It does seem to be the case that even by simply threatening to raise interest rates (known in industry parlance as *jawboning*), the RBA can impact consumer confidence significantly. Of course, nobody knows what the future holds in terms of inflation rates. One thing that may be implied by the historical graph is that there is a higher likelihood of there being periods of high inflation than there is of us seeing a prolonged period of deflation.

Property values will fall at some point... and then rise again

Read Internet forums and commentary on property and you will probably find a thousand reasons why there will supposedly be a crash. Many of the people who make these comments are those who have been unable to get on to the property ladder, and are thinking in a short-term manner and hoping for a crash. Of course property values will fall at some point, as is the case with all growth asset classes. But while the Australian economy is an inflationary environment and the population continues to grow apace, you can also be certain that values will be higher in the future.

Remember that in Australia, we have a definite culture of home ownership with around 70% of us owning (or at least paying off) our homes. Somewhere around half of Australian homes have no debt at all against them, which tends to make the property market more stable – interest rate movements have a diminished impact upon those with no mortgage debt.

When you read of a possible impending crash, remember these reasons and resolve to invest for the long term, and your fears will be alleviated. Stick to investing in properties and suburbs that are in continually high demand and ask: what are the chances of property prices being cheaper in 30 or more years from now? Short-term fluctuations need not worry you unduly.

Applying this to the Kelly Optimization Model

You may have heard the phrase 'Don't bet the farm on a sure thing because it is not a sure thing.' What this means is that the Kelly Optimization Model is a tool best used conservatively, so based upon my own opinions, I should not have more than 60% of my portfolio in Australian property. Because I believe that the leverage offered by property provides such a significant advantage over other asset classes, I invest in property overseas too. I don't necessarily advocate that others invest in overseas property, for reasons I will explain later, but it works for me.

Here is what my own personal target portfolio looks like.

Figure 5.6 – My target portfolio

Asset Class	Target %
Australian residential property	30
UK residential property	30
Direct investments in Australian shares	15
Ethical FTSE Tracker Fund, direct UK shareholdings	15
Cash/fixed interest investments	10
Total	**100**

Note: my self-managed superannuation fund is invested in shares and property, and therefore I have not split it out for the purposes of this table.

Naturally, this balance will be different for everyone, and should be based upon your opinions, favoured asset classes, age, risk profile and so on. As property investment generally involves taking on debt, it is worth pointing out that the target asset allocation refers to percentages of net worth rather than gross asset values.

You will note from the table above that at present there is only a small place in my target portfolio for fixed interest investments. This is because, being in the first quarter of the *Game of Money*, I have time on my side, and believe that growth asset classes such as property and shares over time are the best way to create wealth for me. As I get older, there will surely be a place for more conservative investment classes. Traditionally, it is said that as you approach retirement age you should hold less of your net worth in volatile assets such as shares, and more in fixed interest investments such as bonds and term deposits.

My approach is to aim to have 30% of my net worth in Australian property and 60% of my net worth in property overall. While this may sound a little aggressive, I am somewhat diversified within that asset class in that I plan to continue holding a number of different types of property in different states. Remember that Warren Buffett was prepared to invest well over 40% of his available capital in one company, that company being Coca-Cola[10].

While I personally invest in England and in Australia, I would suggest that there are two very good reasons for Australians to choose Australian property over overseas property, these being taxation benefits and population growth. While investing overseas works for me because I was born in England and spend a fair amount of time there, it is generally advisable for Australians to invest at home. It makes the most sense.

Shares also represent an excellent asset class for an investor who is in the first quarter of the *Game of Money*. If you have time on your side, you can ride through some of the rough periods, and over time shares have historically given an excellent rate of return. For this reason, I aim to maintain an exposure to shares with around 30% of my net worth via index funds and direct holdings in shares.

I prefer Australian shares to UK shares for direct shareholdings in companies for a few reasons, the main reason being simply that I know more about Australian companies than I do about their UK counterparts. I do not have a lot of inclination to spend time learning about two stock markets, and don't much enjoy checking stock-market prices around the clock either.

I am an advocate of index funds as an easy and efficient way to get started in investing in equities. Index funds are cheaper than managed funds because you do not need a fund manager to pick the shares for you. If you invest in an ASX 200 index fund, the index will simply hold the top 200 companies by market capitalisation and liquidity. Index funds clearly also have tremendous diversification, because for as little as $500 you can hold a small share in all of these sizeable companies. Index funds aren't too exciting, as they only mirror the index, but as Buffett says, 'When dumb money acknowledges its limitations, paradoxically, it ceases to be dumb.'

Regarding ethics, I prefer to invest in ethical index funds. I am also considering whether to stop investing in mining companies going forward, as I don't believe it is a terribly ethical industry. It is a difficult dilemma though, as I hold shares in one of the mining giants, a company that is a cash-generating machine. An ethical index fund will generally avoid investing in companies that are involved in, for example, munitions, alcohol or gambling. You have to make your own decisions on this. An ethical index fund may not perform at exactly the same rate as the XJO index (in many instances they have performed better, but this may not always be the case -'unethical' industries are often heavily regulated and thus protected from new competitors), but we all have our own rules and codes of conduct. Ultimately, it is up to you to decide.

Some would argue that you don't need to hold much cash, as it is a drag on your portfolio. This is true to an extent, but cash does have a role to play. Firstly, cash does earn interest (although the interest is taxed and the cash never attains any capital growth). Secondly, cash reduces your risk in case of capital being required urgently for unforeseen expenditure. And thirdly, cash has a hidden opportunity value in times of stock-market distress.

When share markets tank, banks often stop lending to all but the AAA-rated companies (who often don't need the loans anyway), and therefore companies are forced to liquidate their own assets for what has become a scarce commodity: cash. In turn, this means that the investor who has cash available can be ready to capitalise on some wonderful opportunities. We also need cash to live, and being forced to liquidate investments at inopportune moments is not a desirable outcome.

In reality, a target portfolio such as this can be flexible. If the All Ordinaries index (XAO) surges back up above 6,000, I would become more defensive and look to move some of my direct share portfolio into cash or term deposits. On the other hand, if the XAO plummeted to around 3,000, I would be moving a significant portion of my cash into shares. It pays to be flexible.

Note that such a model is designed to be revisited *at least* every 12 months or so. If there appears to be a heightened risk of prolonged deflation, then we should consider rebalancing to incorporate assets that hedge against deflation (silver and gold are traditionally popular, although gold prices at the time of writing are close to the highest they have ever been). At other times, the stock markets may become overpriced and we will want to reduce our exposure to equities, and so on.

Property, however, is something I like to hold through the lean periods. As such a high percentage of Australians choose to own homes, property prices do not generally react to downturns in the same way as shares – most people have confidence in the long-term upward trend of property prices and elect to sit tight through such periods.

So what should your target portfolio be? Obviously, I cannot tell you that. It depends on your own preferences, prejudices and attitude to risk. For younger investors aiming to be financially free at a young age, below are some examples of financial profiles. Some people would advocate specialising and being 100% in property or shares. I don't suggest that, though there is no doubt that this can work. You must simply be very cognisant of the risks.

As many people have no investments at all outside of their own home and a superannuation balance, the default position is that many of us have one property as a place of residence and some exposure to the stock market via our super fund. Conventional wisdom suggests that we should get the best-paid job we can and then somewhere around the age of 30 take out the most expensive mortgage we can afford to buy a house. This approach can pay off handsomely if you live long enough to pay off the mortgage, but it does ensure that you will be working until somewhere close to retirement age. In order to attain financial freedom more quickly than that, I am going to suggest a different approach.

Why not consider shunning buying your own home to live in and renting instead? Part of the problem with buying a hugely expensive house to live in is that you never seem to have enough left over at the end of the month for anything, let alone building a sizeable portfolio of investments. Renting is often significantly cheaper than buying a property, partly because interest rates tend to be higher than rental yields, and partly because the landlord retains responsibility for repair costs, strata fees and insurance. Renting can afford you the luxury of investing heavily instead of being tied to a huge monthly mortgage repayment.

If you were to rent instead of buying a property to live in, there are limitless choices as to where you can allocate your assets. Let's take a look at a few examples.

Figure 5.7 – Possible asset allocation examples (%)

	Moderate	Aggressive	Very aggressive
Australian Property	40	50	60
Australian Shares	20	30	40
International Shares	10	10	-
Diversified Funds	10	5	-
Fixed Interest	10	-	-
Cash	10	5	-
Total	**100**	**100**	**100**

Shown above are just a few of the potential options. The traditional growth assets are shares and property, so a more moderate approach would be to consider some fixed interest investments (e.g. bonds) and some diversified funds. The most aggressive approach would be to shun diversification and invest exclusively in property and/or shares.

The neat thing about this approach is that because you have not lumbered yourself with a huge mortgage, you can instead take out multiple mortgages and have tenants pay them off for you.

Investing in one asset class

Although I am bullish on Australian property, I would not advocate investing solely in one asset class. Many property books refer to equities or fixed interest investments in a dismissive manner, but it is perhaps preferable to be flexible. Ultimately, I am not a property or a share investor; I am simply an investor. Stock-market meltdowns can offer amazing opportunities to the adaptable. Investing in one asset class can pay dividends in the long term, but the road will necessarily be a more volatile one. There will be years and possibly even decades where the investor might see minimal or even negative returns.

As noted, some authors advocate investing in property only. One problem with this is that most prime-location residential property in Australia generates yields that do not cover the mortgage payment and other costs and therefore the property can cost the investor dollars each month. A portfolio that consists of only property can therefore begin to cost the investor significantly. This can be countered by continually borrowing more and refinancing mortgages upwards, but that is not an approach I would necessarily recommend.

Another alternative is to seek out properties that generate a positive cash flow, a strategy I discuss in more detail later in the book. My favoured approach would be to invest in other asset classes in addition to property, such as shares (or bonds if you prefer) that *pay you money* in the form of dividends (or interest) rather than costing you money.

Summary of asset allocation

The choice of asset allocation is a very personal one. When considering the best-performing growth asset classes, some folk have a natural preference for shares, while others have a natural tendency towards property. The choice does not necessarily matter – indeed, you are more likely to succeed in an asset class that you have an interest and affinity for – but the power of focus is important.

Carefully diversifying your portfolio across a raft of assets may reduce your risk, but it is not going to help you to be financially free quickly. Instead, to escape the rat race, it is necessary to apply some focus to your favourite asset class. If you are starting without a large pool of capital, it is my belief that the power of leverage afforded to you by property creates the best chance for the average investor to generate wealth quickly.

That was a brief discussion on asset allocation. Now let's consider exactly how to invest in the main asset classes in more detail.

Practical Action Points

- Consider which asset class interests you most – is it investment property, or are shares your favoured vehicle? While I tend to believe that property affords the average investor the best chance of achieving financial freedom, it is also true that you are likely to be a shrewder investor in an asset class that interests you.

- Further consider which asset class and investment style suits better suits your personality. Do you visualise yourself taking an active or passive role in your investing? Are you a fast thinker tending towards frenetic activity, or are you considered and conservative?

- Consider subscribing to magazines or online investor commentary. For investment property, *Australian Property Investor* is a fine publication. There are several useful magazines that cover share and fund investing too.

- Join your local library! You don't have to pay top dollar for investment books. You can find many of them absolutely free at the library.

6
WHY
PROPERTY?
'The Best Investment On Earth…
Is Earth'

6

Investing in earth

The quote in the chapter title comes from Louis Glickman. Historically, a huge amount of the world's wealth has been derived from the earth itself, specifically from two places: minerals and real estate (or property, as we normally say in Australia). John D. Rockefeller was possibly the richest individual in history adjusted for inflation, and he was a chap who knew a lot about wealth. Like many of the world's wealthiest people, Rockefeller generated huge wealth from minerals – oil in his case. He was the first American to be worth more than $1 billion dollars[1].

Australia is a country in which much wealth is generated from minerals. We can start up exploring companies to seek resources, but this is not a path that is open to most average investors. It takes a high level of skill and experience to start up a company, raise funds from investors and begin exploration. Residential property in Australia has increased in value over the long term too, and property is an asset class that is accessible to the average investor. If we are able to identify the emerging demographic trends, then we can profit from this to generate wealth.

Rockefeller once said that people who have a job are too busy working and earning a living to make money. What he meant by that is that creating wealth is about using other people's time and money to work harder for you, rather than working harder yourself. The asset class that gives the average investor the best chance of not being average is property.

Price history of Australian capital cities

The tables below provide a snapshot of the price history of residential property in Sydney, Melbourne, Brisbane, Adelaide and Perth from 1985 to 2005. Prices have continued to increase throughout the global financial crisis, and are significantly higher today in all states and cities. I would emphasise that I haven't cherry-picked a time period, specific cities or property types here; this is simply the direction in which property values have moved over time in Australia: upwards. Other cities and even regional areas show a similar trend over time. Despite what some people try to claim, property prices have increased relentlessly over the years.

Figure 6.1 – Australian median house prices ($)

Year	Sydney	Melbourne	Brisbane	Adelaide	Perth
1985	89,300	74,400	60,200	73,900	50,500
1990	184,300	140,000	103,000	100,500	97,500
1995	199,300	146,600	132,500	112,800	125,400
2000	315,000	253,000	149,200	135,000	157,800
2005	537,800	356,800	306,600	270,800	277,000

Source: Real Estate Institute of Australia[2]

Figure 6.2 – Australian median unit prices ($)

Year	Sydney	Melbourne	Brisbane	Adelaide	Perth
1985	67,100	58,100	57,100	59,200	36,900
1990	138,300	111,200	88,500	77,500	76,800
1995	154,800	114,100	107,000	92,600	87,900
2000	315,000	253,000	149,200	135,000	157,800
2005	370,300	294,900	238,300	204,900	220,600

Source: Real Estate Institute of Australia[3]

Remember that these are *median* prices. As investors, we want to pick the premium investment properties that will *outperform* the median growth of the market.

It is amazing to me how dismissive many people are of investment property as a vehicle for growing wealth, and I have tried to understand why this is the case. One theory I have comes from noting that if you look at a spreadsheet of median property values over history, the individual increases year on year don't seem particularly big. This is partly because we are looking at historic numbers, and the figures therefore naturally look smaller to us. And yet, if you look at the price of property in 1960, the values are so cheap as to be scarcely believable. It is the cumulative effect of the increases – the compounding growth – that makes property such a devastatingly effective asset class for investors. It is death by a thousand cuts for the doomsayers.

Consider this quotation from one of the books on property investing in Australia:

'It is obvious that property doubles in value every 7 to 10 years[4].'

Quotations such as this are guaranteed to infuriate the many thousands of Australians who are struggling to get on to, or cling on to the property ladder. Almost every time the *Sydney Morning Herald* publishes a property article online, dozens of scornful posters are quick to make the point that property cannot continue to rise in value more quickly than household incomes *ad infinitum*, and that prices will soon come crashing down. In fact, they may have a point, depending on which properties are being referred to.

The people who make these continually bearish comments about the prospects of property may often be those who are not property owners themselves. In other words, they want property prices to fall so they can buy themselves, which is natural enough. The property price debate rages on and on, with most people relying on gross oversimplifications in order to support their preconceived notions.

In cheaper outlying areas, I would have to agree that it is simply not possible for the price of all property to continue to outperform the rise in household income. Eventually, there will come a critical point where the properties become unaffordable, even if prices are propped up by cash-flow investors, because many people in the more remote suburbs are reliant on linear income in the form of one salary. In prestigious suburbs, home owners tend to have more equity and diverse income streams, and are less likely to be wholly reliant on a salary, so the dynamic is somewhat different.

However, the doomsayers who predict a massive Australia-wide property price collapse are likely to be wrong. This is not just my view; the man who should know about these things (one would hope), the Governor of the Reserve Bank of Australia, noted that people who are predicting a property price collapse often know very little about property economics, and often do not own property themselves, so they are simply hoping for a crash. In many cases, all of these things are true. The banks, who are financing much of the property market, the government and the RBA all have a vested interest in there not being a property price crash, and this is just one of the reasons I think it is unlikely.

Part of the problem with this debate is that the bullish property investors are not being specific in their predictions. Do they mean all property will double every 7 to 10 years? Or are they referring to investment-grade properties in blue-chip suburbs with good transport access to the CBD? What inflation rate are they expecting? If a property doubles in value in 10 years but the inflation rate has averaged 7% per annum, then effectively the increase in value has only matched inflation (for the record, I don't think inflation will average 7%; I merely use this as an example).

A similar statement comes from a property book by Chris Gray, property investor and author, who noted in 2005 that property values in Sydney had doubled every seven years since 1969 (he has the numbers to back it up)[5]. Chris Gray and I have a lot in common: he was born in England, he worked for Deloitte and he is bullish on blue-chip Australian residential property. He stated in his book that if his properties continued to increase by 10% per year, his $3.5 million portfolio would be worth more than $50 million by the time he is 65[6].

If you bought property in Sydney in, say, early 2004, you will know that the market has not increased by 10% per annum and therefore doubled over the past seven years. In fact, property prices showed no growth for around five years, and the values have only increased by a fraction of the supposed 10% rate as I write this in 2012. What Gray is saying is that because the median property price doubled in value every seven years in Sydney between 1969 and 2004, he therefore expects it to continue to do so in the future, over the long term[7].

Gray reiterated the point in a later book showing in a table how $10 million of property could be worth $80m after 21 years[8]. His logic is that history is the best indicator we have towards future trends[9]. Warren Buffett does caution us to be wary of past performance as being indicative of future performancein finance (wittily noting that if history books foretold the future, the richest people would be librarians).

Of course, another way of looking at the past performance of the Australian property market might be that property prices have been outperforming inflation and household incomes for so long that the market may now have a prolonged period of cooling, and therefore flat or falling prices. Short of the Reserve Bank abandoning its inflation target, I don't believe that property prices could perpetually increase at a rate of 10% in Sydney – the median price of a house would be getting close to around $5 million in 20 years' time if that were to be the case. That probably won't happen, in my view.

To allow such a phenomenal historical price growth, certain trends have had to emerge. There are many more two-income households now than there were in the 1960s, banks now lend far higher multiples of salaries (and during profligate times even lend 100% of the value of the property) and the population of Australia has grown sharply, which has increased demand. It is also a bold prediction to state that property will rise in value by 10% per annum when prevailing inflation rates are far lower than they were in previous decades, the RBA having introduced its stated target range of inflation in the early 1990s. We also need to assess future demographic trends to make an assessment of where we think the market will head next.

Chris Gray also went on to say that if he is half wrong and his portfolio is only worth $25 million when he is 65, then this will still be better than most superannuation funds[10]. Now, this sheds more light. What Gray is talking about is a *margin of safety* in his prediction. He is betting on a 10% per annum growth for his portfolio, but if the growth is only 5% per annum, he will still be well ahead of the pack[11]. There is still inflation to be considered here, so it is worth noting that if inflation rises at an average of 3% over the 28 years, then the $25 million will be worth less than half of that when measured in today's dollars.

Prices are determined by supply and demand

There are many theories about what makes property prices move, but in the simplest terms, there are two factors that determine price: supply and demand. These factors are themselves affected by a myriad of smaller factors such as availability of financing, affordability and tax laws, to name but three.

So, what is my opinion on this? Well, the markets have a tendency to make monkeys of those who try to make forecasts. I will not make a definitive forecast, but instead I'll look at the fundamentals of the market and the probabilities in order to make investing decisions.

Here are just a few of the fundamentals to consider:

- Demand: the population of Australia is predicted to increase dramatically to somewhere close to 30 million by 2040 (refer to Figure 5.4)

- Demand: the majority of immigrants will be heading for the capital cities, in particular to Sydney, Melbourne, Perth and south-east Queensland (see Figure 7.7 in Chapter 7)

- Supply: statistics on this vary significantly, but it is generally acknowledged that Australia has an acute shortage of dwellings in certain areas and is not building enough new properties to house the expected numbers of immigrants; this is especially true in some landlocked city areas

- Expected inflation: the target inflation rate of the RBA is 2 to 3%, although core inflation is slightly above the target at the time of writing

- Demography: generally, the population is marrying later, living in smaller two-income households for longer, and the younger generation overwhelmingly want to live near the CBDs of cities

- Population density: the increasing population will mean denser traffic, and rising fuel prices will increase the importance of transport links to the CBD.

My opinion is that property will continue to increase in value, but we are unlikely to see the relentless double-digit growth that we have seen in past decades. Crucially, credit growth is extremely unlikely to continue to expand at such a dizzying rate, and it seems to me that the RBA is likely to be far more hawkish on inflation than governing bodies of decades gone by. I also feel that the events of and fallout from the sub-prime crisis of 2007-2009 may force the world's central banks to adopt a slightly different approach – rather than only focussing on controlling CPI and turning a blind eye to asset-price inflation, they may take a more active role in the controlling and deflation of asset bubbles.

For these reasons, I rationalise that the most obvious proxy for future property market growth is likely to be the growth of household incomes: logically, the more people have to spend on their residence, over time the more they will spend (though immigration may make the growth rate slightly higher).

Over the last decade, median household income has increased at a rate of somewhere close to 6% per annum, but this has been partly fuelled by a significant increase in the number of two-income households. Looking forward, it is reasonable to believe that the rate of increase may be somewhat lower, perhaps nearer to 5%, and consequently median dwelling price growth is likely to be somewhat lower than it has in the past too.

While this might be a reasonable assumption to make for a longer-term average, it is worth noting that in the short term property prices rarely move in such a uniform manner. History shows us that growth asset classes are likely to spend long periods with values either flat or falling before seeing a period of accelerated growth. As property investors, we want to remain invested through as many of these boom periods as we can.

It should also be noted here that when Chris Gray states that property has doubled in value every seven years for over three decades, the average rate of inflation was significantly higher than the RBA's target rate of inflation for the future. Between 1960 and 1990, the average rate of inflation was 8%, wage growth was 9.7% and property growth was around 11% (thus outperforming the CPI by around 3%)[12]. Whether or not we have such high rates of inflation in the future remains to be seen, but we should note that the RBA's target rate of inflation is now far lower than historical levels.

Property price growth is not the conspiracy that many people think it is. Much of the increase in property values over time is simply driven by the inflationary nature of our economy. Things will cost more in the future than they do now. As Jan Somers points out, the average male weekly earnings in Australia in 1990 were only $578[13].

So, based on these and other fundamentals, am I more in the Chris Gray camp, or the camp of those foretelling a property price collapse? Unfortunately for the doomsayers, I believe as Gray does that our property prices are likely to be heading upwards when we consider a reasonable time horizon. In future decades, Australia's property prices are very likely to be far higher than they are today. It would be lovely to think that in the year 2050 we could be strolling down to the Sydney harbourside to pick up a luxurious $600,000 apartment by the water, but I simply do not foresee that happening.

The question is, if median property price growth in the future is only somewhere around 5% instead of the 7–10% that has been seen in the past, is property still an asset class we should invest in? For my money, the answer is an emphatic **YES**.

Remember that, as property investors, we are not too concerned with median price growth. We want to significantly outperform median price growth through investing in harmony with market cycles, picking properties that are in continual high demand and selecting properties that we can add value to through renovations. Specifically, in Australia I will be investing in two-bedroom, two-bathroom units (and sometimes even one-bedroom units) with parking that are close to the CBDs of Sydney, Melbourne and Brisbane. I will be seeking investment-grade units in the blue-chip lifestyle suburbs that have transport hubs or links for easy access to the city.

Nobody knows what the future will bring, but if the median price of property grows by 5% per annum over future decades, as a property investor I will be looking for my portfolio to outperform the median growth by at least 2% per annum. I believe that these suburbs and types of properties will achieve that because they are highly sought after as a result of their local resources and facilities. Units in desirable suburbs are also impacted less by affordability issues than some of Australia's housing stock.

Leverage

The biggest advantage that the property investor has is the power of leverage. It is almost impossibly difficult to save your way to wealth, but if you can borrow funds to invest in wealth-producing assets, you can become financially free far more quickly than you may imagine. The property investor can use millions upon millions of dollars from the banks to his advantage if he or she so wishes. And I, for one, do exactly that.

When you first start out in investing, you may need a deposit of somewhere between 5% and 25%, depending upon the prevailing economic climate and the lender's appetite for risk. In more heady days, I once managed to buy property with a 0% deposit. As you take on more debt, lenders may begin to see you as a higher risk, and insist upon a 20% or more deposit to mitigate their risk.

Compounding

Does the gap between expensive properties and cheap properties appear to become ever larger to you? Well, this generally is the case, for the same reason that the difference between the price of a two-litre carton of milk becomes ever larger than the price of a one-litre carton of milk. It is simply inflation and compound growth at work, and the gap grows ever larger. Consider this table showing the value of a $1 million property that increases in value at the rate of 10% per annum:

Figure 6.3 – Compound growth on $1 million at 10% per annum

Year	Value ($)
0	1,000,000
1	1,100,000
2	1,210,000
3	1,331,000
4	1,464,100
5	1,610,510
6	1,771,561
7	1,948,717

You might intuitively expect an asset that increases at a rate of 10% per annum to double in value every 10 years. However, due to the power of compounding, the asset would only take 7.2 years to double in value. Note that the difference in value between years 0 and 1 is $100,000, but the difference in value between years 6 and 7 is $177,156; each increase is greater than its preceding equivalent.

You may also have heard reference to the *Rule of 72*, whereby if we divide the number 72 by the compounding percentage rate we can calculate the number of years it takes the value of an asset to double. Therefore, an asset than increases by 7.2% per annum will take 10 years to double in value, while an asset that increases in value by 10% per annum will only take 7.2 years to double in value. The implication of this is that it is very important to target the highest capital growth rate that can be achieved, as the difference it can make to wealth over time is enormous.

It is the combination of LEVERAGE and COMPOUND GROWTH that turns so many ordinary Australians into millionaires through property.

Some thoughts on inflation...and deflation

Inflation rates may appear to be relatively moderate when they hover around 2% or 3%, but the power of compounding works its deceptive magic on inflation rates too. We can all remember when goods cost far less than they do now. As property investors, we do not worry unduly about inflation provided that it remains a positive figure and the assets that we have purchased over time outperform the inflation rate.

That said, when inflation becomes too high, we will inevitably be beaten with the Reserve Bank's interest rate stick. Inflation can serve to increase the values of property, which works in our favour, while the actual values of our mortgages stay fixed at the value at which we took them out. As share investors, we must be cognisant of inflation too. When we are investing in shares for the long term, we want to be certain that the capital growth we achieve is greater than the rate of inflation, and that we attain a reasonable rate of return in excess of this.

Fund managers worry about deflation. This is probably partly because of the short-termist method in which fund performance is measured, with an emphasis on quarterly growth. However, if we were to enter a period of prolonged deflation, then we, as property investors, should be concerned too.

Theoretically, in a developing economy the price of goods should get cheaper as companies become more efficient. We sometimes see this in the electronic goods industries, where new products such as the latest personal computers and plasma screens are initially very expensive, but become cheaper over time. However, it seems to be human nature to expect prices to increase over time, as companies and individuals gradually increase the amount they charge for services and products.

Certain publicity-seeking individuals get a lot of press through claiming that Australia is going to mirror Japan and head into a downward spiral of deflation with plummeting property prices. In my view, this is not a smart comparison. Japan's population growth has been falling for several decades, and the population actually began to *fall* after the turn of the century.

The Japanese Health Ministry expects that the overall population levels will contract by around 25% by 2050[14], and this is one factor that has caused Japan's growth in gross domestic product (GDP) to be very poor. Housing demand in Japan has therefore been declining, as you might expect if your population, and therefore the demand for property, is in decline. This is a very strong contrast with the situation we have in Australia, as noted earlier.

The impact of deflation on the Japanese economy has been catastrophic, and many property owners have been left with properties that they cannot afford to sell, such has been the fall in their value. It is the severe nature of the impact of deflation on the Japanese economy that leads me to believe that we are actually more likely to see high inflation rates than deflation in Australia, as the Reserve Bank errs on the side of caution.

We should consider the risk of deflation when investing in property, while recognising that the long-term historical trend has been one of inflation, and the Reserve Bank has clearly stated that its intention is for this to continue. We should therefore assume that the RBA will utilise whatever powers it has at its disposal to aim for a steadily inflationary economy.

Practical Action Points

- Investigate how much a bank will lend you for a mortgage. A mortgage broker can help you to find this out, and many brokers do not charge you a fee (instead earning their commissions from banks).

- Calculate how expensive a property you could afford to buy and service. Remember to include the costs of stamp duty and conveyancing/legal fees.

- Consider what type of property you could afford to service. If you have a relatively low disposable income, you may want to consider properties with a strong yield.

- Read property investment books: the best author for the Australian market, in my opinion, is Michael Yardney. If you are going to be investing in Australia, stick to books that are written by Australian authors. Reading books by authors from overseas is at best confusing and at worst may result in financial loss.

- Research and understand how property cycles work, and resolve to use the cycles to your advantage.

- Check your credit history. Lenders will consider any black marks against your name that you may have picked up for late payment of debts or other misdemeanours. Visit www.experian.com to do this. If you have a poor score, it will serve you better to know about it, and you may be able to take corrective action.

- Start saving a deposit by diverting funds to a new high-interest savings account.

7

HOW TO BUILD A
POWERHOUSE
PROPERTY
PORTFOLIO

7

Tread the right path

As is the case with any successful investment strategy, building a powerhouse property portfolio requires a plan, discipline and patience. In his book *Real Estate Riches*, property investor Dolf De Roos says that there is no right or wrong way to invest in property[1]. You have to admire the diplomatic nature of that statement, but it's definitely not true! There are dozens of wrong ways to invest in property. I should know, as I have made a fair number of the mistakes myself over the years. Fortunately for me, by reading about and learning from the mistakes of others, I was able to take a shorter route to financial freedom. You can do the same. Read as much as you can!

Start with the end in mind

Starting with the end in mind is one of the habits of highly effective people as noted by motivational author Stephen Covey[2]. Successful property investing is about knowing why you are investing in the first place, and so it is wise to set yourself some kind of specific and measurable target. Of course, the target may change as you progress along the way.

I previously noted that a target of a property portfolio of $3 million to $5 million in value, if backed up by a portfolio of dividend-paying shares and index funds, would be an excellent launch pad for escaping from the rat race. Depending on where you hail from and your background (and indeed the year in which you are reading this book), this may seem either very high or perhaps not high enough. My thought process is that a portfolio of $5 million will increase in value by $500,000 in a year (and thus so will my net worth) if a 10% per annum capital growth is achieved. In more modest periods of growth, a 5% per annum capital growth would still see the value increase by $250,000 in a year. You need to have a think about some numbers, and about what kind of growth is relevant to you.

In terms of properties to invest in, for me the best method is to start at the top and work down: choose a country (I recommend Australia), then the state that is likely to see the next boom, then a city (in my case, I go for the capital cities), then a well-located suburb, then the best property type and street for attaining capital growth in that suburb.

Invest through two property cycles...and then more

A property cycle is reasonably simple to identify in retrospect – it will involve a period of flat or falling values, followed by an increase in confidence and a period of increasing values until the market becomes overheated and returns to flat or falling values. The exact timings of the cycle, however, will not be completely predictable. The economic cycle is discussed in a little more detail later in the book.

It generally takes two full property cycles for an individual to generate significant wealth through a buy-and-hold investment strategy. The theory is that we buy a small number of properties, after the first boom period we refinance and buy several more properties, and after the second boom period our wealth will have increased very significantly. The idea is almost ridiculously simple in nature, and yet as a percentage of the population, very few people achieve this goal. It really can be as easy as that: don't sell your properties and incur needless capital gains tax, wait for them to increase in value, refinance them, and buy several more.

While at times I pretentiously like to think of myself as a highly sophisticated investor in the mould of a Soros or a Buffett, the truth is that most of the wealth I have created has been simply through buying prime-location investment property and holding it for the long term. My wife bought her first house in 1997, a property that tripled in value over the following eight years. We have refinanced this property several times and over the following years acquired property after property in prime locations and outstanding capital growth suburbs. When many of the newly acquired properties then experienced booms in value, we were financially free. While wealth creation can at times seem complicated, it is often the case that the very simplest ideas are also the most effective.

Australia or overseas?

There is nothing inherently wrong with investing overseas. I have dual nationality, and I find that it sometimes makes sense for me, as the current hugely positive cash flow I have from my UK properties neatly balances the moderately negative cash flow I currently have on my Australian properties. Investing overseas also gives me some diversification against a severe drop in Australian property values. Finally, the strong Australian dollar made investing overseas irresistible to me. However, looking overseas might not be for everyone, because there are also difficulties in investing in overseas property. It is logistically more difficult due to the distances involved, financing can be tricky and other risks are introduced such as sovereign risk and foreign exchange risk. It should also be noted that there is a plentiful supply of outstanding investments in Australia, which reduces the need to look elsewhere.

I have mentioned UK property in conversation before and had people tell me that property prices in England are forever doomed and have collapsed beyond repair. They certainly fell during 2008 and 2009, which meant that I managed to pick up a property in 2010 (in Colchester in the UK) for over 25% less than it had changed hands for in early 2007. However, to conclude that the prices there are forever doomed is incorrect, and typical of a short-sighted viewpoint. Residential property moves in cycles, and after the collapse of several UK banks, many lenders will not currently lend more than around 80% of a property's value, which has removed many buyers from the market (though I recently read that one major bank is reintroducing higher loan percentages).

People tend to have short memories in respect of these matters. Back in the late 1990s and early 2000s, the UK property market was delivering double-digit returns, year after year after year. As I mentioned earlier, my wife's first house, bought in 1997, *tripled* in value in eight years, and even when the global financial crisis hit, the property maintained its value. Clearly, prices do not continue in that vein forever, but nor will they stay flat forever.

Despite this, I do not necessarily advocate investing overseas for most Australian investors. For a start, there may be significant tax advantages when investing in Australia for citizens of this country, mainly in the form of negative gearing, which I will discuss in more detail later. Then, there is the forecast population growth, which underpins the market to a large extent. Australia is a nation of property owners, which also tends to keep prices buoyant. Buying property here is easier, too, and we do not expose ourselves to foreign exchange risk. There are so many fine investments to be had in Australia that it is not necessarily smart to look overseas unless you have a specific knowledge of a country and have reason to believe that you will get better returns elsewhere.

Commercial or residential?

The short answer is that I recommend residential property as a more appropriate class than commercial property for most investors. There are a number of reasons for this. Commercial property can generate higher yields, but this may often be at the expense of robust capital growth, and it is capital growth that creates wealth. Commercial property growth rates are also likely to be more volatile. In times of economic recession, prices may fall and you may experience periods of vacancy as small companies fold. Vacancy rates for residential property are impacted less by economic downturns, as we still need a roof over our heads, and the Australian rate of home ownership is high.

Time horizon for investment

People have differing views on this, depending upon their age and their investment strategy. As I am in the first quarter of the *Game of Money*, when I buy a property I consider it to be a 30-year investment, so I want it to deliver me the best capital growth and cash flow over that time period.

Therefore, I am not trying to spot a moderately undervalued property in a cheap outer or regional suburb in the hope of making a quick 10–20% capital gain. Instead, I want to invest in the best suburbs that will deliver capital growth year in year out for decades to come. In my view, the most reliable method is to invest in top lifestyle suburbs close to the CBDs of capital cities. In the long term, these properties deliver better cash flow as well, so over the life of a 30-year investment there is no question that these are the best properties to invest in.

Of course, there are many different strategies for property investment. Some people renovate properties hoping for a quick profit. If you are approaching your later years, you may be more interested in generating a higher yield than in the capital growth of the property. A higher yield may also be desirable if your income is low. Note, however, that this is a book about attaining financial freedom as quickly as is reasonably possible: if you want to do this, you must attain capital growth to bring you wealth and, importantly, to allow you leverage into further investments. Targeted capital growth can sometimes be at the expense of a higher yield.

Not selling

Neither my wife nor I have ever sold a property. That is so fundamental to this book, I am going to write it again in large type:

'In over 15 years of buying properties, we have never sold one.'

Had we sold properties, paid the associated selling costs and capital gains tax, and then invested in other locations incurring more stamp duty and legal fees, I am positive there is no way we would have been able to give full-time work the flick at such a young age.

Theoretically, one could time the market, selling after a boom and investing counter-cyclically in another location, but in practice this is not as easy to do as it sounds. What if you sell a property that has doubled in value only for it to boom in value again after you have sold it? Property has a wonderful knack of continuing to grow and compound, and while we try to predict property cycles as precisely as we can, the cycles are never completely predictable. Even if we hold on to property for more than one year, the capital gains tax in Australia eats into sales profits, as do agents' fees and commissions.

In theory, it is a smart idea to wait until the peak of a property boom, sell your investment and move your funds into another booming investment, be it in property, shares or another asset class. In practice, however, it is difficult to time markets perfectly in this manner, and therefore I advocate holding on to your investment properties indefinitely. Provided you have chosen investment-grade properties in the first place and avoided investing in 'lemons', you will continue to reap the benefits for decades to come.

Growing wealth through property is fundamentally very simple: buy at the right price and as close to the bottom of the property cycle as possible, add value to the property through renovations, wait for the capital growth, refinance and return to step one. This way, we never incur capital gains tax on sale, and the power of compound growth becomes ever greater as we extend our portfolio. Think of the wealth that your parents' generation could have created over the last 30 or 40 years had they followed this very simple strategy. They would be millionaires over and over again.

However, the statistics show that the majority of property investors never own more than one or two investment properties. This is often due to a mistaken belief that the only way to realise profit from property is through selling. Instead, we can borrow against the increased value of the property to reinvest in further properties or to pay for (moderate!) living costs.

Returns from cash flow or capital growth

Whether it is better to invest for capital growth or cash flow is an old debate. Sometimes, there may tend to be an inverse relation between these factors in Australian property. Generally, cheaper properties in outer suburbs and regional centres have provided a significantly higher cash flow or yield, but the capital growth may have sometimes been lower (hence why remote property is still cheaper). Conversely, properties in the inner and middle-ring suburbs of the capital cities may have seen greater capital growth, but now produce lower rental yields.

Some will counter this argument with statements such as 'Over the last 10 years, certain properties with high yields have seen greater capital growth than those in inner suburbs.' As a Chartered Accountant (who often had to manipulate figures), I am inherently sceptical of statistics with a carefully selected timeframe and with such caveats attached. It is a simple fact that the prestige suburbs have historically outperformed cheaper outlying suburbs over the long term. This is obvious if you think about it. The prices in Vaucluse, Point Piper or Darling Point in Sydney did not get to where they are now with moderate capital growth.

That said:

> 'The key for us today is to ascertain where
> the growth of the FUTURE will be.'

I would never argue that regional centres and outer suburbs cannot achieve capital growth that is superior to that of inner suburbs over certain periods of time, for that would be untrue. The fact is, I am not that interested in which areas have produced the best capital growth in the past; I am only interested in which properties will generate the best capital growth over the next few decades.

There are a number of key trends developing in Australia:

- Very significant population growth, with most of the immigrants heading to our capital cities
- Younger generations wanting to live close to the CBD in lifestyle suburbs
- Houses becoming increasingly unaffordable
- A growing tendency towards unit dwelling and two-income households.

I therefore formulate my argument that the best investments in Australia for the next 30 years will be high-quality one-and two-bedroom apartments in our major capital cities, in suburbs offering a fantastic lifestyle with easy transport access to the CBD. I would always favour buying the best-available investment properties at a fair price over buying inferior-grade properties in poor locations at a tempting cheap price.

Capital growth creates wealth

Let's start with a fact: wealth is mostly created by capital growth. Simple mathematics dictates this. You could find a property with a high yield, but once the mortgage repayments are made and tax is paid on the excess rental income, there won't be a huge amount left over. On the other hand, capital growth on a property creates an unrealised capital gain, and the gain will never be taxed if you don't sell the property; it can simply be left to compound and compound into the future. In short, it is very hard to get rich from $5, $10 or $20 per week in cash flow, but if you can invest in a quality property that doubles in value, you are on the path to wealth.

A dedicated capital growth investor might ask you to consider this hypothetical 'growth' property with a 10% per annum capital growth and 5% yield:

Figure 7.1 – $500,000 property: 10% capital growth, 5% yield

Year	Value ($)	Rental Income p.a. ($)
0	500,000	25,000
1	550,000	27,500
2	605,000	30,250
3	665,500	33,275
4	732,050	36,603
5	805,255	40,263
6	885,781	44,289
7	974,359	48,718
8	1,071,794	53,590
9	1,178,974	58,949
10	**1,296,871**	**64,844**

Then consider this hypothetical 'cash flow' property with a 5% per annum capital growth but a massive 10% yield:

Figure 7.2 – $500,000 property: 5% capital growth, 10% yield

Year	Value ($)	Rental Income p.a. ($)
0	500,000	50,000
1	525,000	52,500
2	551,250	55,125
3	578,813	57,881
4	607,753	60,775
5	638,141	63,814
6	670,048	67,005
7	703,550	70,355
8	738,728	73,872
9	775,664	77,566
10	**814,447**	**81,444**

Of course, there has never been and never will be a property that has behaved in precisely this manner, but the example does demonstrate a useful point. While the yield of the cash-flow property might be tempting in the short term, in the long term the capital growth of the growth property is far more important, and the yield of the growth property increases over time with inflation too. Project this trend forward 50 years and the difference is mind-blowing. I have not done this, as the numbers begin to look unrealistic to our brains, which are programmed to understand values in today's dollars. It is difficult for us to imagine paying millions of dollars for investment properties in the future, just as it must have seemed impossible in the 1960s to imagine the prices of today. Think of how many times we see terraces advertised for sale in Paddington in Sydney (or equivalent suburbs in other cities) that last changed hands for $50,000 or less and now command asking prices in the millions.

Naturally, the above tables present an oversimplification of the argument, but they serve to demonstrate the main point: wealth comes from capital growth. In his book *From 0 to 260+ Properties in 7 Years*, Steve McKnight details how he replaced his reasonably modest salary by buying and selling (i.e. not buying and holding) with a business partner some 260 cheaper cash-flow-positive properties, predominantly in outer suburbs and regional areas[3]. This is a great achievement, but it perhaps provides an example of how many property transactions you may need to be involved in to start generating meaningful wealth from the actual cash flow of the properties.

Given that reportedly only one in 200 property investors own more than five properties (and most property investors never make it to their third property), the odds of significant numbers of investors replicating McKnight's great success are low. He is an abnormally smart guy too. McKnight went on to sell his properties as the market peaked, and is now more into running his website[4] and investing in commercial property and US property. If you are investing for cash flow, you need to be aware that when markets boom in value, higher interest rates may see your properties generating a negative cash flow if you have not fixed your mortgage rates.

McKnight explains that his suggested strategy is to time the market, take the capital growth and then move on. If you are able to do this, it is a strategy that can definitely reap dividends, though I have found the buy-and-hold approach a far easier approach to wealth creation. I also believe that buy and hold is a strategy that gives the average investor a greater chance of success – far too often, 'underperforming' properties are sold by impatient investors only for the properties to be worth far more down the track. Just as average investors tend to be poor at timing the share markets, so it is in property.

Despite the points made above, it should be noted that no capital growth investor in his or her right mind would ever argue that a negative cash flow from a property is a good thing. The tax benefits (explained later) are helpful, but should not mask the fact that losing significant chunks of money each month is not smart investing. Therefore, my recommendation is to find the best capital growth areas and properties you can find, but to minimise the cash-flow loss as far as possible. If you can achieve this, you will find that over time, the yields will increase with inflation (properties tend to produce negative cash flow when capital growth has been experienced but rents have not had a chance to catch up).

An example: when my wife bought her first property in Cambridge, England in 1997, she bought in what would be termed a traditional capital growth area. Her townhouse is in a desirable suburb of a beautiful city and is only walking distance from the city centre with its train links to London. She definitely could have invested in surrounding towns or distant outer suburbs that provided a higher percentage yield from lodgers, but as she was living in the property herself, she went for the desirable inner suburb.

Roll forward to 2012, and despite having refinanced, the rent she receives from this property is 60% higher than the principal-and-interest mortgage, so it is generating an enormous positive cash flow. The capital growth in the property was also phenomenal, as I previously noted, the property tripling in value very quickly. Meanwhile, capital growth in the outer areas has lagged way behind this rate of growth, and yields have not kept pace either. Ultimately, it pays to invest in properties that are most in demand.

With property already expensive in Australia, it is absolutely crucial to invest in properties that are in continual high demand. If there is risk in property as an asset class, I believe it is in buying properties in poor suburbs, where property owners have only linear income streams and demand for properties can be fragile. There is also a risk in investing in areas that may become oversupplied.

Techniques for minimising cash-flow loss

Despite the issues I noted in the previous section, I will say that when I quit my full-time employment, an interesting change began to happen. I suddenly began to resent the properties I owned that were generating a negative cash flow. Those that were generating a positive cash flow – which basically equated to those located in the UK – I looked upon as golden investments. They needed little or no attention, and put extra cash in my pocket at the end of each month, instead of causing me annoyance. Make no mistake, having a positive cash flow in your portfolio is an excellent thing, and ultimately it must be the outcome that we aim for.

The yield from residential property varies significantly depending upon the location and the type of property concerned. If you have a target of a property portfolio with a value of $5 million, you could purchase one house for $5 million in, for example, the suburb of Centennial Park in Sydney. The capital growth over the long term might be great, but if you are receiving a low rental yield of only 2% or 3%, then the negative cash flow could send you broke very quickly. This is an extreme example of why cash flow is important.

Here are some of the techniques that can be used to minimise a cash-flow loss.

Interest-only loans

It is common when purchasing a principal place of residence to take out a principal-and-interest loan in order to get the loan paid off. For investment properties, however, sometimes it is preferable to take out an interest-only loan instead. I have a mixture of both in my portfolio.

There are arguments in favour of both types of loan. Those who do not have the discipline to save may prefer to take out a principal-and-interest loan in order to help build up equity. And I suppose that in times of extremely high interest rates, you may believe that you would not be able to match the interest rate through the returns of an alternative investment. There is, however, something curiously circular about paying down a loan only to redraw it in the future (if that is your intention during the growth stage of your investment life). An interest-only loan has the benefit of requiring a significantly lower monthly repayment.

The reason why I believe interest-only loans are generally a superior product for investors is *flexibility*. It is now possible to take out an interest-only loan that gives the option of paying off lump sum amounts of the principal with no penalty. As an investor, I want to get the highest return on my capital that I can, regardless of which asset class I obtain the return from. If the interest rate on the loan is very high, it may be smart to transfer funds against the principal of the loan, although generally I believe that I can obtain a higher return on my funds in the stock market than the rate being charged on my investment property loans.

If you believe that you need a principal-and-interest loan to force you to make repayments rather than spending the cash frivolously, that is fine, but perhaps you should consider working on your discipline too!

Low strata fees

A common mistake made by investors is to purchase a unit that on the face of it appears to be good value, only to discover that the strata fees each quarter are cripplingly high. Some of the old warehouse-style properties around Darling Harbour seem to offer incredible value, but the buildings inside are falling to pieces, with no sinking fund to cover the astronomical cost of repairs. Even on small two-bedroom units, strata fees can run higher than $2,500 per quarter. If you are investing in units, it is often wise to steer clear of properties with expensive amenities such as swimming pools, saunas and gymnasiums, and those employing a 24-hour concierge service.

Some might argue that a house is a better investment than a unit due to the absence of strata fees, but generally only a relatively small amount of a strata fee goes towards administration, perhaps 20% or less. The majority of strata fees are spent on costs such as repairs, maintenance of common areas and building insurance. Provided you are investing in units with sensible strata fees, you will not be too far out of pocket compared with the equivalent costs of house owners.

Claim depreciation allowances

As a property investor, it is important to take advantage of depreciation allowances. We can claim deductions on our tax return for the depreciation of certain items in an investment property, which can add to a cash-flow loss for tax purposes or sometimes turn a negative cash flow into a positive one via a tax refund.

Some investors try to prepare depreciation schedules themselves, but I would advise against this, as the ATO will not look favourably upon any inaccuracies. Instead, engage a qualified surveyor to prepare the schedule for you. They may charge you up to $500 for the schedule, but you will be able to use the schedule for many years to come, and their fees will be tax deductible too. Surveyors often guarantee that they can save you more than the cost of their fees, and over time they will do so.

Renovations

Giving a property a cosmetic facelift or rejuvenation can add 10% or 20% to the rental income, and significantly reduce or eliminate a cash-flow loss. Full scale renovations may, if you have the relevant skills, add greater returns to both cash flow and capital growth, though there may be a risk premium if you are inexperienced. I like improvements of a more cosmetic nature such as repainting, carpeting and in some circumstances installing a new kitchen and bathroom.

Traditionally, more serious renovators have aimed to spend around 10% of the cost of the property on renovations, aiming for 25% capital growth on the total cost of the investment (i.e. purchase price plus renovation costs). A longer time horizon or a bigger renovation may warrant seeking a higher return as compensation for the risk. In a cosmetic renovation, the investor may simply want to improve the value of the property by $1,500 or more for every $1,000 spent, and significantly increase the potential rental income in the process. Note that the residual un-depreciated value of certain qualifying assets that are scrapped may attract a tax benefit, and therefore it is important to prepare a depreciation schedule both before and after renovations.

Figure 7.3 – Example: simple cosmetic renovation

	$
Purchase Price	300,000
Kitchen upgrade	10,000
Bathroom upgrade	10,000
Carpeting	5,000
Painting	3,000
Garden	2,000
Total cost	**330,000**
Revaluation	**345,000**

The key to a successful renovation is planning and budgeting. The number of 'investors' who buy properties for renovation with no plan – a detailed budget of costs and expected resale value – is very scary. By the way, a budget should not be based solely upon the amount of the money in your bank account! A detailed and realistic budget with a decent contingency is a vital starting point, and will automatically put you a step ahead of a huge number of amateurs.

Blocks of units

If you are looking to make a high-value purchase for an investment, and by this I mean one that runs into the millions of dollars, it may be wise to consider buying a block of units. One of the advantages of this is that you can make a high-value purchase without sacrificing too much in the way of rental yield (expensive houses can produce low yields and cost the investor dearly in terms of cash flow).

A sound strategy may be to find a 'pack' of 4, 6, or 12 (or even more) units that are in need of a cosmetic renovation and then add value to them. There is a big potential upside in buying a block of units at a good price and upgrading them (perhaps through rendering or by adding extra bedrooms). It is important to buy at the right price if this is your strategy, for valuing a block of units is not necessarily as straightforward as valuing an individual unit.

Inner suburbs? Or outer suburbs and regional centres?

Personally, I have a strong inclination towards inner suburbs with a proven history of high capital growth and high demand. You may often hear pundits say that if such properties have even a small negative cash flow, we are introducing a risk into our investment that the capital growth fails to compensate for. I disagree. In an inflationary economic environment, rents will continue to rise in the future, and I have more faith in securing capital growth in top-quality suburbs located close to capital city centres. Investing in regional areas may secure a higher yield initially, but may leave you more exposed to the risk and opportunity cost of poor or negative capital growth.

Around the turn of this century a spate of literature became available on the subject of investing for cash flow, possibly stemming from the *Rich Dad Poor Dad* approach to investment in US real estate. Positive cash flow in your portfolio is a wonderful thing, and something all investors must surely aspire to. However, what is not smart is chasing yield by investing in areas of low demand. Positive-cash-flow books and magazines began touting investment anywhere from remote outlying areas, such as Cairns, to tourism properties in Noosa or the islands off Queensland.

An example of a highly successful positive-cash-flow investor is Margaret Lomas, who noted in her book *How to Maximise your Property Portfolio* that if you spread your investments over a wide range of areas, then some of the properties should attain some good growth[5], and that theoretically the number of positive-cash-flow investments you can own is unlimited (though the banks' appetite for lending may be finite). Can this approach work? It definitely can, and Lomas is living proof of that, with 38 properties in her portfolio. In the same book, Lomas noted that she owns a property in a small city in northern NSW[6], which I thought was an unusual choice, until I checked the 10-year capital growth figures for the city, which blasted the returns on, say, Sydney out of the water for the corresponding period.

Margaret Lomas is one of the finance authors whom I believe does have integrity. Being a positive-cash-flow property investor, Lomas invests mainly in outer-city suburbs and regional centres, which is not a strategy I go for myself, but you can't question her results, integrity or disclosure. Her first book, *How to Make your Money Last as Long as You Do*, sold very well, and she subsequently wrote around half a dozen books on the subject of how to invest in positive-cash-flow property. In one of those books, Lomas disclosed that she had invested in property worth $1 million and shares worth $50,000, having invested in a number of international initial public offerings[7].

I wouldn't necessarily recommend investing in international IPOs if you have a small portfolio of shares, but you can't question the integrity of the disclosure. In any case, Lomas has gone on to build a very large portfolio of properties, so I doubt she worries about it too much! I also respected that when a property that Lomas had previously described as one of her greatest investments in Cairns subsequently turned out to be a dud, the author was totally open about it and disclosed as much. I particularly admired that, because so many finance authors try to portray themselves as being far more successful than they really are and as never having made a mistake. Every investor makes mistakes, and the best investors are often those who have made the most mistakes and learned from them.

I suppose the lesson here is that there is certainly more than one way to skin a cat, and that if you do not earn a high income, aiming for a higher-yield property might be an option for you. I would only caution that if you are aiming to take a positive-cash-flow approach, stick to towns and cities of a reasonable size with growing populations and a high demand for the type of property you are investing in. You should also be aware that physical growth of an area may not correspond to capital growth if there is more land that can be made available for release. In my view, property is unlikely to attain the same stellar levels of capital growth that have been seen in past decades, and therefore we must exercise caution.

Poor investments

I have met a number of people who have bemoaned the fact that they invested in shiny new investment properties on the Gold Coast or in Cairns, only for the values of their properties to fall. In my view, the values did not necessarily fall, they were simply overpriced properties in the first place that were sold to willing buyers from interstate, many on two-tier marketing schemes. A key lesson is that just because something is labelled as an investment, this does not necessarily mean it is any good.

I believe that places such as Cairns do not make for good investments, unless you can time them very well, for the simple reason that there is insufficient demand or population growth to produce great capital growth. I recall that my former employers Deloitte had an office in Cairns, but closed it because 'the place only runs on retirees and tourism' – their words, not mine! There is also a risk that if you invest in areas such as these, rather than prices falling dramatically, they simply do not grow very much, which is the risk of opportunity cost. If we wish to escape the rat race to financial freedom, we simply must attain capital growth.

Tourism-style properties I would just avoid altogether if you are taking a buy-and-hold approach to property investment. Do not confuse a good investment property with somewhere you would like to retire to. While we might get a higher yield and growth in good years, in times of recession we can be left with vacancies, tumbling prices and very few willing buyers.

As I write this, there are news stories in Queensland of prices in Noosa having fallen by a quarter and of luxury properties selling for land value. The Gold Coast has been absolutely hammered by around 40% in some areas too. For the purposes of balance, it should be noted that if you are aiming to time the market in speculative areas such as tourism properties or the Gold Coast, then theoretically you can make a very tidy profit. Please, just note the risks. Personally, I am far more comfortable aiming for properties with a continual high demand and holding them for the long term.

In some respects then, my view is opposite to what you may hear elsewhere. I believe that contrary to what some believe, investing for positive cash flow is not necessarily any less risky than investing in traditional capital growth properties (provided that any negative cash flow is not too high). I remember several years ago reading articles in property magazines about young investors investing in towns they had never heard of because they had found properties with a positive cash flow. If ever there was a poor strategy, this is it.

Quite apart from the fact that vacancies, itinerant tenants and repairs can quickly lead to the cash flow becoming negative, what happens when the interest rates rise significantly? The cash flow may become negative anyway, and if certain regional property prices are being propped up by cash-flow investors, then prices can drop sharply too. Property prices in remote or regional areas may be more susceptible to interest rate rises than those in wealthier suburbs, partly because of cash-flow investors propping up prices, but mainly because of the linear nature of income in lower demographic suburbs.

Finally, be very cautious about investing in regional centres that are highly reliant on one or two industries. We should learn this from the property meltdown in the United States (though the property crisis in the US was exacerbated by a proliferation of sub-prime debt too, of course). A city that is highly reliant on one industry may be a dangerous place to invest. Cash-flow investors were touting the NSW south coast as a smart place to invest until recently; it remains to be seen how dramatically the thousands of recent BlueScope redundancies in the Illawarra region impact the housing market there.

One other point of note on investing primarily for cash flow: high yields are often obtained from niche investments such as serviced apartments, holiday lets, student or retirement accommodation or commercial lets. These are specialised investments, often with variable demand. The high yield that is offered may be achieved at the expense of capital growth – and remember, it is capital growth that creates serious wealth.

I look for properties in landlocked areas where land cannot be released for new development, thereby causing an oversupply. It is also wise to steer clear of investing in CBDs where huge new towers of units can create an over-supply of properties. The population of Australia is growing, and a high proportion of the new population is moving to our capital cities. Look for units that are in high demand and are not impacted by poor affordability.

How much, not how many

You may sometimes hear of investors noting that they have ten individual properties, only to discover that they are worth around the same as your one property in Sydney or Melbourne. Ultimately what matters is the value of the property we own, not the number of individual titles.

It is not uncommon to hear of investors picking up properties for as little as $50,000 or less. The advantage of this might be that cheaper properties in outlying areas may generate a positive cash flow. The thing to be wary of is that cheaper properties are usually cheaper for a good reason. As investors, we need to choose properties that are in high demand and will outperform inflation. If a property only rises in value in line with inflation, while we will slowly create some equity, we will still only be left with a cheap property at the end of the process.

Of course, I do note here that not everyone can afford to buy in capital cities, and in this case it can be good to buy in cheaper areas such as regional centres. If this is to be your strategy, I would again caution to look for towns and cities with a reasonable-sized and growing population, and to be wary of areas that are reliant solely upon one industry (such as mining towns).

One of my centrally located properties in Sydney is worth around $750,000. A cash-flow investor might argue that it is better to hold fifteen $50,000 properties rather than the one that I hold because they will generate a higher yield. That may be one reason in favour of the cash-flow properties. However, these are some of the reasons why I prefer the more expensive property:

- I can still attain a yield of 5–6%, which may be lower, but is still a fair return

- Diversification versus focus: just as it is harder to significantly outperform the average growth of the stock market with ten shares than it is with one, it is harder to outperform the median property price growth with fifteen regional properties as opposed to one excellent property in an outstanding location

- Fewer properties equate to less time spent on administration

- I will get better and more desirable tenants

- I can aim for superior capital growth.

While it might not be politically correct to say so, it is a simple fact that cheap properties attract less desirable tenants. My centrally located properties attract professionals who have never missed rent payments, caused any damage or noise problems or left me with any vacancies at all. Sometimes, they even ask permission to redecorate the units or install new appliances. The yield may be a slightly lower percentage, but the tenants themselves cause no headaches at all.

Most importantly from my perspective, I can choose a property from any suburb in any city in Australia to target the greatest capital growth. I am not limited to only those suburbs that generate a few extra dollars in yield.

Negative gearing and cash flow: examples

In Australia, we currently have negative gearing tax benefits. On certain investments, we may be able to deduct interest repayments (as well as certain other expenses directly related to the investment) from our taxable income. This is of particular benefit to property investors who have properties that generate a negative cash flow, whereby the rental income does not cover the investment loan interest and other expenses.

Higher-rate taxpayers have tended to gravitate towards property investment as a means of reducing their tax bill. While this may be a sound idea in principle, remember that it is never a good idea to purchase an investment solely for the purpose of making a tax loss.

You do not necessarily have to wait until June 30 and beyond to receive the benefit of the reduced tax. If you believe you will be due a refund of tax at the end of any given financial year, you can complete a PAYG variation form to reduce your tax deductions. Engage your accountant if you are unsure as to how to complete the form, because there may be a penalty if your estimates are inaccurate. Your accountant may charge you up to a couple of hundred dollars for helping you, but these fees should be tax deductible.

It is better to have funds in your account where you can put them to work for you than to have them sitting in the ATOs overflowing coffers until August or September. When it comes to tax time, remember to claim those depreciation allowances!

Examples of cash flow on properties

Here are three numerical examples to show the difference between a property where the owner has taken steps to reduce the cash-flow loss and a property where the owner has simply bought an investment property with no regard to the cash flow. For the sake of simplicity I have not included lots of detail, but I have tried to make the examples realistic in terms of the included figures.

Property 1 – Mick: the cash-flow investor

In the first example, Mick has bought a house for $150,000 on the NSW south coast using a 20% deposit. He has chosen a property in this area principally because he can obtain a high yield of 7.25%. As a result, the property generates a positive cash flow after the depreciation allowances are factored in.

Figure 7.4 – Cash-flow property

	$ per annum
Rental income at 7.25% gross yield	10,875
Mortgage repayments – interest-only loan at 7.50% on $120,000 loan	(9,000)
Insurance and repairs	(1,000)
Property management, admin fees	(1,500)
Cleaning costs	(350)
Loss per annum before depreciation	(975)

By putting down a 20% deposit, using an interest-only loan and choosing a regional property with a high yield, Mick has picked a property that nets only a small loss per annum. However, if he has picked a property with good depreciation allowances, he will be able to add these to the loss calculated above on his tax return, and the total loss (which is deducted from his taxable income at his marginal rate of tax) could result in a tax refund or saving that results in an overall positive cash flow for the year.

There are a few things to note about choosing a property for its yield. Firstly, it is very important to ensure that there is a demand for this type of property from renters. If not, then there could be periods of vacancies, and this is frequently a problem when investors choose seasonal tourism properties for the potential high yield.

It should be noted that properties in some regions are historically cheap for a reason, and that is that there is a plentiful supply of land and a lower demand for it. While it is perfectly possible to attain a short-term capital growth spurt if you identify an undervalued or growing area, these types of properties are perhaps unlikely to outperform the more desirable city suburbs in the long run.

Often, inhabitants of regional centres and outlying areas only have linear income from one source (i.e. their job), which limits the potential capital growth compared with more affluent suburbs. Therefore, this approach is perhaps best suited to an investor who is concerned about short-term cash flow but is also prepared to hold the property for the long term to negate any drops in value that may be caused by a recession.

Note that while the property in the example is more or less breaking even now, if interest rates rise significantly, this will no longer be the case, and the property will be generating a loss. This risk can be hedged by taking out a fixed interest loan, but there is generally a premium charged for fixing interest rates (unless the yield curve is inverted – meaning that the futures markets expect interest rates to fall).

The superior cash flow may mean that the investor can afford to hold more of these types of properties, which may be of significant benefit to lower-income earners. We should remember, though, that an investor will generally be limited by how much a bank will lend him or her, and therefore if a property fails to grow in value, there is an opportunity cost attached to this.

Property 2 – Richie: the cash drainer

In this example, higher-rate taxpayer Richie has taken an interest-only loan of $540,000 at 7.5% interest to purchase a unit in Dover Heights, Sydney for $600,000, using a 10% deposit. This property earns a reasonable enough 5% yield but is an old property with poor depreciation allowances. As the property has a heated swimming pool and areas in various states of disrepair, the strata fees are a painful $2,000 per quarter.

Figure 7.5 – Negatively geared property

	$ per annum
Rental income at 5% yield	30,000
Mortgage repayments – interest-only loan at 7.50% on $540,000 loan	(40,500)
Strata fees $2,000 per quarter	(8,000)
Property management/admin fees	(3,000)
Repairs and cleaning costs	(2,500)
Loss per annum before depreciation	(24,000)

This property is costing Richie $2,000 every month (and if he was using a principal-and-interest loan, the cash-flow loss would be significantly higher). While there will be a handy deduction on the tax return, which could be increased further with depreciation allowances, even a higher rate taxpayer like Richie will only save tax at the marginal rate of 45%, and the remainder will be a cash-flow loss straight from the hip pocket. If Richie can soak up the loss, then a reasonable capital growth rate per annum may still see him get ahead. However, he may be limited in how many of these properties he can afford to hold, especially when the interest rates increase, as one day they surely will.

Property 3 – Susan: the experienced growth investor

In this example, Susan has taken an interest-only loan of $540,000 at 7.50% to purchase a $600,000 unit in Vaucluse, Sydney, using a 10% deposit. Following a cosmetic renovation, the rental yield has been increased to 6% and the strata fees are a more manageable $500 per quarter. This property was built in 1995 and qualifies for handy depreciation allowances. Repairs and property management costs are the same as for the property in the previous example.

Figure 7.6 – Investment-grade property with cosmetic renovation

	$ per annum
Rental income – 6% yield due to renovation	$36,000
Mortgage repayments – interest only loan at 7.50% on $540,000 loan	(40,500)
Strata fees $500 per quarter	(2,000)
Property management/admin fees	(3,000)
Repairs and cleaning	(1,000)
Loss per annum before depreciation	(10,500)

It is very important to understand the tax implications of the loss under the negative gearing tax rules. Note that due to depreciation allowances, Susan can show a *significantly* higher loss on her tax return than the cash-flow loss she has incurred, perhaps somewhere closer to $20,000 than $10,000. Depending on the marginal rate at which the taxpayer is able to save tax, this could be a very good result (if Susan was earning a high salary this saving could be almost half of the loss; if she was on a lower salary it may be 30% of the loss). Susan has shown that investing in high-capital-growth areas does not have to cost the investor a significant amount each month. The negative cash flow would be reduced further or even negated completely if a larger deposit was paid, such as in the first example.

As time passes, the rental income will increase with inflation and will minimise the loss further, until eventually the property becomes cash-flow positive in its own right. Do note that in this example, the loan is at an interest rate of 7.50%, and history has shown us that rates can and will run far higher than that.

These examples are slightly oversimplified, and they may even be slightly conservative, as in the early years of ownership you may also be able to claim certain borrowing expenses as tax deductions, such as[8]:

- Stamp duty charged on the mortgage

- Loan establishment fees

- Costs for preparing and filing mortgage documents

- Mortgage broker fees

- Fees for a valuation required for mortgage approval

- Lender's mortgage insurance (taken out by the lender and billed to you).

Of these three examples, I tend to lean towards the type of investment shown the third example. Susan has not compromised on the location of the investment, carefully choosing the best possible suburb for potential capital growth, with a choice of investing anywhere in Australia. Susan has then done everything she can (except for putting down a bigger deposit) to minimise the cash-flow loss. In my view, if we take this approach to our property investing, we give ourselves the best chance of obtaining capital growth without sending ourselves broke with huge negative cash flow.

I appreciate that this approach may be best suited to younger investors. Investors at different stages of their lives may wish to chase yields and invest in other areas. That is fine, but it is not the approach I would advocate for achieving financial freedom at a younger age.

I also appreciate that for some people, even the smallest negative cash flow may be too hard to stomach, and therefore they may prefer to invest in a positive-cash-flow property. That can work as a strategy, but I will say it one last time: do remember to look for towns and cities with a *reasonable and growing population, continual strong demand* and a *good potential for long-term growth.*

One final point on negative gearing is to remember that there are no guarantees that the rules will stay this way forever (the rules were removed once before in Australia before being hastily reintroduced). While the negative gearing rules are undoubtedly fantastic for property investors now, no investment should ever be taken on for the purpose of making a loss. Investors in the US thought that the negative gearing rules there would last forever, but they did not.

Do also consider that if you give up your full-time employment, losses on your property are of no use to you unless you have other income against which to offset them, therefore acquiring *only* negatively geared property may not a great strategy for you over the long term.

Types of residential property

There are many different types of property, and many different names for them: townhouses, terraces, cottages, Queenslanders, maisonettes, apartments, studios…it can certainly be confusing. Essentially, however, there are two types of property that, as investors, we are interested in: houses and units (sometimes known as flats or apartments).

There are a number of special types of property that you may be interested in if you are chasing higher yields. These may include tourism property, retirement property or student rental units. These types of properties may generate a higher yield but, as noted, this can sometimes be at the expense of good capital growth (in much the same way as commercial property can sometimes generate higher yields with lower capital growth).

Historically, it has generally been true that houses have performed better as investments than units. It is my view that this trend may no longer continue, a theory I explore in more detail below.

Houses and units – supply and demand

There is an elegant and long-held theory that houses perform better than units, because land appreciates while buildings depreciate. The logic is based on the fact that houses tend to have more land area than units, and therefore they outperform in terms of capital growth.

This is a neat theory, but it is not necessarily true. In common with all commodities, property prices are driven by supply and demand. It is also not necessarily true that buildings depreciate if you consider the replacement cost of buildings and materials. Materials and building services tend to increase in an inflationary economy, so a federation house that was built in Paddington decades ago would not actually have cost an awful lot to build when considered in today's dollars. And you will intuitively know that the small amount of land under a unit on Sydney Harbour could be of more long-term value than a quarter-acre plot just south of Alice Springs. If you think about it, there are remote towns and rural areas where land costs virtually nothing, and it never will be of much value, because the demand is very low.

If you want to see an example of how limited supply and massive demand can affect prices, take a look at the value of a house in Hong Kong. The house price-to-income ratio is among the highest in the world. You don't need to calculate the actual value; just take a look at the number of '000s and you will get the gist. With a population of seven million and only a tiny number of houses on the island, the in-demand commodity becomes almost priceless.

Therefore, as property investors we must aim to identify the properties for which there will be the highest demand in the future. As noted, historically there has been a higher demand for houses than for units. However, this may not continue to be the case, with affordability issues beginning to impact house prices and more people electing to live close to the CBD in units, or 'apartments' as they like to now call them. I have heard the CEO of Residex, John Edwards, discussing the movement towards units and the corresponding growth in unit values[9]. It will be interesting to see how these trends change over the next few decades. For ongoing information, take a look at RP Data's monthly reports online, as these closely track house and unit trends.

Incidentally, the re-badging of medium-density dwellings as 'apartments' was a stroke of marketing genius. It is amusing to listen to the young people of today proudly waxing lyrical about their 'fabulous downtown apartments'. Where I grew up in Sheffield in England, studios were known as bedsits and flats were just known as 't'flats'. Had anyone dared to call them *apartments*, they would have soon been enthusiastically and probably physically corrected!

Overall, it boils down to picking the properties that will be in the greatest demand. Houses may be in greater demand in some areas and units in others. One final consideration is that there may be a lot of hidden value in a house, such as the potential for renovation or extension. Better still, you may be able to buy a cheap old house and knock it down, replacing it with a block of units. Now *that* is adding value.

Demographic trends

'I don't skate to where the puck is.
I skate to where the puck will be.' – Wayne Gretzky

The quote is from champion ice hockey player Wayne Gretzky of the Edmonton Oilers, and refers to the manner in which he set himself apart from his peers: anticipation. We can apply the same logic to investment. Property investors should first consider where the planned millions of immigrants are likely to reside.

Figure 7.7 – Projected population growth by city ('000)

	Sydney	Melbourne	Brisbane	Perth	Adelaide
Actual June 2007	4,334	3,806	1,857	1,544	1,158
Projected June 2026	5,426	5,038	2,681	2,268	1,385
Projected June 2056	6,977	6,789	3,979	3,358	1,652

Source: Australian Bureau of Statistics (central case of three series quoted)[10]

We can draw a number of conclusions from this. Firstly, if we own properties in Sydney or Melbourne they are likely to perform tremendously well over the next few decades, as the projected population growth is huge and there is so little land available for release. Brisbane's population boom is also likely to make it an outstanding location for investors over a similar timescale.

Adelaide may perform solidly, and I like the place to visit, but as a younger investor with a long time horizon in mind, I am less inclined to invest there myself – there is the potential for some land to be released, and the projected population growth is comparatively a little lower. Perth is a bit of a wildcard for me. Mining booms could potentially make Perth an amazing place to invest, and it has suffered a market correction after the financial crisis. The Australian Bureau of Statistics projects that by 2056 the population may be as high as 4.2 million or as low as 2.8 million[11]. In other words, nobody really knows what will happen in Perth, and only time will tell.

The population forecasts show significant growth for some of the other state locations too in certain cases. The problem, of course, is predicting where the new boom areas might be. You can certainly try to pick the next boom areas if that is your preferred approach. Personally, I don't feel the need to take on the risk of opportunity cost, preferring to consider that the amount of capital the banks will ultimately lend me could be finite. Being heavily invested in Sydney, I know that the population will increase rapidly, and it is increasing *right now*. These are not trends that will only affect us after several decades; they will begin to affect us immediately. History has shown that there is often a strong correlation between population growth and price appreciation, and this is especially the case where available land supply is limited.

I have seen numerous surveys published by newspapers concluding that the kids of Generation Y have no interest in living anywhere further than 30 minutes from the CBDs of our capital cities. I am naturally sceptical as to the veracity and thorough nature of such surveys, but the trend does seem to be emerging that youngsters of today are far less inclined to spend time commuting to their places of work, even if that means that they can only afford to rent a small property.

There has been a definite trend over the last few decades towards an increasing number of two-income households. Couples are having children later, and are choosing smaller properties to live in during their twenties and early thirties. Statistics on these factors are notoriously difficult to pin down, but if you live in one of the capital cities, you do not need me or anyone else to tell you these things because you can see the trends with your own eyes.

Young professionals of today are far more inclined than ever before to live in units (apartments!) that are close to the CBD. It is entirely normal for both halves of a cohabiting couple to go out to work and to delay having children until they are well into their thirties or even beyond. Another trend that seems to be emerging is that even after having a child many couples elect to remain living in a unit rather than moving out to the suburbs. Singles, too, seem to be increasingly happy with a small space, so long as it is theirs. These trends are surely driven by the unaffordable nature of much of our housing stock.

Transport hubs

An inevitable consequence of a growing population is that there will be more traffic on the roads. Something I learned from London is that properties that are close to public transport in cities with traffic problems are hugely sought after. This trend is already unfolding in Sydney, where it can take two hours or more to drive into the CBD from the outer areas of the city. Unfortunately, our train service is also very slow, so this again suggests to me that suburbs closer to the CBD are becoming increasingly desirable.

As I write this, I note that Qantas recently announced redundancies that have been effectively caused by the rising price of fuel. To date, in Australia we have been lucky in that the government has not raised massive excise on the price of fuel (compare our fuel prices with those in the United Kingdom, for example). Given the rapacious nature of many government policies and a growing awareness of the effect of fuel on our environment, I do not foresee such leniency in the future. This suggests to me that suburbs near transport hubs may be superior suburbs to invest in.

Climate

I am certainly not an expert on climate change, but we should use common sense when deciding where to buy property. In Australia, I steer clear of buying properties in areas such as Campbelltown and Penrith where the yields might be attractive but the climate is extremely hot in summer and cold in winter. I do not know whether Australia will be significantly impacted by climate change over the coming decades, but I do know that these areas will always be of secondary choice compared with suburbs closer to the ocean (though not those at risk of flooding). We should take care, too, to avoid where possible areas that are especially prone to flooding, fires or other natural disasters.

Summary of demographic trends

Briefly summarising all of the above demographic trends leads me to believe that the best investments for the *next* 30 years will be those in the capital cities: Sydney, Melbourne, Brisbane and perhaps Perth. I believe that there is a strong case for the properties that outperform median price growth being two-bedroom and even one-bedroom units in desirable lifestyle suburbs, with easy public transport access to the CBD.

Investing with the market cycle

You may have heard the old maxim 'It's about time in the market, not timing the market.' While this may be true to a point, there is no question that by timing the market cycle we can supercharge our returns from capital growth.

If we buy at the very peak of a property cycle (or indeed a share-market cycle) we are likely to experience falling prices and then a prolonged period of little or no price growth while the market corrects itself. We should not underestimate the effect that this can have on an investor's portfolio. Property cycles, of course, do not move because a set number of years has passed or in any totally predictable manner, and the period of flat values can last for a long time, perhaps even more than a decade, which is a very significant chunk of an investor's lifetime.

The idea of the economic or investment clock first appeared in London's *Evening Standard* newspaper in 1937[12]. Printed on a mock-up clock face was an interpretation of the economic cycle from the peak of the boom (12 o'clock) to the depth of the downturn (6 o'clock) and back to the boom period again.

Figure 7.8 – Economic or investment clock

Time	Economic environment	Explanation
1 o'clock	Rising interest rates	To steady growth and inflation
2 o'clock	Falling share prices	Falling profits and confidence
3 o'clock	Falling commodity prices	Construction decreasing
4 o'clock	Falling overseas reserves	Funds passed between Central Banks
5 o'clock	Tighter money	Debt harder and expensive to source
6 o'clock	Falling property values	Property downturn

Time	Economic environment	Explanation
7 o'clock	Falling interest rates	To stimulate economy
8 o'clock	Rising share prices	Increasing profits and confidence
9 o'clock	Rising commodity prices	Construction increasing
10 o'clock	Rising overseas reserves	Funds passed between Central Banks
11 o'clock	Easier money	Debt easier and cheaper to source
12 o'clock	Rising property prices	Boom

Naturally, as property investors we aim to invest counter-cyclically so that we buy when confidence and prices are low in anticipation of the boom period ahead. Over time, you will learn that residential investment property is an asset class that is very sensitive to interest rate movements. Most leveraged property owners in Australia have variable-rate mortgages, and therefore affordability and confidence are inexorably linked with the Reserve Bank's interest rate policy.

If the state in which you live has recently experienced a significant property boom, it can definitely make sense to invest in another capital city. This has the advantages of helping to reduce or negate land tax (if you have a portfolio with a high land value), diversifying the investor's risk across different regions and, especially, allowing the investor to take advantage of the cyclical nature of property markets.

The effect of buying at the bottom of the cycle can have a marked effect on the price we have to pay for an investment property. I once bought a Sydney harbourside property that was originally listed for $675,000 before the asking price was dropped to $645,000. After I made an offer of $575,000, we eventually settled for $582,500. That is the difference that buying at the bottom of the market, when others are fearful, can have on purchase prices. After less than two years, the property was worth significantly more than the initially requested $675,000, and I had still not so much as added a lick of paint to the place.

Infrastructure

I remember that after I had settled on that property on the Pyrmont harbourside, just a few metres from the water, I watched a TV discussion where a budding investor phoned in and said that he was planning to buy a unit in Pyrmont, only for the presenter to tell him in a sombre manner that he should instead be investing in a suburb 45 km west of the CBD. Ostensibly, I assume, the reason was to chase a higher rental yield, but 'new infrastructure' in the outer suburb was given as a major reason.

I knew a fair bit about the suggested outer-western Sydney suburb in question, as I used to have a client there back in my auditing days. Some of my former work colleagues still talk in hushed tones about how, during a warehouse stock count, the mercury nudged 57 degrees. I do not profess to know too much about the infrastructure plans out there, although I do remember taking two diabolical hours to drive from Sydney on the F4 freeway. I tried the train, but it was even worse, taking two and a half hours, my annoyance compounded by being accosted by a couple of dangerously confused-looking chaps in the train station. My lesson that day was that smart suits, laptops and dodgy train stations are not a happy combination.

It pays to be healthily sceptical when cash-flow investors cite 'infrastructure developments' as the main reason to invest in a remote or regional area. However, an area such as Gladstone in Queensland was a no-brainer because of the proposed resource projects in the area and the potentially huge ensuing growth. I can also certainly understand how, for example, the train link being extended right through to Lilyfield from the Sydney CBD might benefit investing in Lilyfield.

However, to say that infrastructure might benefit us investing nearly 50 km from the CBD...to me, that sounds like confirmation bias. Along similar lines, you may also hear investors promoting certain areas by citing meaningless statistics that are not readily comparable with anything: '16% of homebuyers in the area are aged between 33 and 39, and own an average of 1.26 cars per household.' OK, that's fine, but what does it mean?

Just as I need to be wary of always assuming that a centrally located property must outperform a distant suburb or regional town, cash-flow investors should be careful to avoid searching for reasons why a higher yield property must always be better. I've seen myself do this very thing with share investments, buying the share on intuition first and then looking for reasons why it is a good investment afterwards. It is almost like researching in reverse order. Smart investors should find a potential investment and then search for all the reasons they can find *not* to buy it.

I do know that Pyrmont was, and is, an exciting place to be invested in. The area may have had some bad press after several thousand units sprung up around Darling Harbour just over 20 years ago. Although these units initially commanded premium prices, the subsequent 7% yields suggested that perhaps the new units then depreciated a fair amount, which is a risk of new developments. Some developments of older warehouse buildings ran into strata scheme problems that have seen values slide. The surrounding area probably took a while to get 'up to scratch' too, which would have contributed to this. Now, however, there is everything young professionals could want in the suburb: harbour views, bars and restaurants, easy access to the CBD...you name it, Pyrmont has it.

In terms of infrastructure, Pyrmont has had the $780 million development of Star City Casino, there is a proposed $50 million redevelopment of the Sydney fish markets and a proposed redevelopment of the Sydney Exhibition Centre, to name but three things. Across the Pyrmont Bridge, the top end of the CBD has undergone a huge reawakening, the new Westfield Shoppingtown is thriving, and down at Barangaroo there is an amazing transformation due in the coming years. Having seen the growth in the area in recent years, my only regret concerning buying the property there is that I didn't buy three more of the darned things.

Remember that someone will always disagree with your strategy whatever it may be, and at some point you will just have to have the courage of your convictions and take action. I bought a two-bedroom, two-bathroom, one-car-space unit of 100 square metres on the Sydney harbourside because I know there will always – and I mean *always* – be a demand for that type of property. You will achieve more than those who preach doom and gloom and never invest in anything. I should note here that I wouldn't necessarily recommend investing in Pyrmont now, as property values seem to have caught up somewhat, and better opportunities may exist elsewhere.

Value of property to buy

There are a number of theories on this, but I like to buy property that is reasonably close to the median price of the suburb I am investing in. This should ensure that there will always be a reasonable demand for the investment property provided that the right type of property for the suburb has been purchased. Some argue that investing in the lowest quartile of the market is better, due to the higher yields. It's down to personal choice.

Personally, I tend to look for investments in outstanding suburbs that young professionals want to live in. In Sydney in 2012, this might mean around $600,000–$800,000 for two-bedroom units and $400,000–$600,000 for one-bedroom units depending on the size of the property and the location. In Brisbane, for example, the figures might be a fair amount lower, particularly as the 2011 floods seem to have dented confidence in Brisbane.

Renting or owning your place of residence

We are usually taught by our parents that it is smart to buy our own principal place of residence and pay if off as quickly as we can. This is by no means bad advice. The conventional logic is that we will need somewhere to live in our later years, and if we have a mortgage-free property, this will aid our retirement plans.

It is also assumed by most people that the long-term direction of property prices is upwards, so that even when we pay the bank many thousands of dollars in interest for the mortgage, we will be compensated by the appreciating property price. Obviously, there are emotional benefits to owning your own property too; being able to adapt the property to our own needs is important to many people. The downside to this approach is that many people take on mortgages that cost them such a high percentage of their post-tax salary that it leaves them with precious little left over each month to invest with. If you want to be financially free, then you may want to consider a different approach.

It is generally cheaper to rent a property than it is to buy one, and we can use this to our advantage. In the case of luxury properties, rental yields are often so low that it is far better to be the renter than it is to be the landlord in terms of the monthly cash flow that changes hands.

My suggested approach is to shun the massive mortgage on the principal place of residence and instead invest in multiple investment properties. We can then use the tax benefits (negative gearing) of being a landlord to our benefit, get millions of dollars of assets working for us and have tenants to subsidise the mortgages for us. When we have built a large amount of equity, then we can consider purchasing a place of residence. The awesome thing about this approach is that you can have your cake and eat it too. You can live in a premium suburb and a superb property that is rented, while investing elsewhere to create your fortune. You can truly have the best of both worlds.

Risk profiles

Property investor and expert Chris Gray is an advocate of renting your place of residence and investing elsewhere, and on this point I totally agree with him. He is a fine example of an investor to compare my risk profile with, as he openly discusses all aspects of his property investment strategies with the financial press. I recently read an article where Gray explained that he now has $7 million of debt in his property portfolio and he has a loan-to-value ratio (LVR) of approximately 70%. This is a highly geared portfolio. Gray is so confident on property values in Sydney's eastern suburbs that he probably has 100% of his portfolio in property.

I wouldn't necessarily advocate this as an approach, because it does involve having all of your eggs in one basket. Sometimes, share markets and other investments throws up great opportunities. However, be aware that some argue that you should have all your eggs in one basket…and then watch that basket very closely!

As he invests in negatively geared properties selected for capital growth, Gray says that even with interest-only loans his properties generate a negative cash flow of between $100,000 and $200,000 per annum dependent on prevailing interest rates. He also spends a fair sum on renting his own place of residence (and on renting his cars from the luxury car company The SuperCar Club – renting rather than buying luxury cars can be another handy strategy, if cars are your weakness!).

Gray is a gregarious personality who loves his pinstripe suits and cars, and his personality is borne out in his investing style. I do not profess to be a psychoanalyst, but if I am a half-decent reader of personality types, then he will not reduce the gearing ratio of his property portfolio. Instead, he will simply continue to grow his portfolio for as long as he is able to, even if it means taking out loans at commercial rates. I would also bet that this strategy will create massive wealth over the next 30 years.

Not everyone would be comfortable with a risk profile like this. The structure of the portfolio means that in some years he would need cash flow from his business and from borrowing against the increasing value of his portfolio of around $300,000 just to stay afloat.

By contrast, my approach is more leisurely. The LVR on my UK properties, for example, is under 50%. In other words, I have a lot of equity available to expand my portfolio, and in time I will do so when I have finished travelling. I am essentially less aggressive, and do not want to put myself under financial pressure with a large negative cash flow. The trade-off, of course, is that this strategy is likely to grow wealth at a slower rate.

Again, this risk profile reflects my personality type. While I was often fairly abrasive and outspoken in my younger years, I am a far more passive and mellow individual now. Since I quit my full-time job, I am more comfortable driving my RV around barefoot and not cutting my hair for months on end than I am in a Hugo Boss suit. It's horses for courses.

The living-off-equity strategy

Living off equity (LOE) from investment property is a controversial strategy. Using some basic numbers, the principal idea is that you could build a property portfolio of, say, $5 million in value. Then, if you have selected high-performing capital growth properties, these may appreciate significantly each year. In a booming year, the value of the properties may increase by 10% or $500,000, and the investor can borrow against this increased value for living costs. In a less profitable period of the property cycle, the portfolio might only increase by 5%, but even then the value of the portfolio would still have increased by $250,000.

There is one big benefit to this strategy, and that is that money that is borrowed is not taxable income, and therefore if the investor borrowed $150,000 this would be the equivalent of a pre-tax salary of closer to $250,000[13].

Naturally, the downside to this strategy is that the investor is taking on ever-more debt, and is totally reliant on the market continuing to increase in perpetuity. This is why this strategy is risky. There are property groups that advocate building a portfolio of $3 million[14] and retiring forever on the ensuing 10% per annum equity increase. One should be very wary of a strategy that is solely reliant on always borrowing more for your living costs, especially as interest on loans for living costs are *not* tax deductible. You always need to be flexible. In my opinion, it is definitely preferable to have other income streams from sources such as dividends, interest income, part-time businesses or contract employment.

I advocate taking the principals of the LOE strategy and then modifying them to a more conservative approach. Building a substantial property portfolio is a fantastic means of building wealth, and I believe that when refinancing property, it can certainly make sense to borrow a buffer to cover any cash-flow shortfall on further properties purchased, and even some moderate living costs. However, I do believe that we should not be totally reliant on living off equity as a strategy, and that is why I recommend developing your financial education to bring in income from other sources as well.

A plus to quitting your full-time job is that you are totally free to develop other streams of income. There is nothing to say that you can't work on a part-time or contract basis, trade shares for income, invest in high-yielding stocks or bonds, or start a part-time or full-time business. There are a myriad of options that we can use to support our income. In my opinion, being reliant on borrowing more forever is a dangerous strategy, and I would not recommend it.

Escaping the rat race – better exit strategies

Although I have noted that it is possible to profit from your property investment without selling properties (through refinancing and drawing a line of credit), there are other methods than you can adopt to realise the benefits of a successful portfolio of investments.

One option is simply to wait until the cash flow from your properties is very strong. Over time, inflation causes rents to increase until eventually the rental is higher than the associated costs of holding the property. Therefore, if you hold all of your properties for the long term, they can start to generate healthy returns, allowing you to benefit without selling. Alternatively, you could simply invest in cash-flow properties in the first place, though as I have mentioned, there may be a risk that the capital growth may be less than spectacular.

Some investors prefer a different approach, and choose to sell a few of their properties and pay down the debt. Meanwhile, they can retain a number of properties that have very low holding costs and continue to generate rental yield. Yet another option is to sell all of your property investments and invest the profits in investments that generate income, such as shares or bonds. Do remember though, that if you take this route there may be capital gains tax and selling costs to pay.

There are infinite options and strategies available for the educated investor, so you need to find the plan that works best for you. The right choice for you will reflect your own risk profile, lifestyle requirements and preferences. The most important thing is that you give yourself choices in the first place by building an asset base that grows wealth. Property investment may seem complicated – there is a lot of information crammed into this chapter – but so much of it is just common sense. Find properties in continual high demand, add value to them and own them for as long as you can!

Are my property views a little old-fashioned?

As previously noted, I have a belief that the best performing properties in Australia over the next two or three decades are likely to be units located close to the CBDs of capital cities with excellent transport links. Is that an old-fashioned view? Well, perhaps a little, although I would prefer the phrase 'time-tested'!

I've heard all the 'new' theories, of course. Investors who invest primarily for rental yield – cash flows – might sometimes hold one or more of these views:

- Due to the advent of the Internet, more people will choose to work from home and live away from the cities

- Regional commercial centres will replace the obsolete CBDs and commercial properties in the cities will fall vacant

- Residential properties near the city centres will fail to grow in value, while those in outer suburbs and regional centres will surge in value.

These are nice theories, but I don't agree with them. That's cool: it would be a boring world if we all agreed on everything. Besides, we'd all be trying to buy the same properties. It is said that in the USA, which is at the forefront of technological development, a huge percentage (perhaps some 40% of the workforce) have the potential to work from home, yet only around 2.5 million consider their home to be their primary place of business. When the property crash hit, some regional areas in the USA were hit phenomenally hard. Of course, there is much conjecture here, but we must go with our instincts. Vacancy rates in the inner- and middle-ring suburbs of Sydney, I note, are presently very low indeed, which suggests to me that the performance of residential property will remain strong.

As I grew up in England (which has some more-developed property markets), I've heard similar theories before. Thirty years ago, we heard that nobody would live in London anymore; they would simply glide in to work on slick high-speed tilting trains from Edinburgh, Birmingham, Leeds and Newcastle. What happened to that? Well, we got 'the wrong kind of leaves on the track', a frankly terrifying number of derailments, British Rail quietly dropped its 'We're getting there' advertising campaign, and in 1993 it was privatised and broken up.

Then, around 20 years ago, the advent of a newfangled thing dubbed the 'information super-highway' meant that we'd all work remotely and nobody would ever have to set foot in London again. Prices would drop in London and the prestigious suburbs would plummet in value as their proximity to the City and West End hubs would become redundant.

Well, that didn't happen either. In fact the 1990s and early 2000s saw the longest property bull market imaginable. A huge boom in credit growth saw values rising dramatically everywhere, but interestingly it was prices in prestigious areas (Mayfair, Kensington, Holland Park, Bayswater, Chelsea – suburbs close to the City) that went absolutely gangbusters – to levels people never even believed possible. These days, a one-bedroom flat in Park Street, Mayfair, will set you back around £1.3 million, if you can find one available. You'd be lucky to even find a two-bedder for sale.

New commercial centres?

Now, this did happen in England. But interestingly, the big new commercial centre was not in Luton or Stansted. Instead, it was only a few short miles from the existing City district, at a place called Docklands. Of course, you were quids in if you owned a house in the Isle of Dogs, especially after the British National Party councillor (an imbecile by the name of Derek Beacon) finally got punted. Property values in quality suburbs near the City did not fall, however – quite the opposite, in fact.

In Australia, we should consider looking for new second, third and fourth CBDs springing up and consider whether investing nearby would be worthwhile. Business parks away from the main CBD may become increasingly popular due to cheaper leases.

Ugly ducklings near the City can become swans

When I first went to London, there was an invisible line on the eastern edge of the City that seemingly warned: 'Middle Class: Do Not Cross'. However, as more people than ever wanted to live near the City, 'ugly duckling' suburbs such as Bethnal Green and even Whitechapel (once home to the notorious Kray twins and the famous Blind Beggar pub) became 'trendy'…ish. People would increasingly rather live in a two-bedroom flat in gangster territory than in a three-bedroom off-the-shelf house in distant Watford.

What for Australia?

What does this mean for Australia, if anything? If you can predict where the new commercial centres will be, you could do very nicely (I'm looking at buying in Newcastle, but mostly I'll just stick to the capital cities). Perhaps Parramatta will become a big 'third CBD' for Sydney; who knows? It should be patently clear by now that I am certainly not saying that by investing in outer suburbs and regional areas you can't prosper handsomely, for that is certainly not true.

However, I do also believe that (to take the example of Sydney further) with massive population growth, the values in prestigious suburbs such as Vaucluse and Dover Heights will eventually jump to levels we can't even think of today. Only those will family wealth and substantial equity will be able to buy (not the case today – excellent two-bedroom units still change hands in the $600,000 bracket). There is a risk that lower demographic suburbs reach an affordability barrier as families tend to only have linear income in these areas. In prestigious suburbs, inhabitants often have business and investment income and equity in their properties, which can push values to higher levels.

Practical Action Points

- Use a mortgage broker to help you obtain the best available bank loan terms.

- If you wish to go it alone rather than joining an investment club or using a buyer's agent, there are plenty of 'how to' books available that step through the processes of buying property. Do remember to only consult books that are specific to the Australian market, as processes are markedly different in other countries.

- When buying investment property, your goal should be to find the best capital growth asset you can find. These may be prime-location one- or two-bedroom apartments in the inner and middle-ring suburbs of capital cities. Remember to consider transport links, and to invest in harmony with the property cycle.

- Before buying, prepare a schedule of expected rental yield and associated holding costs for the investment property. Remember to include estimated depreciation charges and likely tax rebates. An accountant can help you with this if you are unsure of how to calculate the figures.

- Use a solicitor/conveyancer to review the key documents of any property purchase. Ensure you use a solicitor with property experience.

- Read strata reports and all documentation relating to purchasing property *yourself*; don't rely on others to spot problems, as they may fail to do so.

- Always remember that reported median price growth is only an average. As property investors, we want to significantly *outperform* the averages by:

  - Buying the right property at the right price

  - Investing in high-capital-growth suburbs

  - Investing in harmony with the property cycle

  - Finding properties in which we can manufacture equity through cosmetic renovations.

8
AUSTRALIAN RESIDENTIAL
PROPERTY SPECIFICS

8

Specific points on property investing

In this chapter, I will briefly discuss a few more of the specifics of investing in residential property in Australia. I will keep it brief, because it is nearly time to consider other asset classes for growing wealth.

Financing

I have already mentioned my preference for interest-only mortgages. Some argue that principal-and-interest mortgages are a better option, as by paying down the principal it is possible to build equity. However, as it is possible to take out interest-only mortgages that allow additional repayments to be made without additional charge, to me it does not necessarily make sense to tie oneself into a principal-and-interest mortgage. With an interest-only mortgage, I am free to invest my funds elsewhere in order to achieve higher rates of return, or if I believe this is not possible, then I can still make payments to reduce the mortgage.

One of the key decisions we need to make when financing property is whether to fix interest rates. Fixing interest rates often means that we incur a premium, in the form of an interest rate that is somewhat higher than the currently available variable rate. Therefore, taking a fixed rate could be seen as a gamble as to whether rates over the period for which we have fixed will be, on average, higher than the variable rate. Of course, it is impossible to know. Forecasting is a futile exercise, as there are simply too many factors involved. The best thing we can do as investors is ascertain the facts and risks facing our own portfolio and make a balanced decision based upon them.

In general, I prefer to roll with the punches and take the variable rates that are on offer. While rates can and will go very high at points in time, investors often find that these are also the periods where prices have been increasingly rapidly, which should be some compensation. We should also remember that rates do not stay high (or low) forever. However, taking out all variable-rate mortgages does potentially leave me exposed if we do have a period of particularly high rates, and for this reason I do have some fixed-rate mortgages as well.

Viewing before buying

Some property writers suggest that not only do you not need to view a property before you buy it, it is actually advisable not to. The theory is that if you view a property you may become emotionally attached to it or emotionally involved in the purchase, and act illogically as a result. They may cite examples of properties they have bought that would not be acceptable or inhabitable to themselves, and therefore they become tempted to spend unnecessary money on new carpets or paintwork. The argument is that you can do all the research you need to remotely. I understand the logic, but disagree. Why would you not want to use all of the tools at your disposal?

I have bought a property in this manner before, having bought a place in England while I was otherwise engaged in Australia. I sent a family member along to view the property on my behalf. The property has performed fine, but when I finally did view it I discovered some things that I had not considered about the changing nature of the town's demographics.

I would suggest that while there is not necessarily a problem with buying a property sight unseen, if you are prone to becoming emotionally involved in a purchase, perhaps it is your emotions you should work on rather than preventing yourself from looking at a property. This is only a skill like any other, and one that can be learned.

Renovations

There are many different ways to make money in property, renovating being just one of them. I generally undertake mainly cosmetic renovations such as new carpets, new bathrooms, minor repair work, and painting, for example. As noted, as a rule of thumb an investor should aim to add $1,500 or more of value for every $1,000 spent on a cosmetic renovation. This ought to allow the investor to increase the rent by 10% or even 20%, which is an excellent way to minimise any negative cash flow on a property.

Although I tend to undertake cosmetic rather than major renovations, one thing I have learned from television is the importance of budgeting (as an accountant, I should already know this, of course). Often on television shows we see people buying properties above the price at which there is any margin for profit. With the increasing popularity of these shows, there seems to have been a trend in the market place whereby 'renovator' properties have become almost as expensive as renovated properties.

The financial plan for a major renovation needs to include the purchase price, a detailed expenditure plan or budget (including any mortgage payments and rental income if applicable) and, importantly, a contingency for overruns and unforeseen expenditure. Too often, the budget is taken to mean simply how much money is available, but this is a disaster waiting to happen, often resulting in the use of multiple credit cards or loans from family members.

One thing that I have heard experienced renovators say is that they wish they had held on to their properties rather than repeatedly flipping (quickly reselling) them. This mirrors the strategy of not selling that I referred to previously. Fortunately, having never sold a property, I have not experienced this, but it must be incredibly galling to have sold a property only to see it double or triple in value in future years.

Strata fees

As noted previously, it is sometimes argued that houses are superior investments to units because of the lack of strata fees. Before we come to the same conclusion, we should consider what strata fees go towards, which are mostly costs that house owners may also incur: general building repairs and maintenance, building insurance and administrative overheads. Normally, no more than 20% of the fees paid should be spent on administration.

That said, we should be extremely wary of expensive strata fees. Some old properties may be in dire need of repair, and so they raise special levies and charge vast quarterly strata fees. Avoid these like the plague, as old properties with structural issues, for example, can be bottomless pits in terms of required expenditure. Other properties to avoid may include those with expensive heated swimming pools.

'We should always thoroughly read any strata reports or relevant information on strata schemes and sinking funds that may be available.'

Whatever happens, do not rely solely upon a solicitor to commission a strata report and identify any potential issues. In my experience of buying properties, I have only come across two problems of any significance in strata reports, and the solicitors I used missed them both (they weren't quite so *laissez faire* when it came to chasing up payment of their invoices, of course). You should use a professional to review documents, but a lesson I learned the hard way is that you should also read the strata reports and other paperwork yourself. My experience of solicitors has shown them to be of little use, but perhaps I have chosen ordinary solicitors. I suppose that, as with auditors, you only discover a solicitor's true worth when there are problems to be found.

Property management

It is possible, of course, to manage your investment properties yourself without the assistance of a property manager. You might decide to do this in the early days of your investing in order to save money. However, if your goal is to have more time and more freedom, it makes sense to employ a property manager or management company. There also comes a point where your own time becomes worth more per hour than managing a property is worth. The same applies to many areas of investing, and your life in general. I would never have paid for a carwash when I was 17, for example, but now I feel that the time saved can sometimes be worth the cost.

Property management should be simple – find a good property manager and keep hold of him or her for as long as you can. Despite what you may have read in books promoting share investing, management of your property portfolio should not be time consuming, costly or stressful. In England, property managers are expensive and can charge as much as 12–15% of the rental income in fees. In Australia, we are fortunate that the monthly fees tend not to be nearly as high, but property managers can charge very steep fees for re-letting a property, even if the property is only let to the same tenant.

Having experimented with a couple of different property managers, I have now found one that I trust to do a good job. He is authorised to make expenditure on my behalf up to a pre-agreed limit because I trust him to do the right thing. I would estimate that the time it should take you to manage a property portfolio is as little as an hour per month, and you should set aside maybe a couple of hours to collate the information for the annual tax return. With email and mobile phones, it is really not that difficult.

Tax

Property investment has significant tax implications, so let's very quickly summarise them. Firstly, the loan interest and certain expenses on a qualifying property investment may be tax deductible: if your properties are loss-making, you may qualify for the benefits of the negative gearing rules, which can reduce the tax payable on your salary income significantly or even completely negate it.

'It is recommended that you discuss this with your tax advisor.'

You do not necessarily have to wait until the end of the tax year to receive these benefits. By estimating the income and expenses on your properties and completing a variation form you may be able to reduce the rate at which your employer deducts tax from your salary at source (all the way down to 0% in my last paid work – this makes a heck of a difference to your net pay). Remember to claim your depreciation allowances too.

There are tax implications, too, if you sell a property, in the form of capital gains tax. It is strongly recommended that you use an accountant who has skills in dealing with property investors. Their fees are generally not prohibitive, and are tax deductible themselves. Importantly, skilled accountants may save you from paying significant amounts of unnecessary tax.

As we have already seen, one of the greatest things about property investment is the tax you don't have to pay on unrealised capital gains. By never selling your properties, you can continue to grow your portfolio without ever triggering a capital gains tax liability, and this can make a huge difference to your wealth creation capabilities.

Ethics

In all forms of investing, I believe it is important to act in harmony with one's ethics and personality. As mentioned, one of my rules in property is that I never let out a property that I would not be prepared to live in myself. I sometimes read of investors who will not spend money on repairs, and buy properties that they personally would not go close to. This is a matter of personal choice, of course, but I am a strong believer in karma. I believe that over the long term, wealth is created by giving more value than you receive in whichever field you operate in.

The last thing I would want to be is an investing slumlord, flatly refusing to make property repairs. This approach is likely to create headaches in the form of vacancies, unruly tenants, vandalism and damages. I have heard first-hand some real horror stories of tenants destroying properties and then disappearing, leaving two months of rent unpaid. Thankfully, I have not experienced this, and hopefully will never do so.

Getting a valuation

Obtaining an independent valuation of any property you intend to purchase is a very sound and very sensible idea. While a valuation may cost around $500, and you may be reluctant to pay this amount up-front (especially as there may be no guarantee of completing the purchase), the potential savings to be made from not paying too much for the property will be many times larger than this fee. Take the short cut at your own peril. Enough said.

Unit sizes and types

My ideal unit investment has two bedrooms, two bathrooms, a reasonably sized balcony, a kitchen and lounge area, is around 100 square metres in size and has a parking area with a storage cage. Sometimes, however, the funds may not be available to buy the perfect unit. At such times, I believe it makes sense to consider a one-bedroom unit in an outstanding suburb, rather than aiming for an inferior two-bedroom unit in an ordinary suburb. A one-bedroom unit should ideally still be above 50 square metres in size and have a functional modern layout.

I avoid studio units, as the future capital growth on such property may be questionable. Banks often do not like lending on properties under a certain number of square metres, and may insist on a minimum 20% deposit – so be careful before making an offer on a property that you may be unable to finance.

As a general rule, smaller blocks of units may be preferable to larger developments for the simple reason that the larger supply and availability of units similar to your own can reduce the value of your property. Smaller developments of four to twelve units may be the best bet if you are considering investing in medium-density property.

Off plan property

Buying property off plan has become increasingly popular over the years. In times of rapid capital growth, buying off plan can be a useful way to extend a portfolio if an investor does not have a full deposit or approved mortgage ready. Executed well, buying off plan can allow an investor to profit from capital growth even before the property they are buying is built.

There is something undeniably attractive about a shiny new property, and sometimes it is noted by investors that the depreciation allowances on new properties are attractive, and this can indeed be the case. Remember, though, that the depreciation allowances are high precisely because new stuff does depreciate quickly, and that can include your property's perceived value. There can be stamp duty savings in buying off plan, where the stamp duty is levied on the land value only. However, there are most certainly risks involved in buying off plan and, to me, these usually outweigh the benefits.

It would take a lot of space to list all of the risks of buying off plan, so I will mention but a few. Firstly, developers may not always be the trustworthy and reputable crowd that you are hoping for. The property you believe you are buying in the flash brochure may not look much like the product you end up with, and the finish may be of poor quality to boot. In times of recession, it is even possible that the property never gets built if the developer falls on hard times.

One of the most significant points to note is that the developer is most certainly going to build a fair profit margin into any property development, and that margin will be built into the price of any off plan property you buy. Similarly, any attractive brochures and adverts you see in the newspapers will ultimately be funded by you, the individual property buyer.

There is also a hidden opportunity cost in buying a brand-new property, and that is that you forfeit the opportunity to purchase any property at what might appear to be 'under market value' (I use inverted commas because there is an argument that whatever you pay for a property can be construed to be the market value, as by definition no-one has been fully prepared to pay more than you for it) or a property that you can add value to through renovation.

One thing to be wary of when buying off plan is that when you are arranging your finance, the valuer of the property may not believe it to be worth as much as the developer's asking price. If this is the case, you may find that obtaining full finance for the purchase is not possible. You may be able to use this as leverage to negotiate the price down slightly, but don't bank on it. Remember that everything is negotiable, even if the brochure says it is not. Sometimes, the price may not be negotiated downwards, but added extras can be included – a storage cage in the car parking space, for example.

I have only bought one off plan property, a unit in Erskineville in Sydney's inner west. I already loved the village atmosphere of the suburb, one of my best buddies had moved there and we liked a couple of the local pubs (mind you, we liked pretty much any pub that served cold beer in those days). I also really liked the fact that the suburb was only two stops and 4 km from Central Station on the train line, ideal for young professionals. It seemed to me to be an excellent suburb for investment, being so close to the city and with many appealing lifestyle factors.

At the time, I deemed the risk to be relatively low, as I could readily compare the purchase price with similar units in the area, and there was less than one year between my purchase and the building completion. While the property has always been tenanted and has shown excellent capital growth, I would probably not buy off plan again. This is partly because there is no opportunity to add value to a brand-new property through renovations, but mainly because there is just too much unnecessary risk involved. A sophisticated share investor would expect to buy a risky asset at a significant discount to compensate for the risk. When you are buying off plan, developers instead demand a premium. Besides, why buy based upon the developer's pictures of what a property might look like when there are thousands of opportunities in existing properties?

Buyer's agents

Just as you can pay a fund manager to buy and sell investments for you in the stock market, you can enlist a buyer's agent to oversee the process of buying investment properties for you. Some of the processes that can be delegated to a professional buyer's agent include:

- Arranging a meeting with a mortgage broker/financial planner/accountant

- Locating property for purchase that meets your criteria

- Engaging a solicitor for the buying process

- Arranging pest and building inspections

- Engaging an independent valuer to ensure you don't overpay for a property

- Attending the auction process on your behalf or negotiating the purchase price

- Some buyer's agents will also project manage a renovation for you if that is your plan.

Buyer's agent fees can sometimes be quite expensive, perhaps $15,000 or even more for the purchase of a quality city property. While this is a lot of money, the theory is that if the agent can buy you a property that performs better than one you could have chosen yourself by, say, 1% per annum in capital growth terms, then they will have saved you their fees in just the first few years post-purchase. Perhaps more importantly, a professional buyer's agent should give you the peace of mind that you haven't purchased a complete lemon of a property.

If you are planning to use a buyer's agent, look for one with a good track record of buying quality properties at a fair price for satisfied clients (*Empire* in Sydney might be a good place to start). There's nothing wrong using a team of experts to make your life easier and to create wealth - that is exactly what this book is all about.

Other ways to invest in property

There are many other ways to invest in property, such as wraps (vendor financing), options (agreements with the owner of the property) or buying A-REITS (shares in listed property trusts). I am not going to waste valuable space going into all the various techniques, because I simply don't believe that they are necessary. In my opinion, the best way to make money from property is simple: own a series of outstanding properties in outperforming suburbs and never sell them. The combination of leverage and compound growth should make you wealthy enough over time that you don't need to consider more unconventional property practices and short cuts. This is how many of the big fortunes are made.

Property investment clubs

A final word on property investment clubs. You may have seen adverts for property clubs. I've looked into some of them before, and I do believe that for some people the support they offer can be very helpful. Remember, though, to be healthily sceptical at all times. Some 'clubs' are not clubs at all; they are profit-making proprietary limited companies that exist to make money from investors.

The usual format is that the club will invite you to a free seminar, where you may be fed the usual line that property always increases by 10% per annum and that property is the only place you can build serious wealth. Personally, I disagree with both of these statements, but let's stay on the point here. The idea is that the club will then have a series of properties to sell you that they have researched on your behalf. There are some questions that I would recommend that you ask yourself before you get involved.

Do you need the support?

The most significant thing that a club can offer you is support. If you are intimidated by the processes of buying property or obtaining finance, then a club can definitely help you with this. I am just going to add one very important rider here:

Do not be pressured into taking on more debt than you can comfortably afford, and do not be pressured into buying property when you are not certain that is what you want to do.

Do you know that the research is genuine?

Investment clubs will tell you that they have carried out hours of careful research to bring you the best available properties. You must be sure that you know this is true before you buy anything. The sceptic in me says that a club will try to sell you any property for which it earns a commission, and then justify the location and property type afterwards. I say this based on some of the properties I have seen for sale in the most unlikely remote locations. In some cases, I believe that these are simply properties that developers cannot get rid of.

Clubs may allow you to have the final choice of property, and I do believe that the person who is best qualified to make decisions about what is most appropriate for your financial future is you. By definition, nobody will know more about your cash-flow situation, your future earnings potential and your risk profile than you do yourself. And you can be absolutely certain that nobody will care about your money as much as you do.

What commissions does the club receive?

Some clubs receive 5–6% or more of the sale price as a commission from the developer. Of course, they will be at pains to stress that commissions are not received from you. Remember, though, that if a developer is willing to offload property to you by paying a club to sell for them, then you may have effectively overpaid for the property. The property may take years to increase sufficiently in value to cover a 6% commission, so consider whether you may be better off finding property to buy yourself; then, you will have the opportunity to negotiate better deals.

Summary

In summary, I am not saying don't join an investment club; I am just saying that if you do, go in with your eyes wide open. Clubs often exist to make profits by selling properties and receiving a sales commission, not just to make your life easier. If you feel confident enough to invest in property yourself, then that may be the way to go. If you feel that you need the support – and clubs can certainly offer this – then by all means join up.

Practical Action Points

- Find a good property manager and hang on to them. The major estate agents (such as Ray White or LJ Hooker) have property managers, or you may wish to consider some of the more boutique agencies (such as *Empire* in Sydney) for a more bespoke service.

- Research market value rents to ensure that you generate an appropriate yield for the property you own. The best websites are www.domain.com. au and www.realestate.com.au

- Engage a property valuer before buying any property. This simple action may cost you a few dollars, but it could potentially save you many more.

- Property clubs can have a role to play if you feel that you could use the support of like-minded people. As always, do your due diligence and do not be pressured into buying any property that you are not completely comfortable with.

- If you are not confident in the process of buying property yourself, consider using a buyer's agent for peace of mind. Buyer's agents do not usually come cheap, so ensure that you do your research before engaging an agent, and be certain that you thoroughly understand their proposed fee schedule.

9
AUTOMATED FUND
INVESTMENT

9

Investing in funds

I appreciate that starting out in share investing can be a stressful experience for those who have not done it before. If you have not experienced loss of investment capital, then the emotions involved when a share price takes a downward turn (and this will happen) can be difficult to deal with.

An excellent way to start out is to invest in an index fund. Index funds offer great diversification and require little in the way of initial capital. If you adopt an averaging approach of paying in the same amount of capital each month, then short-term market fluctuations need not worry you at all. This seems especially relevant in light of the great volatility of global share markets over recent years.

Why funds?

Investing in equities and other asset classes does not necessarily have to be stressful, time consuming or difficult. We can simply delegate the responsibility to the professionals (for a fee) or accept returns that are equal to the market by investing in an index fund.

Investing in a managed fund can give you the benefit of instant diversification, and allows you to invest in products and vehicles that may not be available to you directly with a small pool of cash. Fund managers will charge you for the privilege, however, in some cases as much as 2% per annum, and we need to decide whether the value they are adding is worthy of the fees. Are the fund managers significantly outperforming the general stock market over a period of time?

Investing in managed funds can be fine, but you must be sure that the fund manager is earning his fees and that the balance of the fund is congruent with your own financial plan. If you are like me and in the first quarter of the *Game of Money*, you might wish to choose a growth fund with a high exposure to Australian and international equities, but you might want to choose a less aggressive or more balanced fund if you are in your fifties or sixties. It must always be remembered that ultimately, nobody else will care as deeply about your capital as you do yourself.

I am naturally inclined towards the investment style of an *accumulator*. I love investments that I do not have to time 100% correctly, and my preferred timescale for holding an investment is indefinitely. This is why I have such an affinity towards averaging into index funds. There is nothing too exciting in the short term about investing in an index fund, as by definition the fund can neither outperform nor underperform the market: its returns can only mirror the index to which it relates.

However, an index fund is very efficient, as you will not be charged expensive fees to have a manager frenetically turning over your portfolio in a vain attempt to top the returns tables for the next quarter. Such activity simply triggers unnecessary capital gains tax and generates untold transaction costs.

Managed funds

When you open your superannuation statement at the end of the year, has the fund grown at a rate that significantly outperforms the stock market? It never seems to, does it? And yet, you are paying fund managers handsomely to manage your money for you. The fees may be well hidden in the details of the statement, but make no mistake, they are deducting them. Even a well-trained monkey could match the returns of the stock market by simply buying an index fund, so what are the fund managers doing to justify the fees that they charge you in good years and in bad? It is a very valid question.

The main reasons why the vast majority of funds do not outperform the market are:

- Transaction costs from high turnover of portfolios
- Capital gains within the fund on stocks sold
- Market impact
- The bid/ask spread
- The commissions siphoned off by the fund managers themselves.

Each of these points will be considered in a little more detail in Chapter 13, which looks at how to maximise the returns on your superannuation.

The individual investor can hold a tremendous advantage over the fund managers if he knows what he or she is doing. A large fund is limited in the positions it can take due to liquidity issues. On the other hand, the individual investor can move freely in and out of even the smaller and mid-cap stocks with relative ease.

Some people may try to tell you that it is not possible to outperform the stock market over time without luck due to what is known as the *efficient market theory*: that all publicly available information is quickly reflected in the price of a stock by rational and self-motivated profit-makers. Frankly, that is codswallop. While the market is frequently efficient, it is not always so. Since when have human beings been rational? The answer is 'never'.

Provided that we are prepared to take a long-term view, we as individuals can most assuredly outperform the stock-market index. The chances of a stock moving up or down tomorrow may be 50:50, but even by simply avoiding underperforming sectors or industries we can begin to move ahead of the average return. Here's another way to outperform the market: when Warren Buffett buys a significant percentage shareholding in a major company, buy shares in that company. Can it really be that simple? Well, yes, although Berkshire Hathaway is only compelled to provide limited disclosure on its holdings at certain times. Buffett has nearly half a century of investment experience in picking outstanding stocks and buying them at the right price. Plenty have made fortunes following in his footsteps.

Exchange Traded Funds

The advent of Exchange Traded Funds (ETFs) and Listed Investment Companies (LICs) has made investing in funds an easily accessible option for investors. Exchange Traded Funds are simply investment funds that are traded on the stock exchange, much like stocks.

What we must ultimately assess is whether the returns of a managed fund justify the fees we will inevitably be charged. While we should acknowledge the diversification a fund can offer, I believe there can be benefits to picking your own stocks. For one thing, learning to choose our own stocks by starting small is an invaluable way to continue to increase our financial skills and education, it encourages us to learn money-management skills and it helps us to understand the emotions experienced through investing.

ETFs are one of the fastest-growing products in Australia, with several billion dollars already under management. Here is a brief summary of the pros and cons of ETFs:

Figure 9.1 – Advantages and disadvantages of ETFs

For	Against
Easy to trade	Specialist ETFs may be illiquid; may not always be easy to find a buyer/seller
Real-time pricing	Bid/ask spread may be wide for illiquid ETFs
No minimum investment amount	Brokerage costs each time you trade
Cheaper than managed funds...	...but there are still fees
More tax efficient (less turnover, can choose when to incur capital gains)	
Share-market ETFs pay dividends with franking credits	

Ultimately, funds are going to invest in shares, property, fixed interest investments and cash or cash equivalents. Therefore, you must weigh up whether it is worth paying someone else to do that for you, or whether you would be better served investing directly in these assets yourself. One of the easiest and most efficient ways we can invest in share markets is through index funds.

Index funds

My wife started investing in an ethical FTSE index fund (she is a hippy at heart, despite her capitalist choice of career) in 1997, and we continue to pay a monthly contribution even today, more than 15 years later. Index funds mirror the index you have chosen to invest in. You cannot outperform or underperform the market, you will simply match it. One of my other half's funds is a UK ISA and attracts no tax, making it a simple and efficient investment tool. If only all young people could start contributing a small amount each month into an index fund, they would make a tremendous difference to their financial futures.

One of the neat effects of such an investment strategy is the application of what is sometimes called *dollar cost averaging*. Essentially, what this means is that if you contribute the same dollar figure to the fund each month, when the index is low you purchase more units and when the index is high you purchase fewer units. This gives peace of mind, as you do not have to worry greatly about timing the market. Provided you have chosen an index with a long-term upward trend (such as the stock market itself) then over time you will do very nicely indeed, without paying a fund manager to create transaction costs in trying to outperform the index.

Where you have the option to do so, it may be desirable to reinvest any dividends. Remember what Anthony Robbins said: the speed at which you generate wealth is directly related to the rate at which you reinvest your gains.

What about your superannuation fund?

Most super funds are invested via fund managers. When I first started working in Australia, my attitude was appallingly relaxed, and I ticked the box to sign up with the fund manager recommended by my employer without doing any worthwhile research at all. Just as shareholders end up with the management they deserve, so it is with our super returns.

If you have a super balance of around $100,000 or more, you should at least consider whether to set up a self-managed super fund (SMSF). If this sounds like a lot of effort, it really need not be, because the process of setting up an SMSF is very simple, and the management of the funds themselves can take as much or as little of your time as you wish. Of course, fund managers try to discourage self-management by implying that there is a certain mystery to their art, but the reality is that the majority of fund managers do not even beat the returns of the overall stock market: they simply add no value at all.

There are some limitations as to what you can and cannot do with an SMSF, so this is a subject best discussed with an advisor. Alternatively, there is a wealth of information available on the subject on the Internet. You will need to have an approved strategy for your fund, and there are number of very important rules that must be adhered to.

I left my super fund with a fund manager for six years, but after one too many years of uninspiring returns that were reduced by carefully hidden fund management fees, insurance premiums and taxes, I finally cracked and decided to take control myself.

One day, I was reading a financial magazine and noted that the super fund I was invested in had only returned 3% per annum over the more than five years that I had been invested in it. In other words, the fund had barely matched the rate of inflation. By the time I was able to transfer the balance across to a new account for my SMSF (this can be a time-consuming process, and can take months) the stock market had fallen sharply and wiped out a fair chunk of those returns too. The period my funds had been under management did encompass a market crash, but a long period of stock-market recovery as well.

Instead of allowing our super funds to creep up at this painfully slow rate, my wife and I decided to pool our respective balances via a holding trust structure (this is a requirement for pooled superannuation funds and may cost a couple of thousand dollars to be set up by a tax accountant) to buy an investment unit.

Of course, another alternative would be to invest your superannuation directly in equities yourself. If you follow this approach, the portfolio will need to be reasonably diversified to limit risk and volatility, but you will have the pleasure of not having paid a fund manager to try, but often fail, to even match the performance of the stock-market index. As taking control of your superannuation is such an important topic, I look at it in more detail in Chapter 13.

Practical Action Points

- Make a standing payment into a new high-interest savings account to kick-start building your capital.

- Carry out research into the types of funds that might suit you, and consider your preferred asset allocation. In particular, look for low-cost funds – Vanguard Investments Australia may be a useful place to start.

- There are a great many sources to use for your research. Start with the financial press, trade magazines and the Internet.

- If you have a significant superannuation balance (by 'significant', I mean one that perhaps runs into six figures), consider whether you would benefit from self-managing your super. If your balance is lower than this, the administrative costs of switching to an SMSF may prove to be prohibitive, so instead concentrate on building your balance first. See Chapter 13 for more on SMSFs.

- Also consider whether you might buy investment property with your superannuation. There are advantages and disadvantages in doing so, therefore it is important to consider all of the factors by researching the process via books or the Internet. The rules relating to super do change, so ensure that what you read is up to date.

10
BE THE NEXT
BUFFETT?
Value Investing in Shares

10

The 'Sage of Omaha'

The doyen of value investors is undoubtedly Warren Buffett, and the returns he has achieved with his colleagues at Berkshire Hathaway over the decades prove it. There is a stack of books available that profess to teach you how to invest like Buffett, and there are untold thousands of investors who try. The premise is simple enough: pick a few outstanding companies, place a meaningful amount of your net worth in each of them and hold on to them for a long time.

One of the ironies is that these investors often hang on every word of the 'Sage of Omaha', and yet they fail to heed what he says about picking your own stocks – he says that amateur investors should leave it to the professionals[1]. Does that mean we should not pick our own stocks? Not necessarily. For one thing, picking your own stocks is more interesting than delegating the responsibility to a fund manager (who will charge you fees and most certainly not care about your capital as deeply as you do). Doing your own research and selecting your own stocks is a superb way to continually improve your financial and investing skills. When it comes to investing, there is a never-ending learning curve.

Perhaps a good test to ascertain whether you are suited to picking your own stocks is to read *The Intelligent Investor* by Benjamin Graham. Then, when you have finished, read it again. If you found the text to be boring or hard going, it may be that you are better suited to investing in an index fund (see Chapter 9), or perhaps to a more technical approach to trading or investing in shares (see Chapters 11 and 12).

Value investing is about finding stocks that are trading below their intrinsic value, investing a meaningful amount in them and holding them until they become overvalued (or until information comes to light that suggests that the company is no longer performing as we want it to). Value investors may choose to invest in fewer companies, preferring to focus on a few outstanding opportunities, and therefore sometimes may also be referred to as *focus investors*.

An interesting point is that women often prove to be better value investors than men. My other half is a far better value investor than I am, although I am constantly trying to learn the appropriate skills. Success in share investing is achieved through committing to always learning how to improve your skills. After the last stock-market crash, my missus picked up a tranche of Wesfarmers (WES) shares for $14 and did not even look at them again until the price was over $30 when she cashed them in for a 100% return in less than two years. She did the same thing with Wotif.com (WTF), buying at around $3 and then selling when a buying frenzy saw them become overvalued at well over $7.

Value investing can be as simple or as complex as we make it. My wife viewed Wesfarmers as a diversified company comprising big familiar names such as Coles and K-Mart, and took a position at a cheap share price. By her own admission, she probably did little more than observe a sound management, an impressive range of brands and a cheap price-earnings ratio. Wotif.com was a company with a website that she has used and loved for years, and she saw it as a company with a *brand moat* that protected it from competitors – it could become the biggest and best-known brand in the discounted and last-minute accommodation and flights industry.

I would probably have tried to over-analyse Wesfarmers. It is so complex and has so many strands to its business that I am convinced that they have teams of management accountants who probably don't even understand its complexity. A company like Wotif, I am more comfortable with analysing. It has low debt, generates excellent margins and cash flow, and has the potential to grow at a significant rate. I have invested in this company myself, albeit achieving a lower rate of return.

One of the reasons why my wife is a better value investor than I am is that I am an 'infomaniac'. I like to read all the company releases and annual reports, and check the share prices on a daily basis when I can. By contrast, better value investors are happy to pick a few outstanding companies and disregard share prices for many years, instead focussing on how the company is operating. Some studies have shown that women can be better investors than men for precisely these reasons. These are skills that I am continually trying to develop. Frenetic trading creates transaction costs and capital gains liabilities, and can significantly impact results.

The key lesson for value investors is that over time, a company that generates outstanding operating results and cash flows will ultimately have a share price that reflects its intrinsic value. This is always the case. Where there is no dilution of shareholdings, a consistently improving operating result will eventually be reflected in an improving share price.

'Value investing is about the company's operating results, NOT share price action.'

Value investing goals

The concept of value investing is so simple: invest a meaningful amount of your net worth in a handful of the most outstanding companies when they are cheap, and hold for the long term. It is worth noting here that while I have divided up the sections on shares into several chapters, the principles of making money in shares are the same – buy low and sell high (unless you are short selling – see Chapter 12). And yet relatively few investors make a genuine success of value investing. It seems to me that the reason for this is the targeting of unrealistic goals.

It's related to the old adage of people over-estimating what they can achieve in the short term and massively under-estimating what they can achieve over the long term. A 'newbie' investor might suggest that his target is to buy a new $30,000 Holden with his investment profits, but when you press further you may discover that his starting capital is $30,000 and his timescale for securing the desired profit is six months. Therefore, he needs to achieve an annualised return of 200%, which he will generally not do.

This quotation is taken from one of Warren Buffett's famous letters to shareholders:

'The per-share book value of our stock increased by 13% in 2010. Over the last 46 years...book value has grown from $19 to $95,453, a rate of 20.2% compounded annually.'

Source: Berkshire Hathaway, Letter to Shareholders 2010

As a value investor, it needs to be remembered that Buffett's annualised return over 46 years is 'only' around 20% compounded, according to his own measurement criteria. Therefore, one needs to be wary or healthily sceptical when hearing people make comments such as, 'There is an easy 50% profit to be made', or 'You could definitely double your money here'. The reality is that these returns are generally not made quickly without an increased exposure to risk.

The genius of Buffett's approach is the lack of risk attached to it. By investing in the finest companies when the market has priced them very cheaply and holding them for the long term (instead of relying on short-term market reactions), he all but eliminates risk. Remember the rule of 72: because of the compounding effect, 20% annual growth will *double your capital invested in less than four years*.

It is probably a combination of the required starting capital and the required time horizon of value investing that puts most people off. The biggest hurdle for most would-be investors is short-term thinking. Too often, people place all of their hopes in one or two incredibly speculative ventures. If by chance one of them proves to be a home run, they are still not much closer to wealth, because there is still no financial plan for long-term growth of capital.

The Buffett principles

Goodness, aren't there a lot of books on Warren Buffett on the bookshelves? Buffett is rightly seen as the guru of value investors, and it seems that an awful lot of people want to know his 'secrets'. Discussed below are some of the key principles that guide his investing.

Ben Graham was Buffett's predecessor and mentor, and is considered to have been a value investor. Graham noted in *Security Analysis* and *The Intelligent Investor* that there were three main methods of investing in shares. Firstly, he noted, there was the cross-section approach, which would involve holding a stake in each of the top companies – this is the equivalent of investing in an index fund today, and will entail lower risk but average returns. Secondly, he identified the anticipation approach, the choosing of shares with a seemingly favourable outlook for 6–12 months, seeking out companies with higher than average sales or profit growth expectations.

The trouble with the anticipation approach is that you must guess to what extent the market has factored in growth forecasts, and therefore it is risky. This is how the institutions are investing your super fund today, by identifying growth stocks or value stocks with prospects for immediate capital gains. Since Graham's day, it has been better understood by Buffett that the distinction between growth and value stocks is a little nonsensical. Value simply means the intrinsic value of the company, that is, the future cash flows of the company discounted to today's value. Growth is merely a factor used to determine value.

Graham's preferred approach was a third way. He liked to purchase companies at a price that represented a *margin of safety*, out-of-favour companies trading at below their book value, the theory being that in the event of the company failing and being liquidated, the investor would still be likely to make a profit on their investment. The problem with this theory is that it is only worthwhile to the investor if the company is liquidated on a timely basis, and that does not always happen.

Buffett took on board the idea of a margin of safety as the sensible way to invest, but instead realised that rather than looking at struggling companies and their share prices versus their book values, he should look for companies with superior future cash-generating ability. Buffett learned two important lessons from his early investing – that 'turnaround' investments don't always turn (though Buffett did invest successfully in the floundering GEICO insurance company), and that time is the friend of the outstanding companies and the enemy of the mediocre[2]. So instead of looking for floundering companies at a cheap price, he focussed on finding excellent companies at a price representing a *margin of safety*. Therefore, perhaps Buffett should not be labelled a value investor in the traditional sense.

The Buffett approach is based squarely upon the principles of finding a few excellent companies, only buying them at a price where there is a significant margin of safety, placing a meaningful amount of one's net worth[3] into any purchase that one is committed to and holding for the longer term.

This approach necessarily requires the making of fewer but far bigger decisions. The longer time horizon should, if appropriate companies have been selected, mean that there is lower risk involved in each investment. In terms of the time period for holding an investment, although Berkshire Hathaway has disposed of investments in shorter timescales, it is likely that most of their investment is planned for a period of more than ten years (Berkshire Hathaway does also engage in shorter-term arbitrage transactions).

So if we are to follow a similar approach, what do we need to do?

Firstly, we will need a good amount of capital to invest with. Having the discipline to build the capital needed to start investing can be a problem for some people. We then need to understand how to calculate the intrinsic value of a company, so that we can buy at a significant discount to this value. We also need to know how to identify what is an outstanding company with outstanding prospects, for which a number of measurement criteria can be used. Remember, we only need to identify a handful of top companies to invest in.

Buffett's results have already been mentioned briefly. It is perhaps worth noting that due to the colossal size of the fund now managed, returns will likely be lower in the future. Berkshire Hathaway is compelled to hold shares in more companies than they did previously in order to put their vast capital to work. As a result of the huge success of Berkshire Hathaway and their refusal to engage in stock splitting, *individual* shares in Berkshire Hathaway now cost around $100,000!

According to the classical market theorists, such high returns should be impossible without taking significant risks. Yet Buffett has achieved returns of 20% per annum compounded since the 1960s and has rarely experienced losses. How can this be done?

Here is one prime example: Buffett identified Coca-Cola, a company with an incredible *brand moat* and around a century of operating profits to analyse, as significantly undervalued by the market during a lull in the late 1980s. Remember the Kelly Optimization Model: when the odds are stacked in your favour, you should place big bets. Through 1988 and 1989, Berkshire Hathaway acquired shares in Coca-Cola at a cost of more than $1 billion[4]. By 1998, the shareholding was worth well over $13 billion, as recorded in the Berkshire Hathaway Annual Report[5]. Note that Buffett was not fazed by around 40% of Berkshire Hathaway's wealth being tied up in the shares of just one company[6].

The average investor is not Warren Buffett. While millions of books are sold that list the strategies of the Buffett approach, very few investors have the skill, discipline and patience to perform the necessary research that identifying a few outstanding companies entails. I can only estimate based on my own experience, but my instinct tells me that the percentages are very low.

Blowing away the classic market and portfolio theories

I remember in my early days at accountancy training college in London being fascinated and delighted by some of the classical theories of finance and investment. I am, of course, a genuine nerd at heart. Below is a very short history of three of these theories, and how they apply to value investing today.

Modern portfolio theory

The Great Depression impacted the stock market so heavily and for such a long period of time that had you invested your net worth in the US index in the early 1930s you may not have generated a positive return for well over two decades. Such was the impact of this crash that investors began to question how they could insulate themselves from the impact of such a devastating event should it occur again.

In the early 1950s, Markowitz published his views that saw the genesis of the modern portfolio theory[7]. His view was that higher returns could only be generated by exposing a portfolio to more risk. These days, of course, we are reasonably familiar with the concept of risk and return, but in the 1950s these were relatively groundbreaking ideas. The outcome of these thought processes was that it was considered that the best approach was to identify a level of risk that the investor was comfortable with, and to then construct a portfolio around this risk profile. Previously, portfolios had been constructed on a far more haphazard basis, with stocks being added whenever one was found that the portfolio manager liked the look of.

These ideas have had a tremendous impact, particularly on institutional investors, and today it is not uncommon to see fund managers holding hundreds of stocks in a portfolio to diversify company-specific risk. Focussed value investors such as Buffett refute these ideas completely, and instead hold the view that risk is instead linked to the time horizon for which you hold an investment and the intrinsic value of the company.

If you purchase a share today with a view to selling it tomorrow, your chances of making a gain are close to 50 per cent (or indeed less, if you factor in slippage and transaction costs). If, on the other hand, you identify a wonderful company that meets all the criteria for a successful long-term investment and purchase it at a significant discount to its intrinsic value, the risk is reduced to virtually zero.

Capital Asset Pricing Model (CAPM)

In the early 1960s, a young PhD student by the name of William Sharpe published his thesis on the Capital Asset Pricing Model, usually referred to as 'CAPM' and pronounced 'Cap Em'[8]. This was a classically elegant theory that attempted to show that risk has a mathematical definition. I must have understood the concept reasonably well, because I passed the accounting exam question on the subject with a pretty good mark (while I scraped through the auditing exam by 1%, which should probably have told me something).

The basic concept of CAPM is that the stock market is the main influencing factor on the movement of share prices, and a hypothetical company with a share price that moved perfectly in tandem with the market would be assigned a Beta of 1. BHP Billiton might have a Beta that is close to 1. A company that is twice as volatile as the market would be assigned a Beta of 2, while a company that is half as volatile as the market would be assigned a Beta of 0.5, and so on. This is a useful consideration for market timers, as it may make sense to buy more volatile companies when the market is highly distressed (see the next chapter).

In formulaic terms, the conclusions of CAPM are shown below.

Figure 10.1 – CAPM conclusions

1.	**Beta** = Volatility of stock/volatility of market (>1 is more volatile)
2.	**Volatility %** = (share price high – share price low)/share price low * 100
3.	**Stock return** = Bond yield * Beta * (market return – bond yield)

Don't worry if you do not totally understand these formulas: the important thing to grasp is that some companies (such as BHP Billiton) have a relatively low volatility and their prices tend to move in tandem with the general stock market, while companies with a lower market capitalisation are often considered riskier, have a greater volatility and their prices may swing lower in a stock-market downturn, potentially turning sharply upwards in a stock-market recovery. From this, the conclusion is drawn that the return you receive on a stock can be measured with reference to a low-risk investment (bond yield), the return of the stock market (market return) and the risk of the individual stock (Beta).

From this starting point, Sharpe concluded that when investing in shares, there is a systemic risk that cannot be diversified, this being the risk of being invested in the stock market itself[9]. There also exists a non-systemic risk, a risk specific to the company itself that can be diversified away by holding more stocks. Such theories, while undoubtedly clever, have a habit of being taken to illogical conclusions. In this case, the ultimate conclusion is that the efficient portfolio is simply the market itself: higher returns can only be generated by adding more risk to a portfolio.

This makes for a very interesting university thesis, certainly a lot better than the drivel I was churning out as a university undergraduate, but to me the CAPM model does not make sense. If the risk of a stock can really be measured by its volatility, then a stock that drops sharply in value becomes *more* risky (i.e. buying a share at $25 is more risky than buying it at $50). Basically, this theory only holds up if it is agreed by everyone that the market is always rational, which it most patently is not.

In 2008, a huge crash in the stock market caused prices to drop across all the major companies. It was possible to pick up shares in BHP Billiton, for example, for less than $25. Based upon the theory of CAPM, due to this huge drop in the share price, BHP Billiton had become a more risky investment. Clearly, this is hogwash, and smart investors capitalised on the very cheap prices offered on one of Australia's finest companies. There is less risk involved in buying into BHP Billiton at $25 when the market sentiment is despondent than there is in buying in when the market is exuberant and overvalued. The rampant speculation phase is the time when smart investors will get out of the market.

Buffett dispelled the CAPM theory by first believing and then demonstrating over decades of sustained success that risk is not price-based, it is economic-value-based[10]. Again, his view was that if you can find an outstanding company with the right fundamentals, buy it at the right price and invest in it for the long term, then the risk is negligible.

Efficient Market Theory (EMT)

Efficient market theory was conceived in the 1960s by Eugene Fama, who concluded that all available information was instantly reflected in a share price by rational profiteers, so that without inside information it was not possible to consistently profit from stocks[11]. As a finance student, I was intrigued by this idea of the 'perfect capital market', that the market could somehow rationally process all information into a share price.

However, when I started investing myself, it became evident that, at least with small to mid-cap stocks, if one could rationally consider a market release and, importantly, interpret how the market would react to the information, you could indeed make profits from the market. Moreover, it became increasingly obvious, even to a moderately intelligent fellow such as me, that the market was anything but rational.

Consider this graph of the XAO (the Australian All Ordinaries Index):

Figure 10.2 – Graph of XAO (All Ordinaries Index)

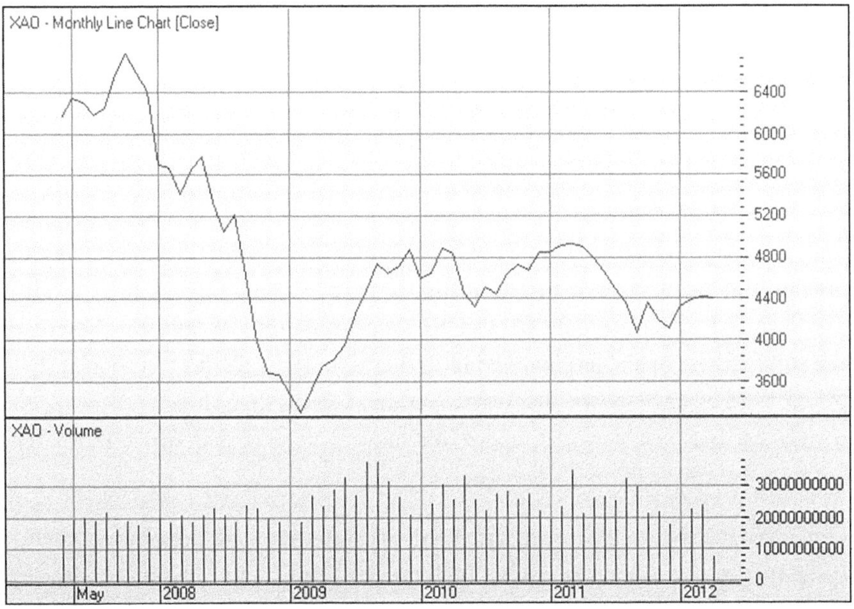

Source: www.asx.com.au

This graph demonstrates the irrational nature of stock markets, which are particularly dominated by two emotions, fear and greed. In the early part of the graph, greed is the predominant emotion. It seems as though, despite the expensive price of stocks, everyone is in the market, not daring to miss out on the upward surge pushing the XAO to around 6,700. Then, the market turns and fear begins to set in, and the market plummets downwards for over a year before bottoming out at around 3,000. Over time, this cycle is seen in the stock market over and over again.

It is quite clear that if one is able to restrict his or her purchases to a time when the market is truly despondent, the odds of success in the long term are improved immeasurably.

Building and balancing a portfolio

Buffett does not rebalance his portfolio if one of his picks becomes successful. The massive success of Coca-Cola led to this one company representing more than 40% of Berkshire Hathaway's portfolio. This success is, of course, not necessarily a reason to sell some or all of the holding. However, it may be psychologically difficult to hold on to a share that has increased sharply in value, there being a strong temptation to 'lock in' some or all of the profit.

One of the reasons why value investing is not as straightforward as it might appear is that it is not simply a case of choosing a handful of companies, buying their shares and then forgetting about them for 10, 20 or 30 years. The process should be an ongoing one. The stocks you hold become the benchmark against which you should compare new opportunities when they come along.

The successful focussed investor should ignore short-term share-price results, because the nature of a focussed portfolio dictates that results will be volatile. The focussed investor would be wise to concentrate on the operating results of the company he or she has invested in, rather than the daily fluctuations in share prices. Studies have shown that over a period of more than three years or so, the correlation between net-operating-result movement and share-price movement becomes a statistically meaningful one[12].

One investing tool that has seen a tremendous amount of bad press in recent years is the method of averaging down. The basic principle is that if you are invested in a company and the price goes down, then you buy more of the stock and in doing so reduce the average cost of your holding. The reason this method has been so openly slated, I suppose, is that financial advisors may have encouraged their clients to continue investing in shares throughout the stock-market crash of 2008 and 2009 until their investment accounts had been absolutely crucified. Naturally, one would not advocate following their lead.

We should note, however, that averaging down can be a useful tool for the focussed investor, providing you have a solid and substantiated belief in the company you are investing in and you believe that there is a huge margin of safety between the share price and the intrinsic value. Indeed, Ben Graham himself talks of such a strategy in *The Intelligent Investor*[13]. In some circumstances, a fall in the share price can offer an opportunity to buy more of an excellent thing at a mouth-watering price[14].

Diversification or focus?

Diversification has been the subject of a thousand university theses whereby students generate vast numbers of theoretical portfolios and test them against market data. All that we need to take from these studies is this:

'It is more difficult to outperform the index with many stocks than it is with a few stocks.'

This is an extension of the Kelly Optimization Model for the value investor. Pick your best investing ideas and place big bets on them, rather than placing one-twentieth of your capital into your twenty best ideas.

The table below shows the diminishing effect of diversification. An investor who invests in two stocks instead of one has significantly reduced the company-specific risk attributed to his capital, as he now has 50% invested in each company rather than 100% invested in one company. Adding a further company to the portfolio means that he now has 33% invested in each company instead of 50%. However, there is a law of diminishing returns at work here. By adding a 13th, 14th and 15th stock to the portfolio, you are only marginally improving the level of diversification.

Figure 10.3 – Diversification of a share portfolio

Number of stocks	% of portfolio in each stock
1	100.0
2	50.0
3	33.3
4	25.0
5	20.0
6	16.7
7	14.3
8	12.5
9	11.1

Number of stocks	% of portfolio in each stock
10	10.0
11	9.1
12	8.3
13	7.7
14	7.1
15	6.7
20	5.0
50	2.0
100	1.0

The number of stocks you want to invest in for the long term will vary depending on your risk appetite, the amount of your net worth you have attributed to investing in shares, your age, the make-up of your portfolio and various other factors. If, for example, you only invest in mining and resources companies (whose prices may move in a correlated manner), you may want to spread your company risk over more stocks than if you invest in companies whose prices move more independently of each other.

Figure 10.4 – Tracking error

Number of Stocks	Tracking Error (%)
1	40
2	20
4	10
6	7
8	5
10	4
20	2
40	1

Source: Online Investing on the Australian Share Market, Roger Kinsky[15]

Tracking error is a measurement of how closely a portfolio follows the index to which it is benchmarked. Thus, a portfolio of one stock might diverge from the index quite dramatically, but a portfolio of 40 stocks is likely to mirror the index return very closely. It is again clear that there is a law of diminishing returns at work here. Increasing the number of stocks you own from two to four provides substantial diversification benefits. Increasing the number from 20 to 40 provides far less.

Ben Graham suggested that for the average investor, three companies might be a good place to start[16]. Buffett himself suggests five to ten. However, it is worth noting that in the late 1980s, the Berkshire Hathaway portfolio essentially consisted of just three holdings (Capital Cities/ABC, Washington Post and GEICO). If 100% of your net worth and capital is exposed to one share market, you might want to have a portfolio of around 10–15 stocks (or even more if you have multiple stocks in one industry). Having tried various approaches over the years, I have found that my best results have come from the more focussed approach.

I now tend to only have around five or six stocks in my portfolio, and spend more time in choosing the companies to invest in. Note, however, that due to being heavily exposed to residential property and overseas index funds, I have only had a relatively controlled portion of my net worth invested directly in Australian equities at any one time.

> 'If you have a high percentage of your net worth invested in one stock market, you may be more inclined towards a more diversified portfolio of shares.'

The idea of a focussed portfolio is not new, and Buffett recognises this. As far back as the 1940s, John Maynard Keynes noted that diversification into numerous stocks you have no particular confidence in may be more risky than focussing on getting to know a few stocks in detail. The point remains valid today: how much confidence will you have in your 10th, 15th or 20th best idea, compared with two or three ideas that you have researched thoroughly and extensively?

A study of any rich list of the wealthiest individuals will show that those on the list have applied focus rather than diversification to attain their wealth. Buffett's focus is well documented. George Soros, though his approach was very different to that of Buffett, also applied focus.

When I was 11 years old, the United Kingdom entered the Exchange Rate Mechanism (ERM) in Europe, a controversial move that was unpopular with many patriotic Brits. The move linked the British pound to the Deutschmark in Germany. All kinds of problems loomed after the fall of the Berlin Wall and the fall of the 'iron curtain', the metaphorical barrier that separated the Communist Eastern Bloc and the nations of Western Europe. After Germany reunified in 1991, George Soros took a massive $10 billion short position against the pound, sensing that it had nowhere to go but down[17].

While I sat in an English lesson at school, the pound imploded on 'Black Wednesday' in September 1992, netting Soros a massive US$1.1 billion estimated profit at a time when his fund's assets were only $7 billion (he had employed huge leverage to take on the full short position). Now that is a focussed approach! Soros identified that he had little downside risk, as little as 4% by his own estimations[18], while the upside to his fund was obviously huge.

Of course, I was too young to understand any of this, being a school student more interested in football. However, the look of panic on my English teacher's face told us that something very serious had happened, and indeed it had. The British government immediately announced an increase in interest rates from 10% to 12% and pledged to raise them to 15% later the same day. It is small wonder that the teacher looked shocked. The government was forced to withdraw the pound from the ERM, earning Soros the moniker 'the man who broke the Bank of England[19]'.

The one-stock portfolio

On the face of it, the one-stock portfolio is madness. It goes totally against the concepts of diversification that are chanted religiously by financial advisors. And yet, in various respects, there is something to be said in favour of this approach. The one-stock portfolio is taking the focussed approach to its ultimate extreme. As a result, performance will undoubtedly be volatile, and may create stress. The one-stock portfolio is not for the weak of heart! On the plus side, you presumably would not be placing 100% of your share portfolio capital into a company you did not totally believe in.

In my professional career, I often worked with executives who, due to share options schemes, were almost totally exposed to one stock. This financial profile is guaranteed to provide highs and lows. Such execs often watch the share price hour in hour out, cursing every fall and taking delight in every upward tick. When the share price moves up, you are likely to hear triumphant comments from the more vociferous types such as:

- Look at us go…we could be the next 10-bagger!

o We're up on a down day. Solid as a rock we are, the Aussie battler!

- Up 3% today and the market's only up 1%!

Of course, on a day when the share price moves down, it's a totally different story:

- This government is pathetic.

o These climate-change greenies make me sick. I get so angry, all they want to do is tax.

- Look at those comments on the Internet chat forums. These idiots don't know what they are talking about...

Take a look at the *BRW Rich List* and note how many of the richest individuals have a huge portion of their net worth tied up in one company (or group of companies). That is to say, a great many of them. Think of Steve Jobs, Bill Gates, Andrew Forrest, Richard Branson, or Frank Lowy. Their worth has been generated through a focus on one specific brand or group of companies, not through wide diversification of their efforts.

At various times, I have been so exposed to one stock that I have been close to employing the one-stock portfolio. This was partly because much of my wealth was in property, and therefore I could take more of a risk with my direct share investments. Of course, I wanted to know everything I could possibly know about my chosen stocks without resorting to insider trading. It is also worthy of note that as your wealth increases, your appetite for risk generally decreases.

Remember that being invested in one stock can be incredibly stressful. Also remember that even great business leaders like Steve Jobs had several ventures that completely hit the skids too. You have been warned!

Picking your own stocks

Buffett, as always, has the perfect analogy for how to pick your own stocks. Imagine you have a lifetime card and you are only allowed to make "20 punches" in it, one for each investment you make[20]. This should ensure you spend an appropriate amount of time analysing an investment before plunging a significant amount of your net worth into it. Perfectly put.

In my view, this is where too many value investors fall short of the mark, and simply do not take the time to learn how to analyse a company. To be truly successful as a value or focus investor, you must be prepared to learn how to analyse companies in detail and perform the relevant calculations.

There is much to be said for picking your own stocks if you are the type of person who can commit to continually learning more about the subject of investing. If you are prepared to look at investment as a discipline for your never-ending improvement, picking your own stocks and learning from your mistakes is an excellent way to develop your financial skills. It certainly helps if the mistakes you make do not cripple you financially, so starting small is smart.

An incredulous Adam Smith (a journalist, not the economist) once asked Buffett how he knew where to begin looking given that there are 27,000 public companies in the USA. Buffett's response: 'Start with As[21].'

There are far fewer listed companies in Australia, and these days filtering software can immediately eliminate many of them as companies that are simply those you should not be interested in. The starting point, as always, is to identify your own goals, and then look for companies that can help you achieve those goals.

If you are going to pick stocks to invest in, it is imperative that you identify and stick to industries and companies that you understand – those that are within your 'circle of competence'.

Fundamental analysis

If done properly, the fundamental analysis of a company is a complex and time-consuming process. There is some truth too, though, in the view that a simple investment strategy is better than a more complex one. As there is so much information readily available on the Internet, it can be daunting for the investor. There can certainly be a law of diminishing returns in analysing information. One approach that can be useful in analysing a company is to try to prove your selections wrong. You will probably not find a reason to invest in a company on page 150 of its annual report, but you may find a reason *not* to invest in it.

A smart fundamental investor learns to think in probabilities. Charlie Munger, the Vice Chairman of Berkshire Hathaway, has said that the essence of his investment strategy is to subtract the amount of possible loss multiplied by the probability of loss from the amount of possible profit multiplied by the probability of profit[22]. This method may be imprecise and necessarily involve much in the way of estimation and assumption, but all investing is about weighing up the probabilities to the best of our abilities, and jumping in when the odds are most in our favour. This approach is especially well suited to *arbitrage* (see the *Glossary of Terms* for a definition).

In *The Warren Buffett Way*, author and fund manager Robert Hagstrom analysed Buffett's investments and demonstrated three ways in which outstanding opportunities can arise:

- A company facing a temporary specific risk (e.g. Wells Fargo)

- Investor indifference (e.g. Coca-Cola)

- A stock-market fall (e.g. Washington Post).

In an ideal world, we would simply wait for stock-market distress and pick up companies very cheaply, as Buffett did with the Washington Post company. However, Ben Graham recognised long ago that stock-market cycles can be very long, and therefore it is not always possible or desirable to wait for a stock-market correction before investing in shares. Often, the value investor is forced to identify companies that the market has failed to price correctly and that are trading below their intrinsic value.

A good starting point for the analysis of a company is performing ratio analysis. I don't want to fill pages and pages of space on this, but I've listed below a few basic ratios and calculations that should be undertaken before you even consider devoting a significant chunk of your net worth to investing in a company. If you don't understand the ratios and/or you aren't prepared to learn them, this is not necessarily a bad thing, but you probably shouldn't be risking much of your net worth in individual stocks if that is the case. Instead, make your life easier and invest in an index fund. Also note that plenty of these calculations may already be done for you on Internet broker sites.

One key calculation is market capitalisation.

> **Market Capitalisation** = number of ordinary shares on issue * prevailing price per share

This represents the value of a company on the stock market, and is calculated as above. This is a very important calculation, as it forms the basis of any assessment of whether a company's share price is cheap or expensive. If you can calculate an estimation of the intrinsic value of company, then you have a basis for a comparison.

Some basic profitability ratios

1. **Return on capital (ROC)** = *after-tax profit/total assets *100*

2. **Return on equity (ROE)** = *after-tax profit/shareholders' equity *100*

3. **Earnings per share (EPS)** = *after-tax profit/no. of issued ordinary shares*

4. **Dividend per share (DPS)** = *total dividend paid/no. of issued ordinary shares*

5. **Payout ratio** = *dividend per share/earnings per share*

6. **Dividend yield** = *dividend per share/share price (in cents) *100*

Dividend yield is usually somewhere between 3–8% for profit-making companies and nil for speculative stocks.

7. **Price-earnings (PE) ratio** = *share price in cents/earnings per share*

The 'Rule of 20' states that a fair-value PE ratio might be 20 minus the inflation rate per annum. Therefore, a 'fair-value PE' might currently be around 17 depending on the nature of the company and its industry.

8. **Price-earnings growth** = *PE ratio/earnings growth*

9. **Total shareholder return (TSR)** = *sum of capital gains + dividends received*

Debt and balance sheet ratios

1. **Interest cover** = *earnings before interest and tax/interest payable on debt*

At least three or four times is often considered to be good.

2. **Debt to equity ratio** = *debt/equity *100*

This should be less than 100%, and lower is generally considered to be good.

3. **Current ratio** = *current assets/current liabilities*

Greater than 2 is good. Less than 1 could be dangerous. For example, a property development company may appear to be worth a lot on paper (high net assets), but could become insolvent due to many of its assets being non-current.

The quick ratio (or what was termed in the old days the 'acid test') is the current ratio excluding stock.

Putting the calculations together: identifying a healthy company

After looking at a company through these calculations and ratios, we want to find companies that:

- Are profitable
- Have a return on capital of more than 8%
- Have a return on equity of more than 10% and preferably rising
- Provide total shareholder returns of more than 10% (preferably over a period of decades) including the dividends
- Have a dividend yield of around 3–5% or more (the dividend being affordable and sustainable for the company)
- Have interest cover of more than 3 times and a debt/equity ratio of less than 75%
- Have a current ratio of more than 1
- Have a PE ratio of 10 to 20 depending upon the industry in which the company operates; the PE ratio should also ideally be in an upward trend
- Have a price-earnings growth of less than 1.

If you told me that performing this kind of analysis is tedious, you would be preaching to the converted! However, to identify a healthy company, it is necessary to understand the basic financials. A huge number of 'investors' simply do not bother to carry out their due diligence, and are therefore probably better termed 'speculators'. The relevant figures can all be found relatively easily via company annual reports and stock-market data sites. Fashions, trends and industries come and go – for example, in days gone by, price to book value (comparison of market capitalisation to net assets) was considered key. These days, price-earnings ratio and price-earnings growth are given far more importance – but the basic rules of analysing the health of a company are constant.

It is important to note that while a PE ratio is a key indicator of whether a company represents good value, this measurement criterion is not absolute. A company with a PE ratio of 3 may be 'cheap', but it is probably cheap because its future prospects are poor. A company in a technology sector with a PE ratio of 50 may appear extremely expensive, and yet if the company or the industry is growing at a phenomenal rate, the PE ratio may be entirely justified.

Analysing companies – Buffett style

Hagstrom noted that there are four categories of fundamentals or 'tenets' that Warren Buffett uses to identify a company to invest in[23].

1. The business

Buffett likes a business that is simple, one that he can understand and one with a consistent operational history[24]. Of course, there are always fast-growing companies with outstanding short-term returns, but the focus investor does not need to chase short-term results, as he is interested in wealth for the long term.

One company that was seen by analysts and commentators as a tremendous innovator was Enron. Management was frequently praised for its innovative approach and yet, in the end, nobody (including the directors) really understood the phenomenally complex series of derivatives used, and when the tide turned the whole group went up in smoke. Buffett was not interested in a company such as Enron, despite its distressed share price, as its earnings were far too unpredictable and not even remotely transparent. He tends to steer clear of technology companies (IBM being a notable exception) for the same reason: he does not truly understand them.

Buffett likes companies with a long and consistent operating history. Coca-Cola is an example of a company in this mould. The company was founded in 1892[25], so Buffett had around a century of trading results to consider in making his assessment of the company.

Importantly, a company must have outstanding long-term prospects and, just as a castle has a moat to protect it from invaders, a company must have a moat to protect it from competitors. Moats are also sometimes known as *barriers to entry*. Some companies have a sound brand moat – that is, customers will only use their company because the brand is too special for imitators to copy successfully. An example of a company with an almost unbreachable brand moat is Harley Davidson[26] – competitors may try to infiltrate their market, but they will never succeed because, ultimately, the customers want to ride a Harley.

Buffett believed that Coca-Cola had a virtually impregnable brand moat. In theory, it should be very easy to attack the fizzy drinks market, as the product itself is extremely cheap to make. However, witness what happened when Richard Branson vowed to swipe a third of Coca-Cola's market through launching the Virgin Cola brand in the UK. The product itself cost him little to produce – just a few cents per can – but the advertising budgets can be phenomenal. Coca-Cola's advertising budget and the expenditure on the creation of its image are mind-blowing, and the company can also threaten to withdraw supply (and its fridges) from outlets that stock other brands[27]. Not an easy market to penetrate, as Branson found out fairly quickly.

Other companies have a barrier to entry in the form of technology. For example, Intel was able to create success as it had more advanced technology in the realm of microprocessors than any of its competitors.

2. Financials

Buffett prefers to look at return on equity and *owner earnings*[28], this being net profit plus depreciation and amortisation less capital expenditures. He feels that earnings per share may be more easily manipulated through opaque accounting. Buffett is clear that net profit does not necessarily equal cash flow, and is wary of companies with increasing capital commitments. Companies with high asset turnover are susceptible to inflation, and we know that there is a risk of high inflation in certain economies. Buffett knows that inflation does not necessarily translate to increased earnings for all companies. In particular, Buffett likes to see a company that earns high profit margins, which is a reflection of his own preference for a margin of safety in his share investments.

Some companies and investors prefer to look at a company's Enterprise Value Add (EVA), a measurement that attempts to demonstrate the margin by which it outperforms its cost of capital. Unsurprisingly, Buffett is not a fan of this method of measurement. The cost of capital is not a particularly satisfactory benchmarking tool, as it favours companies with high levels of debt (which is generally cheaper than equity), and the cost of equity is determined using the Beta from the CAPM model (which Buffett stands in direct opposition to). ***Recent market events in 2008 and 2009 have clearly shown the dangers that can face a company servicing high levels of debt.***

3. Management

There are two schools of thought on whether we can evaluate management. Some would argue that it is a futile exercise, and that the quality of management is reflected in a company's operating results. Others believe that we can indeed assess the quality of management and use this analysis as a tool for improving our investment decisions.

Company management should behave rationally and be honest with shareholders[29]. This is not necessarily easy to measure, but we can certainly review previous annual reports and ascertain whether management have done what they told us they would. Good management will resist trying to bait the institutional investors through releasing only positive news and burying or delaying bad news.

Management should be, but may not be, rational. If a company cannot reinvest its cash profitably, it should return it to shareholders via the payment of dividends[30]. It should resist the temptation to 'buy growth' or invest in low-return projects. I lost count of the number of times I saw management do this in my professional career, watching companies make acquisitions for the sake of making acquisitions. Management can also often be tempted to pursue substandard projects while continuing to justify and draw their executive salaries. A good remuneration policy will discourage this, and therefore one section of the annual report that deserves our attention is the remuneration report.

Ask yourself: in whose interest is management acting, its own or that of the shareholders? So often, it appears that management is only interested in its own remuneration and not the interests of the actual owners of the company, the shareholders. There are too many examples to mention, of course, but note the massive executive offloading of shares during the Enron debacle.

I believe that an example of a company with superior management is BHP Billiton. Whether or not you believe that BHP Billiton is an appropriate company to invest in from an ethical perspective, it cannot be argued that its management is anything less than extremely effective. Note how management deals with challenges such as the proposed resources tax: instead of coming out and fighting every government proposal, they tend to be flexible and speak of the potential benefits of the proposals, allowing them more leverage to mould them to their own advantage. Compare this with, for example, BlueScope Steel's approach to the proposed carbon tax – openly aggressive on all fronts. To an outsider, BHP Billiton looks to have a management that is in control of its own destiny.

4. The market

The Buffett approach then involves calculating the intrinsic value of a company and comparing this with the prevailing market valuation. The intrinsic value of a company is best calculated by projecting its estimated future cash flows as detailed in the section below. It is, of course, impossible to accurately forecast the future cash flows of any company, as there as too many variables. For this reason, a margin of safety is required in the purchase price.

Note that Buffett considers the market and share price last of all[31]. Once he has identified an outstanding company and its intrinsic value, he then wants to know at what price he can currently buy shares in it. He will want a significant margin of safety in his purchase. When evaluating riskier investments, Buffett does not increase his discount rate (refer to the following section), but instead insists on buying with a greater margin of safety.

How to value a company

There is no single agreed-upon approach as to how to find the intrinsic value of a company, and therefore an investor will have to decide upon his or her own favoured approach. It is helpful to remember that when valuing a company, it is far better to be approximately right than precisely wrong. In other words, we want to take a relatively broad-brush approach and buy with a large margin of safety relative to our calculated intrinsic value.

In a sense, valuing a company can be much like valuing a bond or similar financial instrument. A bond has a maturity date and a coupon (rate of interest payment) that can be discounted back to give a valuation for the instrument. In a similar vein, the value investor can look at the expected future cash inflows and outflows of the company to determine the value of the company today.

Of course, future cash flows cannot be known precisely, so they must be estimated. As accountants, we call this a discounted cash flow calculation, which is a bread and butter model for any bean counter who has had decent exposure to the listed corporate environment. However, all such calculations are only as good as the inputs; as the Americans used to say in the early days of computing, 'garbage in, garbage out.'

The main principle of a discounted cash flow valuation is that cash received in the future is less valuable than cash received today, due to inflation, opportunity cost and the risk of the cash flow not occurring due to unforeseen circumstances. Therefore, if a company is to receive $100 one year in the future, at a discount rate of 10% we might say that this inflow has a present value of $91 ($100/1.1). $100 received two years in the future would be worth $82 ($100/1.1/1.1), and so on.

While this may sound complicated, it isn't really, and building a model in a spreadsheet can be done relatively easily these days (indeed, mainstream providers of spreadsheets build NPV tools into their products). Of course, such valuations cannot be precise or accurate, as they are based on a huge number of variables. However, the idea is simply to come to a valuation that is approximately right.

Many investors will rely on short-cut methods to value a company. In days gone by, this may have involved looking at the price-to-book ratio of the company by simply comparing the net assets on the balance sheet with the market capitalisation. This approach is very much out of vogue these days, with investors preferring to look at price-earnings ratios.

A price-earnings ratio (price per share/earnings per share) is a very useful measure, but is not absolute, in that the ratios can vary significantly from company to company and from industry to industry. It can definitely be useful as a benchmarking tool for comparing similar companies, but we should be wary of relying on a current price-earnings ratio, as one year's earnings may be very different from the next (and can easily be manipulated by companies). A more conservative approach may be to look at an average of the last five or even 10 years of earnings.

Some companies go to great lengths to announce 'normalised' earnings adjusted for various one-off expenditures or discontinued operations – indeed, some of the companies for which I wrote annual reports seemed to want to report nothing but normalised earnings every single reporting season. For a price-earnings ratio to be of use, we need to have some understanding of the accounting entries that have impacted the earnings figures being used.

It should be noted that younger 'growth' companies at an earlier stage in the life cycle of a business can trade at far higher multiples of their earnings than larger, more mature companies. Famously, many *dotcom* companies traded at huge multiples of their earnings before the market imploded, indeed many of these companies never made a profit at all, thus making their PE ratios infinite. Instead, we heard references to insane valuation methods such as 'price-per-click' (e.g. number of website views) and other such nonsense. It was always going to end in tears, and anyone who thought otherwise…well, they probably did not know much about the history of stock markets.

The *dotcom* speculation craze was the absolute antithesis to the Buffett value approach of finding an undervalued business with a consistent and predictable operating history. Sometimes, you may hear of fund managers carefully differentiating between 'value stocks' and 'growth stocks' (although Berkshire Hathaway's view is that the distinction is nonsense).

The more thorough approach is to estimate all future inflows and outflows of the company (this may rely upon projecting forward a historic growth rate or a projected future growth rate) and discount the future earnings back to today's present value using an appropriate discount rate. Applying a discount rate to future earnings is a method of compensating for the fact that cash inflows received in the future are more uncertain, and will be worth less in today's dollars than cash that is received right now.

This idea raises a number of questions, such as what growth rate to use (a conservative one is sensible, perhaps a five- or even 10-year average for the company) and what discount rate to use. The discount rate to use in a discounted cash flow calculation is a matter of personal choice. Many advocate using a 'risk-free' rate, such as the rate that might be earned on a 10-year government bond (a government bond being a proxy for a very safe investment, though some may argue that with certain governments being very highly leveraged, government bonds are far from risk-free). This approach can be affected when interest rates are very low, in which case it might be sensible and safe to simply adjust the discount rate upwards and use a rate of closer to 10%[32].

The risk-free rate is simply used to compare one investment with another[33]. If you can attain this rate of return with no risk, why would you invest in a company with specific risk? Instead of adding an equity risk premium to the discount rate, Buffett would instead insist on buying shares in the company at a cheaper price to compensate for the risk[34].

Another question that is often raised when discussing how to value a company is how to treat earnings that are more than, say, five years in the future. One investor might determine that earnings so far in the future are too risky to factor in, and value them at $0 (more appropriate for a young company), while another may take the expected earnings in five years' time and project them in perpetuity (far more appropriate for a mature company such as Coca-Cola).

Of course, both answers are imperfect, and there is no 'correct' answer to such a question. All we can do is apply the best methodology relevant to the company we are analysing: the earnings of Coca-Cola are far more predictable and reliable than the earnings of Facebook or Twitter, for example, which is why Buffett so strongly favours companies with a consistent operating history. Again, we need to look at probabilities.

Owner earnings are generally a better input figure to use than earnings. Owner earnings are calculated by adding back non-cash items such as depreciation or amortisation to earnings and subtracting the ongoing capital expenditure (for new plant and equipment, for example, or warehouses) required to keep the company growing.

These calculations may sound complex if you are not from a financial background, and it is certainly the case that most people take short cuts when choosing companies to invest in, preferring to take a cursory look at the financials and then going with some kind of 'gut feel' about a company. In my view, this is why most people will never be successful Buffett-style value investors: they rely far too much on short cuts instead of being prepared to carry out their research in full.

Ben Graham detailed a series of ratios that he insisted on a company fulfilling in order for him to invest in them[35]. While some of the ratios are less relevant today due to changes in economic trends, the idea of having such benchmarking criteria is a solid one. I wonder how many everyday investors follow such a rigorous approach. The answer is probably very few.

Financial statements

As I have previously been an author of listed-company financial statements, this is my area of expertise, and theoretically I should be able to profit handsomely from my skills. However, we need to remember that identifying undervalued companies is only one part of a profitable investment decision. As financial statements contain historic information, perhaps the key is to be able to interpret this information and use it to determine the strength of the company and, consequently, its prospects for success in the future.

There is something of a law of diminishing returns at work when analysing financial statements. The big-ticket items, the balance sheet, the cash-flow statements and the operating results, are commonly displayed towards the front of the report. As you work through the notes, the information may appear to be holding decreasing significance. You are not going to suddenly pick out a company as a winner based on, say, its financial commitments note. You might, however, decide not to invest in a company because of information hidden deep in the same note.

The buy-and-hold strategy

The buy-and-hold strategy is designed to lower risk by buying companies when their share prices are undervalued and holding them for as long as required until the share prices are more attractive for selling. We should be aware that the market can take a long time to recognise a company's intrinsic value: price and value are linked, but only loosely.

One of the unavoidable consequences of the focussed approach to investing is that returns will be more volatile. A heavily diversified portfolio will tend to move in harmony with the market, but an investor with all of his net worth in a handful of stocks may see his paper net worth fluctuate significantly on a short-term basis. One of the skills, therefore, that a focus investor needs to learn is to ignore the day-to-day gyrations of the market.

One way in which this can be achieved is to buy shares in outstanding companies, hold for the long term, and remove the focus on share-price action as the benchmarking tool for the portfolio. Instead, value investors should concentrate on the operating performance of the companies they have invested in. If a company is operating as intended, then in time the share price should reflect the operating results. Studies have shown that while price and value can move in a seemingly unsynchronised manner in the short term, over a period of three or more years the statistical link between the movements of the two figures becomes far more valid.

While Buffett preaches holding for the long term, we should note that in some of his investments, where he has parcels of securities of a quantum that are not easily marketable, he has no choice in this matter. As smaller individual investors, we do have more freedom to exit investments, and while this ought not to give the investor *carte blanche* to start turning over his portfolio in a frenetic manner, he can continue to survey the market for better investments. A zero turnover of stocks is not necessarily desirable, as there could be an opportunity cost in not capitalising on more appealing opportunities as they come along. In this case, the benchmark for any potential new investment is a comparison against the stocks the investor already holds[36].

One tremendous advantage of a buy-and-hold strategy is the reduced impact of capital gains tax. Buffett refers to unrealised profits (paper profits on shares that have not yet been sold) as an interest-free loan from the Treasury[37]. Consider the following table, where a share trader has doubled $10,000 five times in five trades, each time realising a gain within a year and incurring capital gains tax at an assumed rate of 30%.

Figure 10.5 – Capital gains taxed at 30% ($)

Starting capital	Capital doubled to:	Tax at 30%	Finishing capital
10,000	20,000	(3,000)	17,000
17,000	34,000	(5,100)	28,900
28,900	57,800	(8,670)	49,130
49,130	98,260	(14,739)	83,521
83,521	167,042	(25,056)	**141,986**

In the table above, after doubling his capital five times and paying his due capital gains tax at an assumed 30%, the investor has been left with total capital of $141,986.

Now consider this table, where a share trader has again doubled his capital of $10,000 five times. This time, he has held each trade for more than a year and has thus only incurred capital gains tax at an assumed lower rate of 15% (due to the capital gains tax discount for assets held for more than 12 months).

Figure 10.6 – Capital gains taxed at 15% ($)

Starting capital	Capital doubled to:	Tax at 15%	Finishing capital
10,000	20,000	(1,500)	18,500
18,500	37,000	(2,775)	34,225
34,225	68,450	(5,134)	63,316
63,316	126,633	(9,497)	117,135
117,135	234,270	(17,570)	**216,700**

While he has still incurred tax that has eaten into his gains, his final capital of $216,700 is considerably more than that of the investor in the first example.

Finally, consider the table below of an investor who has doubled his capital of $10,000 five times through one trade that he has held over a period of years. He will pay capital gains tax of 15% on the whole amount of the gain in the final year.

Figure 10.7 – The power of compounding unrealised gains ($)

Starting capital	Capital doubled to:	Tax at 15%	Finishing capital
10,000	20,000	-	20,000
20,000	40,000	-	40,000
40,000	80,000	-	80,000
80,000	160,000	-	160,000
160,000	320,000	(46,500)	**273,500**

While the tax payment in the final year is undoubtedly painful, the final capital of $273,500 is an excellent result, and far outstrips the capital of the other two investors who have traded more frequently. This is the essence of successful value investing, and in many ways it echoes the approach of the property investor who never sells in order not to trigger a capital gains tax liability. The tax bill in year five may be significant, but the final capital balance is a handsome compensation.

Buying cheap from Mr. Market – the margin of safety

Ben Graham's famous analogy of Mr. Market has been widely documented. Graham argues that we should consider the stock market to be a partner who is prepared to offer us a buy/sell price at any given point in time for any security. On some days, he is depressed and negative and offers us very low prices, while on other days he is euphoric and overtly positive, and thus offers us very high prices[38]. The key for value investors is to buy when Mr. Market is depressed and to sell when he is euphoric[39]. We need to use Mr. Market to serve us, and not allow him to be our master[40].

The key for value investors is to identify significant discrepancies between the share price and the intrinsic value of the company we are considering investing in. Valuing a company is an art, not a science, so remember that the goal is to achieve an approximately right result.

The best value investors learn to think in probabilities. As previously noted, Warren Buffett's sidekick Charlie Munger has said that the way the finest investors think is to consider the probabilities of outcomes and then make an interpretation of the likely implications thereof. This thought process is sometimes known as Bayesian Analysis, named after Thomas Bayes[41]. I remember it more readily from Year 9 mathematics, where the teacher called it a 'probability decision tree'.

A word on debt

Another classical theory we learned in accountancy training college in London concerned the role of debt. There was a historical economic theory that stated that because debt generally costs less than equity, and because debt also offers a tax shield (i.e. qualifying loan interest is tax deductible), taking out more debt made a profitable company more valuable.

While this could be true in theory, a number of corporate collapses (e.g. Centro) have illustrated the dangers of high levels of debt and low interest-cover ratios. In economic downturns, companies with high levels of debt can expose themselves to having insufficient cash to meet debt repayments and supplier payments.

When this happens, other sources of finance can become devilishly difficult to source, and the company may find itself the victim of the classic 'run on the bank' (cf. Enron).

Even the most academic of economists would now have to acknowledge that while sensibly used and moderate levels of debt can benefit a company, excessive debt levels bring risk. As we might expect, Buffett does not like risk, and insists on investing in companies with low debt. A company that is generating high margins and bringing in cash has no need to be highly geared.

Leveraged investing

Borrowing to invest is not a strategy that I would advocate for the value investor with a buy-and-hold strategy. Buffett advised on leverage that if you are smart, you don't need it, and if you are dumb you definitely shouldn't use it[42]. He also said that 'we only discover who is swimming naked when the tide goes out[43].' Spot on as always.

Returns from shares come in the form of dividends and capital growth. If we are using leverage to invest in shares, it is likely that we are paying somewhere not far off 10% per annum to the margin lending party. Therefore, we are immediately under pressure to attain a return that exceeds the cost of borrowing. Depending on prevailing tax law, it may be that the interest on margin loans is tax deductible, but the point remains that by borrowing to invest, there is a pressure to outperform a tough benchmark every year, regardless of whether the market is moving up, down or tracking sideways.

The best investors are those who think with the clearest heads, and this is why the simplest investing methods are often the best. Using leverage to invest in shares makes the decision-making process a more difficult one, and clouds our thinking. This is particularly the case when a share price moves in a sideways direction for a prolonged period of time. The leveraged investor can soon begin to fidget and fret that he is not making a return on his investment sufficient to cover the cost of the investment debt. There is then a risk that he closes out of a position just prior to the share price returning to an upward trend. He will have missed out on maximising his profit on a trade in a bid to chase returns to cover his cost of capital.

That's not to say that Buffett does not use leverage himself. He does so on occasion, and he does so successfully. One of the paradoxes of leverage is that it is the availability of cheap funds that can cause bubbles and asset inflation to occur – but history shows us that when the inevitable crash occurs and bargains become prevalent, funds become devilishly difficult to obtain.

One final point on leverage; as Marcus Padley has regularly pointed out in his *Sydney Morning Herald* column, if you have debt on a property and also own shares outside of your superannuation fund, you are in effect a leveraged investor[44]. In other words, you have chosen to invest in shares instead of paying down your mortgage debt.

Why value investing can be difficult

The principles of value investing are simple. So why are so few investors successful? There are numerous reasons, the most pertinent of which I have noted below.

Firstly, the market is frequently (if not always) efficient, and identifying stocks that trade at a huge discount to their intrinsic value is not straightforward for the average investor. Stocks are analysed by many thousands of people, and a prevailing share price usually represents a rational consensus viewpoint of a company's value.

Secondly, I believe that investors take short cuts in analysing companies. I know a fair bit about this because I have been guilty of this myself in the past. There are long explanations in plenty of 'Buffett' books of the key calculations that an investor should undertake in analysing a company. As a Chartered Accountant, performing such calculations should be very easy, so why do I not always undertake research thoroughly and diligently?

The main reason is laziness, plain and simple. Calculating owner earnings and net profit margins for dozens of companies is an extremely tedious process, even for a seasoned accountant. Another reason is potentially a lack of faith that even if we go through the detailed processes, we may still be missing that one key point that the institutional investors have identified with their larger resources. We should not necessarily believe this. We may well be better at identifying outstanding companies than we give ourselves credit for.

Thirdly, value investing with a significant percentage of one's net worth in a handful of stocks is psychologically testing. Focus portfolios are by their nature more volatile than a heavily diversified selection of investments, and in times of stock-market distress the value investor must hold his nerve. No matter how much faith one has in the stock selection process, it is most certainly not easy to watch plummeting share prices and remain calm. The prescribed antidote to this is simply to not focus on share prices, but rather to scrutinise the operating results of the companies you have invested in.

Finally, it seems to me that a majority of investors do not have the discipline or patience for this form of investing. This is a shame, because I believe that most of the successful share portfolios I have seen are those in which the investor has bought shares in the top-performing companies and held on to them for the long term (providing the company is still performing as expected). Too many of us prefer to take a punt on long shots and chase an unrealistic goal of instant wealth, instead of creating a plan to become wealthy ten, fifteen or twenty years from now.

Putting it together – getting started in value investing

Most investors spend far too much time looking at the share price and not nearly enough time understanding and analysing the business. If you are going to be a value investor and hold for the long term, it is important to choose great *businesses* to invest in, so try to imagine that you are buying a business, not simply a parcel of shares.

Look for businesses that are *needed* and those with no close substitute. Commodity businesses have the disadvantage that, by definition, they are producing a commodity, and therefore they can only compete on price. For this reason, Buffett favours *franchise* companies. In this context, a franchise company is one with a strong *economic moat* (or barrier to entry).

In Berkshire Hathaway's 1991 annual report, Buffett notes that an economic franchise 'arises from a product or service that: (1) is needed or desired; (2) is thought by its customers to have no close substitute and; (3) is not subject to price regulation.'

Source: Berkshire Hathaway Annual Report, 1991.

Review the *tenets* that Buffett considers from earlier in this chapter: a consistent operating history, sound financials, an honest, rational and effective management and a share price that represents a margin of safety. Also check that the company does not have a dangerous level of debt that it cannot service easily, or future capital expenditure requirements that will hinder its ability to generate future cash flows.

The key words for me are *future cash flows*. I look for companies with high profit margins and that have the ability to be cash-generating machines. Ideally, you want a company that can consistently grow its return on equity (a growing Earnings per Share is not enough, as companies tend to retain profits). I don't advise as to specific stocks in which to invest, but if you are looking for some ideas on places to start, here are three ideas:

- Major banks – can generate massive profits and pay very handsome dividends to the investor

- Mining giants – although these companies produce *commodities*, they can also generate huge amounts of cash, though the operating results tend to be highly cyclical due to the cyclical movement of commodity prices

- Healthcare companies – a sector I expect to grow in future years with our ageing population.

When you are comfortable that you have done the right research, try to forget about the stock-market share-price noise, and forget about the cycle of the economy too. Buffett thinks of the economy as being like a racehorse – it is going fast or it is going slow, but it's going[45]. Perhaps twice a year, review the companies you have invested in to ensure that they are still on track. If your analysis is correct, the share price will follow.

Don't focus too much on one-year results, as profits do not always fall neatly into one year or the next. Instead, take a longer-term view over several years and look for the general health and cash-generating ability of the company. Try to strip out capital gains and extraordinary or non-recurring items to get a feel for the performance of the core business. Finally, and perhaps most importantly, never stop learning!

Practical Action Points

- Set up a low-fee brokerage account.

- Read as many books on share investment as you can, particularly those that focus on the fundamental analysis of companies. Refer to my recommended reading section at the end of the book.

- Consider which industries and companies you are interested in. You will understand companies in industries you have a feel for more thoroughly, and in turn this will make you a better investor.

- Devise a written investment strategy. This should include your targeted return (perhaps this may be outperforming the index by a certain percentage per annum) and the likely make-up of your portfolio (e.g. how many stocks you will hold, which industries they are likely to be in, etc.).

- If you are looking for ideas on companies to invest in, try looking at mining and resources, the major banks and healthcare stocks. Note that I do not tip individual stocks, and I do not work as a licensed financial advisor.

- To research individual companies, look at the ASX website for company releases (www.asx.com.au) and annual reports (you no longer have to be a shareholder to read annual reports, as they are freely available via the ASX and company websites).

- If you are serious about being a successful value investor, you will need to undertake some ratio analysis of any company in which you intend to invest in order to understand the fundamentals of the business. Much of the information you seek may already be available directly from brokerage websites.

- If you find the idea of starting out in investing intimidating, remember, there is nothing wrong with paying a monthly contribution into an index fund.

- Consider how many stocks your ideal portfolio should include: sometimes less can be more. It may be better to research a few companies in detail than to spread your investments too thinly across a number of poorly researched stocks.

11
TIMING THE
MARKET:
Medium-Term Trading of Shares

11

Timing the market

Regarding direct investment in equities, some people prefer a strategy of timing the market to one of buying and holding. Periodically, the stock market becomes so overvalued that it becomes apparent to sophisticated investors that a significant correction or crash will eventually impact the market. It is impossible to know exactly when such a drop will occur, but through identifying indicators we can certainly become attuned to when the risk has become higher.

The converse is also true. There comes a point in time when the market is so undervalued that shares become extremely cheap to buy. If we want to follow a market-timing strategy, we have to recognise and accept that it is absolutely not possible to consistently pick the precise bottom (or top) of any market, and instead aim simply to buy when the market is cheap and sell when it is expensive. Simple can be better than complex, and this strategy should allow you to achieve your goals.

There are numerous indicators we can turn to that can help us to identify an overheated market (which could mean it is time to reduce our exposure to the stock market):

- PE ratios becoming significantly higher than the long-term average

- Few bargains to be found in the market

- Dividend yields becoming significantly lower than the long-term average

- A lot of new stock exchange floats (including quasi cash box floats – companies with few genuine plans for how they will use the capital they have raised)[1]

- Stories in the press about a new financial era; the 'old rules' no longer applying

- Companies with no recorded profits trading at highly speculative prices

- Increased volatility in the stock market, the new highs being driven by speculation in a narrow field of companies or industries

- Your taxi driver/shoe-shine boy telling you he is starting to get really involved in stock trading and is 'making a killing' (though there is no actual reason why taxi drivers and shoe-shine boys cannot be smart investors).

An approach of timing the market will only work if we minimise our losses in a bear market (a downward-trending market). There is no value in riding the bull market (an upward-trending market) to the very top if we then remain heavily invested throughout the bear market too and lose all of our paper profits. If market timing is to be a vehicle for your wealth creation, you will need to have some protection due to the shorter time horizon of each investment.

Those who favour buy-and-hold will point out the disadvantages of such a strategy: it is not possible to predict market tops and market bottoms precisely, transaction costs will be higher and capital gains tax will eat into returns. There is some truth in each of these points, but a proponent of market timing would counter that through identifying which phase of the market we are in he can maximise returns while avoiding the downside experienced by buy-and-hold investors during bear markets.

I tend to read the vast majority of the investment books that I buy once, and then read them a second time before passing them on to the op-shop. Occasionally, I find books that I want to keep for future reference or to remind me to keep in mind the basics of successful investing. Some classics such as Ben Graham's *The Intelligent Investor* fall into the latter category. The best book by a long way that I have read on the subject of share-market timing for the Australian reader is *Building Wealth in the Stock Market* by Colin Nicholson. It is a relatively short and very precise book, and I have rarely read a book that is better thought out or presented. I have retained my copy and would wholeheartedly recommend that you obtain a copy and read it (refer to the recommended reading at the end of the book).

There is some conjecture in the world of shares as to what constitutes investing and what constitutes trading. Graham notes that *investing* involves a satisfactory return and certainty around return of the principal. Some have said that the main difference is that share trading focuses on share-price action, and perhaps in this respect an approach that is based around timing the market might be construed to be trading.

However, given that the stock market can take many years to run through a cycle, and that a market timer might hold a stock for five or more years, others would say that this is investing. My view is that the terminology in this case is not too important, but the *methodology* you apply to the market certainly is. I will use the term *trading* for the purposes of this chapter.

Dow Theory and participating in bull markets

Dow Theory was an idea conceived by journalist and founder of *The Wall Street Journal* Charles Dow, and it refers in part to the cyclical nature of the stock market[2]. Dow identified how the stock market tends to move in three phases, an accumulation phase, a public participation phase and a distribution phase.

The accumulation phase is a period when investors who are 'in the know' are actively buying stock against the general opinion of the market. During this phase, the stock price does not change much because these investors are in the minority, absorbing stock that the market at large is supplying. Eventually, the market catches on to the moves of these astute investors and a rapid price change occurs, which indicates the second phase. This occurs when the crowd begins to participate. This phase continues until rampant speculation occurs. At this point, astute investors begin to distribute their holdings to the market, and the market eventually begins to fall. Rinse and repeat.

To reduce the risk of loss of capital, market timers need to be cognisant of which phase of the market is prevailing, aiming to be fully invested when stocks become cheap and to decrease exposure when the market is risky and overvalued. Like the value-investing strategy, this strategy also requires patience. Stock-market downturns can take a long time to play themselves out in full. Using the All Ordinaries index as a benchmark, the 1987 crash took some seven years to recover its value, though that seems relatively speedy compared with the glacial 25-year recovery from the famous Wall Street Crash of 1929.

Many see Ben Graham as the predecessor of Warren Buffett and the godfather of value investors. Graham states in *The Intelligent Investor* that we should aim to buy shares when they are cheap and sell when they are overvalued[3], so while he placed a strong emphasis on fundamental analysis, to some extent he was still referring to *timing* the market[4].

It is worth noting again here that while I have divided my discussion of shares into separate chapters – index funds, value investing, timing the market and short-term trading – the fundamental concept is always the same; to buy low and sell high. These ideas are not new. It was more than half a century ago when Ben Graham identified his three methods of investing in shares[5]. Firstly, he suggested that one could employ a cross-section approach by buying shares in each of the top industrial stocks (this is very similar to today's index-fund investing)[6]. Secondly, he noted that one could aim for stocks with a favourable outlook for the forthcoming year or so (the 'anticipation approach' or *timing the market*)[7]. Thirdly, his favoured approach was the margin-of-safety approach, later improved upon by Buffett[8]. Today, we might refer to this as value investing or focus investing.

Graham notes that the difficulty with timing the market is that one has to be able to predict the vagaries of the market, which is very difficult to do. For this reason, when timing the market, it is advantageous to also employ an element of technical analysis in one's trading.

Plans and records

As the old saying goes, if you fail to plan you plan to fail. Many investors may be aware on some level that they should have a written plan, but for various reasons the vast majority of investors do not have such a document.

A good trading plan should clearly identify goals and strategies. Here are just a few tips to consider when you are starting out in trading:

- Paper trade your plans before implementing them in the market with real money
- Set specific rules for entering a trade
- Set specific rules for exiting a trade
- Determine a maximum percentage of your capital to be risked on each trade
- Keep detailed records of all your trades
- Keep a trading diary of your thought processes
- Review your records and learn from them.

Too many investors are all too keen to tell you all about their successful trades, but never seem to have losers. This is normally either because they are not telling you about their losing trades or investments, or because they have let their losing trades ride ever downwards using the theory that the loss is not real if it is not realised. A smart investor generally does not talk openly about his or her trades, as this can have an effect on ego and impair the decision-making process.

We should also keep a record of our trades and investments for tax purposes. For your tax returns, you will definitely require records of share purchases and disposals, brokerage fees and dividends received. Online brokerage sites offer this service as a matter of course these days, but we should take care to review our records to learn from them, both in relation to what we did well and what we can do better. Take note of whether you have a tendency to make any rash trades. We will not learn anything simply by emailing our records to our accountants.

Percentage fall, percentage to recover

Below is a table that demonstrates why it is so important to cut losing trades short.

Figure 11.1 – % fall, % to recover

% by which stock falls	% recovery needed to break even
10	11
20	25
30	43
40	67
50	100
60	150
70	233
80	400
90	900
100	Impossible to recover

What this table clearly demonstrates is that if we lose too much on our investments, we cannot win overall. This is a strong reason for a preference for timing the market over a buy-and-hold strategy. While many would defend the buy-and-hold strategy to the death, it should be noted that essentially, investors such as Berkshire Hathaway do not have much choice. If Berkshire Hathaway builds up an investment of $10 billion in Coca-Cola or IBM, they do not have a parcel of shares that can be traded easily on the stock market. As individual investors, we are generally free from such constraints, provided that we trade liquid stocks. If the market becomes wildly overvalued, we are free to dispose of our holdings and then pick them up again at more attractive prices in the future.

This is a very important point:

'If we allow a share price to fall 50% from when we buy it, we then need it to DOUBLE in order for us to break even.'

It is sometimes far more sensible to cut a losing trade or investment short and swallow a 7% or 8% loss than to let it fall to these depths and pray that the share price will somehow double in order to save us. Remember that just because you have sold a share does not mean that you cannot buy it again at some point in the future if the price and fundamentals again become attractive.

Risks

There are a number of risks facing share investors that apply whether the favoured strategy is buy and hold or market timing.

Specific risk relating to investing in companies can be diversified away by investing in more companies. The number of stocks that you hold should be determined by how much of your net worth you have invested in the market, your appetite for risk and your investment plan in general. Diversification has already been covered to some extent in the previous chapter, where we noted how with fewer stocks held, returns can be more volatile.

There is also the risk of being in the market itself, known as **market risk**. This risk can be mitigated to some extent by exposing more of your capital in the early stages of a bull market (or when the market is perceived to be cheap) and reducing this exposure when the market becomes overheated in the late stages of the bull market. Naturally, this is a skill that takes several market cycles to master, but an awareness of the logic should certainly help the investor to become far more wary in speculative times. The risk can also be mitigated by investment in other asset classes as discussed earlier in the book.

Liquidity risk – *slippage* is the term used to refer to the difference between the price you decide to buy or sell at and the price you end up settling a trade at. The cause of a significant disconnect is likely to be the illiquidity of a stock. Larger companies can see volumes of many millions of shares being traded each day, and therefore at any given point during the market opening the quoted 'last trade' is likely to be within one small tick of the market price at which you could sell. Smaller, illiquid companies may have virtually no buyers or sellers at various points in time.

Brokerage sites now allow you to view the market depth, being the prices at which other investors are prepared to buy and sell. If you are trading a smaller stock, the numbers of willing buyers may be far fewer and the prices between the highest buys and lowest sells (known as the *bid/ask spread*) may be further apart.

If we were to look at the share price and trading volume history of an illiquid stock, we would see a staccato chart containing gaps representing days with very low trading volumes and possibly some days showing no trades at all. Put simply, few shares are traded in these stocks in the course of a normal trading day. Investors should be wary of such stocks: the last-traded price is meaningless to the value of your investment if nobody is willing to purchase the parcel of shares you wish to sell.

Leverage: buying on margin

Just as property investors can use leverage to their advantage, share investors can take on a *margin loan* from an investment lender in a bid to boost their returns.

For example, if you have purchased a $100,000 investment in Rio Tinto shares, an investment lender may use the value of your investment as security to lend you a further $80,000, being 80% of your initial investment. Therefore, as an investor, if you have $100,000 in cash you can purchase an investment up to this level and take on an additional $80,000 loan to purchase more stock (either in the same security or another stock).

One of the curiosities of margin loans is that you may then potentially borrow again against the newly purchased $80,000 of stock to buy another $64,000 (80% of $80,000) worth of shares. And then you may be able to borrow 80% of $64,000…you get the picture. This is one reason why I say that comparing property and share-investment lending practices is more complicated than is frequently made out.

Rio Tinto, BHP Billiton and other blue-chip stocks such as the major banks may attract a loan-to-value ratio of 80% depending upon the prevailing risk appetite of the lending market, while other stocks that are perceived to be of a more risky nature attract lower percentages. In the case of speculative stocks, lenders will generally not lend against them at all.

If the value of your leveraged share portfolio drops, you may be subjected to what is known as a *margin call*. If this is the case, the lender will want you to top up your account with more cash as security for the loan, and if you cannot do this they will insist on shares being sold at the prevailing market price. The lender will not be interested in achieving an optimal sale price on your behalf, only in the recovery of the leverage capital.

I've used margin loans extensively in the past to help magnify returns, but I have come to the realisation that they can be as much of a burden as they can be a benefit. In a bull market, margin loans are very useful, but when the market is trending downwards or is flat, they are a hindrance. I believe that the best trading systems are those that are easy to follow and are transparent. The process of buying on margin adds confusion to the trading system. It also becomes far more difficult to measure a true rate of return, because margin-loan interest needs to be attributed to any stock that has been bought on margin.

Where margin loans become particularly troublesome is in a sideways market. If the market has trended down we are likely to dispose of our holdings, and if the market has been trending strongly upwards we are generally very happy, whether leveraged or not. However, the market can track sideways for long periods of time, and this is where the decision-making processes can become clouded or impaired for the leveraged investor.

The debt-free investor is free to hold on to sideways-tracking stocks for as long as he feels necessary, or until the share-price chart breaks out on the downside. At some point, the stocks may be disposed of if the investor feels there is an opportunity cost, that is, there are better opportunities to be had elsewhere. The leveraged investor has a far more difficult decision to make. For every day, week or month he holds a leveraged investment that does not appreciate, it is costing him or her money in the form of interest charges.

The leveraged investor may therefore be inclined towards taking even greater risks. If there are finance charges of nearly 10% per annum associated with an investment, the investor is 'behind the 8 ball' before he even begins – he must achieve returns sufficient to cover brokerage, slippage and interest charges before he is ahead.

I am a firm believer that the successful trader is one who can operate with the clearest mind, and for this reason I believe that buying with leverage is neither necessary nor desirable. The real beneficiaries of margin loans are the margin-lending institutions and the brokerage firms.

Money-management skills

Money-management skills are arguably more important than stock-picking skills, a theory that some have tried to prove by demonstrating that with their superior trading skills they can still make profits from randomly selected stocks. Trading competitions have shown that the winners are often those who relentlessly dispose of losing trades quickly.

Having outstanding money-management skills necessitates having a clear trading plan and good trading records – and using them. A trading plan should detail what percentage of your trading capital will be risked on each individual trade. If you are aggressive, you might elect for this figure to be as much as 2% or more of your entire capital per trade. If your investment capital in shares represents a high percentage of your net worth, then the figure might be closer to 0.5% per trade (in other words, you would have to make 200 bad trades in order to be wiped out). However, the figure should not go much lower than this, otherwise you will then limit your upside.

When to buy in

In an ideal world, just as with value investing, we would simply wait until the market is exceptionally cheap and pick up a series of shares at bargain prices, then wait for the inevitable profits to roll in. Unfortunately, the real world doesn't always work like that. Firstly, it is never entirely clear when the market is reaching its nadir (or, for that matter, its peak). Moreover, a stock-market cycle can last for many years, and therefore it is not always practical or desirable for the investor to wait for the market to crash before buying in.

As it is impossible to pick the bottom of the market perfectly, a technical analyst may tell you that the best time to buy is when the market is trending upwards through a 'breakout' – breaking through a period of resistance – and not when it is falling downwards, trying to 'catch the falling knife'.

There are any number of tools that can be used to identify when the market is finally trending upwards again after a stock-market crash. Two of the more popular methods are moving average calculations (such as a 50-day moving average) or the Coppock indicator (a technical oscillator that generates a 'buy' signal on an upturn from a market trough). I will not go into much detail here, but it should be remembered that these tools are only indicators of a trend, and should be used in conjunction with our overall assessment of the market sentiment.

Choosing stocks

There are well over 2,000 companies on the Australian Securities Exchange[9], so knowing where to start can be a daunting process for the beginning investor. To know which are the best stocks for you to pick, you first need to be clear on why you are investing and what your goals are, and also clear on which industries you have an understanding of.

The companies that are traded on the stock exchange vary from BHP Billiton at the top end of the blue-chip range, with a market capitalisation of well over $100 billion, to some tiny, valueless companies, the shares of which are almost never traded. The remaining stocks fall somewhere between these two extremes.

There is a huge amount of public interest in stocks at the speculative end of the market, particularly in the shares of speculative resources exploration companies in Australia. This is because many investors and speculators are interested in getting rich quickly by trying to hit 'home runs', that is, finding a company with a share price that rockets upwards upon the discovery of a major new resource. At the other end of the scale, it is recognised that blue-chip stocks are less likely to show capital growth that triples or quadruples the share price in a short space of time.

In the main, I tend to steer clear of out-and-out speculative stocks because of the additional risk they bring to my portfolio. I do not need to hit '10-baggers' to make me wealthy quickly, as I can instead build my wealth safely and securely over time. Speculative stocks can play a part in wealth creation as part of a plan, but they should not be the plan.

For a market timer, these are some of the factors that might be taken into account when picking stocks. Look for companies:

- With a profit-making history of several consecutive years, and preferably with increasing profits – there are plenty of them out there, so why pick those that are making losses?

- With a consistent and growing dividend; dividends are often overlooked in bull markets, but form a very important part of shareholder returns

- With a reasonably consistent operating history

- Which may include some smaller or mid-cap stocks – remember, these can be more volatile, but this can work in our favour when the market is cheap, as they can boom in price (as per the CAPM model discussed in the previous chapter)

- With a price-earnings ratio that is not too high in relation to the company's history or industry averages – we want to buy companies when they are reasonably cheap

- With outstanding future prospects!

- That operate in an industry with outstanding prospects, and an industry that you understand.

Speculative stocks

Like playing the pokies, trading highly speculative stocks is rapidly becoming a national pastime in Australia. If you take a look at the Internet bulletin boards, there appears to be an inverse relationship between the market capitalisation of companies and the relative level of interest in them. The reason for this is simple: many people are looking for that elusive home-run stock or a '10-bagger' that will catapult them into wealth, rather than building wealth slowly but surely.

Of course, there is absolutely nothing wrong with this, provided that you are playing with money that you can afford to lose. There can be a place for trying to hit home runs in any financial plan. However, we should be aware that we may run the risk of ending up like a lottery winner who has no context for investing his funds: we could make a million from one stock, but then go on to lose it and be back to where we started.

There are certainly plenty of stocks out there that can help an investor achieve phenomenal returns if he can choose the right one. Stockbroker, journalist and author Marcus Padley has said that some 12% of the ASX listed stocks would have turned $10,000 into $1 million had we invested in them over a long-enough time period[10].

Sometimes, share investors cite the example of the Westfield Group as cast-iron proof as to why shares are a better investment than property. They will state things such as, 'Had you invested just $1,000 in Westfield in 1960, it would be worth over $100 million today.' To pick just one stock from a couple of thousand on the ASX over a carefully chosen time period and conclude that shares are therefore better than other asset classes is, of course, nonsense.

Just one of the problems with this theory is whether we are able to hold on to a stock after it has doubled, tripled or quadrupled in value. It should be easy with the benefit of hindsight, but in reality investors like to take profits while they are on the table. Other than Frank Lowy perhaps, do you know any investors who invested in Westfield in 1960 and still have their shares today? No, neither do I. The vast majority of Westfield investors over time cashed in their profits somewhere along that long timeline of the last 50 years.

It is often wise to step back and wonder what Warren Buffett would think of an investing approach. In his view, while chasing speculative stocks may see a short-term return, it is no way to build wealth for the long term. An investment plan needs to be sustainable and repeatable. Trying to continually find '10-baggers' and hit home runs is neither of these things.

When to sell

Deciding when to sell a share is almost invariably a more difficult decision than deciding when to buy. Buying shares is the fun part of the equation. Selling shares can involve more difficult emotions, and is rarely as easy to do. In terms of when to reduce overall exposure to the stock market, there are a number of indicators we can look at to identify an overheated or speculative stock market. Variously, these may include high average price-earnings ratios, low average dividend yields, extreme difficulty in identifying any good-value stocks, a proliferation of new floats and cab drivers getting into the market.

Identifying when the market has become a risky and speculative environment is a powerful tool in the investor's armoury. In terms of identifying the right time to sell an individual shareholding, Colin Nicholson advocates a method that compels us to sell holdings in individual shares when the uptrend is broken[11], that is, when the share price falls through a point of previous resistance. By having a prescribed written methodology, he is able to remove emotion from the selling process. Instead, he pictures himself as a 'serial decision maker' who is following and executing a planned process[12]. This sounds like a smart plan to me, and I try to follow it myself.

Another simple method that can be used is to sell any stock that falls by an arbitrary percentage from your entry price, say 7.5%. If the percentage is set too low, then 'market noise' can mean that your stop position is hit just through the day-to-day fluctuations in the market. If you set the percentage too high, then bigger losses become very difficult to make up with profitable trades.

It is probably fair to say that if a share price falls more than 10% from what you bought it for, the stock is not 'cooperating' or performing as you expected it to, and it may be a sound idea to sell it before you hurt your trading account too badly. Choosing a tighter percentage can be a sensible idea. If you never lose more than 7–8% on a trade, you can never hurt your trading account too badly (provided you are holding a reasonable number of stocks, of course). You will be like the Melbourne Storm: if you rarely concede tries in defence, then you must certainly win most of the time.

Note that a share-price chart can be travelling in both an upwards and a downwards direction depending on the time horizon we are looking at. For example, look at this six-month share-price chart for Telstra, showing a very reasonable uptrend.

Figure 11.2– Telstra six-month chart

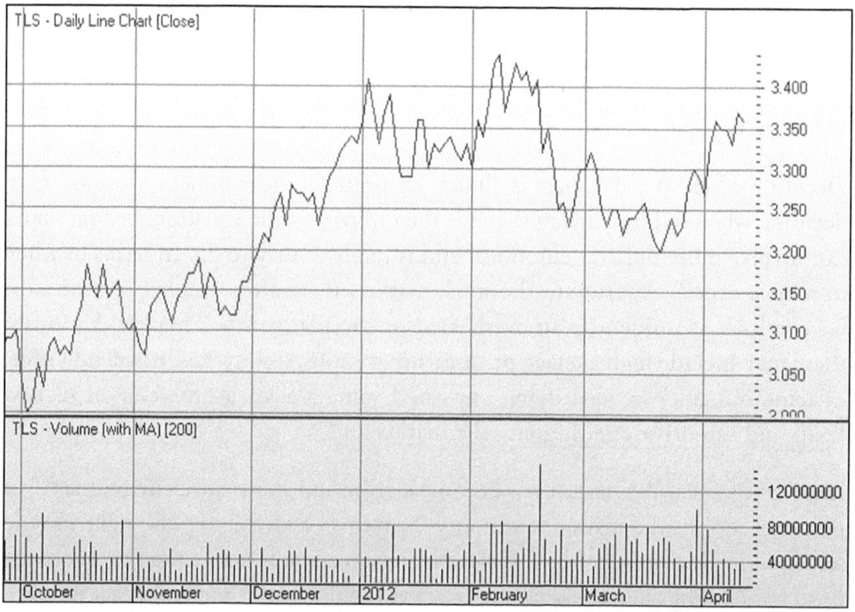

Source: www.asx.com.au

Now consider this 10-year chart for the same share, showing a diabolical performance.

Figure 11.3 – Telstra 10-year chart

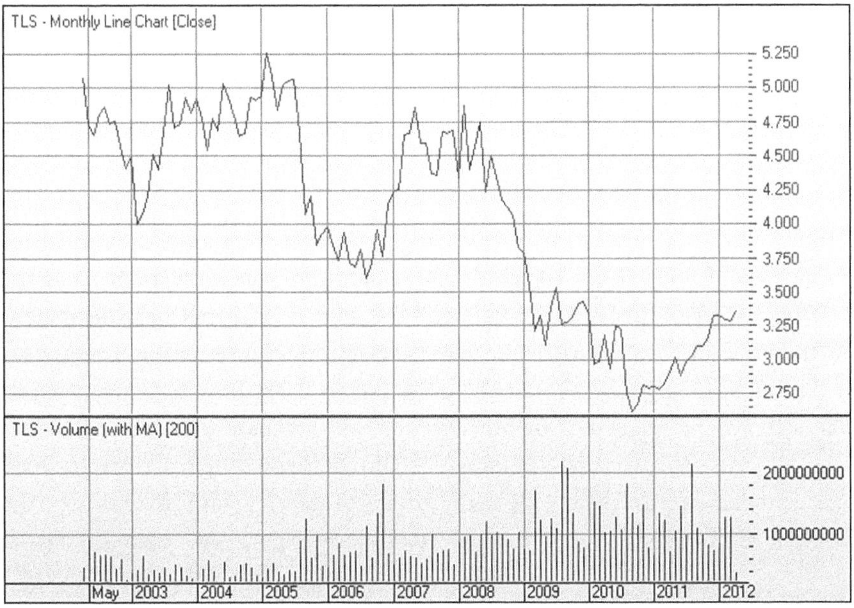

Source: www.asx.com.au

One of the skills for investors to master is learning which time horizons are most appropriate to use in analysing the share-price movement of a stock or of a market.

Above all else, we must not fall into the trap of letting losses turn into 'long-term investments' that drift ever downward. If we do that, then the benefit of our successful investments can be totally negated.

Using sell stops

A sell stop is a tool that can be used to limit downside risk on any given trade. For example, you might purchase a share for $10, but decide that if it falls by 10% then you will sell it. In this case, you would set your sell stop at a price of $9.00.

Stops cost very little in dollar terms, and can be set automatically on your brokerage account. Alternatively, you can record your sell-stop price and trigger a stop manually, provided that you can trust yourself to execute the stop. Note that if you do not access your account each day, it is likely to be a better practice to have automated sell stops in place. If you are otherwise engaged and a particular stock falls sharply, then a painful outcome can result, a lesson I, of course, had to learn the hard way.

It is important to note that if you are using sell stops, the stop should only be moved in the direction of the trade, a point frequently highlighted in his texts by professional stock trader and author Dr Alexander Elder[13]. This means that if you are buying the stock or *going long*, the sell stop should only be moved upwards as the share price increases. Conversely, if you are *short selling* (see Chapter 12) the stock, the stop should only be moved downwards as the share price decreases (rather than panicking in response to adverse movements and sacrificing gains you stand to make).

Online accounts have become increasingly sophisticated, and one tool I have found useful when I am travelling and unable to access the Internet is the *trailing sell stop*. This is a tool whereby the stop is triggered by a movement in the price of a certain percentage and/or volume. For example, I might set a trailing stop whereby should the price fall by 10% from any given point, the sell will be triggered. In other words, as the share price rises, so does the sell stop. This has the advantage of allowing you to participate in share price movements on the upside while always protecting your downside by the prescribed margin.

Psychology of trading

Emotions and psychology are vital to successful share trading. A winning trader should be able to recognise his or her temperament and control it. The finest traders and investors are those who can act in a rational and unemotional manner regardless of whether they are winning or losing. Beginning traders tend to become excited by winning trades and despondent each time they generate a loss. Beginners also tend to suffer from recency bias, their expectations being heavily weighted towards their most recent outcomes.

It is important to recognise that all traders make losses, but the successful ones are those who can close out the position rationally, quietly and unemotionally before moving on to the next trade. To learn more on this subject, I recommend reading *The Psychology of Investing* by Colin Nicholson.

Loss aversion

Studies have shown that humans are likely to be twice as thrifty in an economic downturn or recession as they are extravagant in boom times[14]. This is partly reflective of a recognised trait known as *loss aversion*.

An interesting exercise that is often cited is shown in Figure 11.4.

Figure 11.4 – Ball exercise[15]

Suppose I said you could select one ball from Box 1 while blindfolded. If you picked a smiley face, then I would give you $100,000, but if you picked a sad face, you would receive nothing. Alternatively, you could just take the ball from Box 2 and receive a guaranteed $75,000. Which box would you instinctively go for? Box 2?

Now, what if you had to select one ball from Box 1, and if you picked any of the three smiley faces, you would lose $100,000, but if you picked the sad face, you would lose nothing. Alternatively, you could just pick the ball from Box 2 and automatically lose $75,000. What now? Box 1, perhaps?

If you instinctively agree with the suggested likely choices, don't worry; that is typical human psychology. Now, what if the first scenario was either a guaranteed $75,000, or a three-in-four chance of winning $125,000 and a one-in-four chance of receiving nothing. Still going for the guaranteed $75,000? It's a more difficult choice now, but most people would still take the $75,000.

These are very similar to the instincts that arise when we make winning and losing trades. We are unwilling to take losses, for this would represent admitting that we got a trade wrong or made a mistake. This is completely illogical, because all traders make bad trades – it is impossible not to.

Hyperactive trading

The introduction of online brokerage accounts has had a significant effect on the behaviour of traders. In days gone by, investors may have been reluctant to phone up their brokers several times a day to place buy and sell orders. They may also have been embarrassed to sell shares at a loss, and therefore became disinclined to close out losing trades ('it's a long-term investment').

Now that the human element has been removed, frenetic trading seems to be all the rage, and we see traders making dozens of trades in a day. Studies have shown that women tend to make fewer trades than men, and their less hyperactive approach can result in better trading results. Be aware that if you trade frequently, seemingly insignificant brokerage fees can quickly add up to take a surprisingly nasty chunk out of your trading returns when it comes to an end-of-year review of trading results for tax returns.

The bottom line

Pareto's Law dictates that in many spheres of life, 80% of the outputs are often derived from 20% of the inputs, and for this reason it is sometimes referred to as the 80/20 rule.

Suppose a trader has funds of $10,000 (for the sake of simplicity I have used a small figure – in reality a trader with this sum available may find it a little more difficult to make significant profits due to the transaction costs of trading), which he decides to split into 10 trades of $1,000 each.

Example 1: Expected by beginners

Figure 11.5 – Beginner's expected trading account ($)

Trade number	Profit/(loss)
1	100
2	150
3	200
4	300
5	100
6	50
7	150
8	200
9	500
10	100
Total	**1,850**

This is likely a fair reflection of what a beginner in share trading or investing is expecting his trading account to look like. He is fully expecting to make a profit on every share that he trades. He expects some of the profits to be small, and he will bank others when the profit rises to $500 or so. None of his trades are expected to make a loss.

Example 2: More likely trading results for a beginner

Figure 11.6 – Beginner's more likely trading account ($)

Trade number	Profit/(loss)
1	300
2	700
3	(200)
4	100
5	50
6	600
7	(800)
8	(800)
9	50
10	100
Total	**100**

In reality, this is what the trading accounts of many beginners (and many more experienced hands) may look like. There are a couple of excellent trades in here that have made significant profits and several good trades that have made further gains, but a huge amount of the good work has been undone by two shocking trades. In my experience, many people have trading accounts that follow a pattern similar to this.

Many traders are quick to snatch at profits, but when a trade goes bad they allow it to run further and further downwards, deluding themselves that the trade has become a 'long-term investment'. Remember that if a share price halves, it then has to double in order for the trade to break even (in fact it has to more than double if transaction costs are taken into account).

Due to the effect of letting poor trades run, many investors make little or no progress at all with their share-market exploits, and some generate devastating losses in market downturns and are lost to share trading forever. Many will be very quick to tell you in detail about their successful trades, but fail to mention any losses. By not selling their losing trades, they may not have realised a loss, but you can be certain that they are in the post.

Example 3: Experienced trader's results

Figure 11.7 – Experienced trader's trading account ($)

Trade number	Profit/(loss)
1	100
2	(100)
3	800
4	(100)
5	(100)
6	200
7	300
8	1,200
9	(50)
10	250
Total	**2,500**

This is a hypothetical example of an experienced trader's account. Note that four of the ten trades he has executed have lost money, but the trader has ensured that none of these trades has lost more than 10% of the capital invested. What this trader has done well is not to snatch at winning trades, but allow them to run.

You will note that $2,000 of the overall $2,500 profit has been made on just two of the trades. Another way of looking at this is that 80% of the outputs have been generated by only 20% of the inputs. This is Pareto's Law, or the 80/20 rule, at work.

Tax

If you are to follow the path of timing the market, then where profits are realised, tax liabilities will follow. This is an unavoidable fact of trading life. While value investing may follow a buy-and-hold course that allows unrealised profits to accumulate in a tax-deferred manner, the market timer can create tax liabilities in the current financial year when he sells out of a trade at a profit.

This should not necessarily deter you from following a market-timing approach. Just as a successful profit-making business must pay tax, so must a successful share trader – if you are paying tax, then you must be making money, and that, at least, can only be a good thing. I do not have to worry about the tax implications too much, particularly as I have negatively geared properties that have reduced my tax liability to zero. However, if you are already paying tax in the top bracket, the impact of tax may be more significant.

Learning to read charts

Learning how to read a share-price chart is an important skill for those aiming to time the market, and one which takes time and experience to develop. A successful timer of the market must be able to understand the various types of charts that are available, and to understand how to read charts that cover different periods of time. An experienced reader of charts will easily be able to recognise when a share price is trending upwards, downwards or moving sideways within a range.

Two of the key concepts to understand are resistance and support lines. A support line is formed when a price decreases and then rebounds from a point that aligns with at least two levels of support. Conversely, a resistance trend line is formed when a price increases and then rebounds from a point that aligns with at least two previous points of resistance. Sometimes, share-trading books talk of *floors* and *ceilings* instead of support and resistance, but the meanings are the same.

Successful traders recognise that a good time to buy into a stock may sometimes be when its price has broken through a point of resistance, as this may indicate that the price could continue on an upwards run. On the flip side, it is often wise to steer clear of (or perhaps short sell) stocks with a share price that has fallen through a recognised level of support.

Discipline

In this chapter, I have introduced you to just a few of the ideas that should be considered by a share trader aiming to time the market. Share trading through timing the market, like all forms of wealth creation, requires a determination to succeed, a high level of discipline, measurement of results and, crucially, a determination to continue to learn from your results and experiences.

Practical Action Points

- As always, read finance books that cover the subject of share trading. Anything by Colin Nicholson is an excellent starting point.

- As noted in the previous chapter, in order to trade shares you will need to set up a brokerage account. Ensure that you choose one with low brokerage fees.

- Research historical charts and earnings valuations from the ASX to get a feel for when the market is cheap and when it is overvalued.

- Learn to read share-price charts. Understand how support and resistance lines interact with each other, and how to recognise a breakout from a trading range, particularly breakouts supported by a strong trading volume.

- Calculate your proposed position sizes. What percentage of your capital will you risk on each trade? Conservative is good – perhaps a maximum of 2% of your capital could be risked on each position you trade.

- Consider very carefully whether you want leverage to be a part of your trading plan. Remember that leverage is a double-edged sword – in a strong bull market you may magnify your returns, but in flat or falling markets leverage can be a curse. My rule of thumb would be: if in doubt, steer clear.

- Develop a written trading strategy. When are you going to be fully invested in the market? When will you enter trades? When will you exit trades? What is your targeted return per annum (this could be a set percentage, or a target of outperforming the index by a certain percentage each year).

12
SHORT-TERM
TRADING
OF SHARES
FOR INCOME

12

Thinking differently

In my opinion, much of the writing on share trading is rather boring, although I've still read it all, because I want to arm myself with all the knowledge I can. Even if a book only helps me to decide what won't work for me, I still consider this to be time well spent. I feel that short-term trading of shares for income should only be a small component of a wealth-creation plan. For reasons already noted, wealth is more easily created in tax-favoured and tax-deferred environments than it is in frenetic short-term trading that generates brokerage fees and taxes on profits.

I suspect that part of the reason for the large number of books and trading systems that are available in the bookshops and online is simply that there is a big demand for them from punters seeking the 'Holy Grail', the information or system that will make them infallible share traders.

Many people hold romanticised notions of sitting in their home office closing out a few deals while being free from a boss telling them what to do. What happens to many of these dreamers is that they trade reasonably happily for some time, and then are completely wiped out when the market crashes (as was the case during the global financial crisis). They have little or no protection on the downside, and no plan for when the market turns and begins to head in a downwards direction.

We could summarise a massive chunk of the share trading advice out there simply by saying that to be a successful trader, you need to think and act differently to the majority. This is logical, as the majority of share traders are unsuccessful in what they set out to do. Not only do you need to act differently, much of the time your behavioural traits will need to be the exact opposite to those of the majority, and possibly the opposite of your own natural instincts.

Take a few moments to consider this table, as it contains some very important information on share trading.

Figure 12.1 – Shares traders thinking differently

Regarding...	The struggling majority...	The successful traders...
Losses	**Let losses run** in the hope that they 'come back', thus exposing the risk of one bad trade destroying their trading account	Recognise non-cooperative trades, and relentlessly and unemotionally **cut losses** quickly before they can cause significant damage

Regarding...	The struggling majority...	The successful traders...
Profits	Lock in profits by **snatching** at them quickly	Recognise good trades and **let them run** and run
Position sizes	Take **large** positions, hoping for big wins quickly	Take **small** positions, adopting a reduced exposure to risk to preserve trading capital at all costs – above all else
Adding to trading positions	**Average down** on losing trades or adopt the *Martingale* approach of doubling the position for the next trading position entered into	Enter smaller initial positions, reducing risk, and add to winning trades; known as **averaging up** or *pyramiding*
Upon losing several trades	**Increase** position sizes to hopefully recover losses made on previous trades	**Reduce** position sizes in direct proportion the remaining trading capital

The list could go on, but hopefully you get the picture. The key point is that it has been proven time and again that the winning traders are those who cut their loss-making trades quickly (and all traders have loss-making trades). Over time, the losers will be those who average down on loss-making trades and the winners those who average up on winning trades, halving the risk to their capital by taking a smaller initial position on a trade.

To paraphrase Warren Buffett, the key rules of trading could be summarised thus:

'Rule #1: Don't lose your money.
Rule #2: See Rule #1.'

In other words, take care of the loss-making trades quickly and the profits will look after themselves. Most people focus a huge amount of effort on finding those elusive big winning trades, when what they should instead be focussing on is a constant and unending improvement in their money-management skills.

Too many share traders miss the big picture. Short-term trading can be an excellent way to create some extra income, but you will have to work for it, the income will be taxable and you will incur brokerage costs. While not being answerable to an employer is an attractive idea, it is not necessarily smart to create a stressful new job of trading for yourself. Ultimately, financial independence is about the freedom to do whatever you want to.

When Internet connectivity became commonplace in homes, a number of books on *day trading* sprung up, suggesting a plan that involved something like:

- Trade the big, liquid utility stocks

- Trade the bid/ask spread (buy at bid price, sell at ask price)
- Aim to take one 'tick' (see *Glossary of Terms*) out of each trade
- Aim for 10 successful trades a day that generate a bigger profit than brokerage costs
- Pay the tax on your profits.

The theory is that by doing this, you could grind out a profit of $200 per day, five days a week. To me, that sounds incredibly tedious, and barely a productive use of one's time. There may be better methods of trading shares; the key is to find the one that is most suitable for you.

Where to start

Huge volumes have been written on the topic of share trading, therefore again it is not easy for share traders to know where to start. Developing your own trading style is something that can only be learned through practice and in the real world of the markets. Paper trading – learning to trade through theoretical transactions without real dollars at stake – is an excellent idea and highly recommended. However, if you want to become a successful trader, at some point you will have to put your money where your mouth is.

The best books on trading, in my opinion, include those by Dr Alexander Elder[1], William J. O'Neill[2] and Van K. Tharp[3]. I strongly recommend reading these books in preference to those promoting the latest fad. However, I do not believe that trading can be learned solely from reading books. The reason for this is that one of the key skills is learning to recognise and control our emotions. It is perfectly possible that a trader may make excellent trades and profits on paper, but crumble under pressure when real losses are at stake.

Trading systems

How often do we see trading systems advertised in magazines and at seminars? Answer: too many. If there was a trading system in the world that could genuinely guarantee that it worked, don't you think that it would be used universally? In which case, of course, there would be no profits to be made, because we would all have the perfect trading system. The reality is that trading systems may work some of the time in some markets, but ultimately they will fail.

'There is no algorithmic way to beat all markets all of the time – and if there was, the advantage would soon be arbitraged away.'

I believe that the reason why so many trading systems are available is the same reason why racing-tip phone lines exist: there is a demand for them. Psychologically, people like to believe that they have a system that they can turn to every time, even if it has been conceived by someone with no verifiable track record whom we have never met. It is an undeniably attractive idea, and I believe it stems from the same psychological need that draws me to index funds - it is investing with peace of mind attached. Sometimes this is referred to as investors' search for the 'Holy Grail'. The public demand for complex trading systems that supposedly guarantee success is met by opportunists.

In my experience, the best traders are those who can use *technical analysis* to interpret share price charts and volumes, but are also able to introduce a subjective element to their trading style.

It is important to consider how short-term trading of shares fits in with your overall wealth-creation strategy. Personally, I only use trading as a means of generating income for living expenses. Others dream of financial freedom through the 'job' of being a self-employed day trader. Something to be wary of is that if we only generate income for living, and do not invest money into appreciating assets, we run the danger of not building wealth for the long term.

I recently read a book in which the author noted that he had made profits of $1.5 million over the past decade but, tellingly, later in the book he lamented: 'Where has it all gone?' Just as a salary that is not invested will be taxed, and will not in itself make us rich, so it is with taxed trading of shares. We need to be absolutely clear what our strategy for wealth creation is, and how the trading of shares fits into this strategy.

Technical analysis

Technical analysis could be the subject of a book in itself. Indeed, it has been the subject of many books! There are a huge number of tools available to the technical trader including stochastic oscillators, the relative strength index, moving averages, Bollinger Bands, pivot points…the list is almost endless.

This can be extremely daunting for the beginner trying to determine which of the approaches has more merit than the rest. First of all, it is important to note that while many such indicators are useful, none are infallible, so it is not time well spent searching for the elusive 'perfect signal'.

A technical trader first needs to understand how to read share-price graphs. There is a wide variety of presentational styles, including candlesticks, open-high-low-close charts, point-and-figure charts, line charts and many others. The trader must be able to recognise where *support* and *resistance* levels are, and must understand that these levels need to be tested more than once to be proven and how support and resistance interact with each other over time.

What all technical analysis tools are ultimately trying to achieve is finding a method for deciding when to buy and when to sell. Do be aware that technical analysis does have its limitations. An analyst may tell you that there is definite support or resistance at a certain price level, but in reality he may not *know* that there are willing buyers or sellers at that level. Sceptics may also say that if you gave a technical analyst a randomly created graph of figures they would start to see head-and-shoulders patterns, cup-and-handle formations, double bottoms or a host of other technical signals beyond numbering. There may be an element of truth in that.

Most importantly, we should note that a technical price chart does not predict the future; it is merely a map of what has gone before, incorporating the human emotions and psychology associated with the price of a particular stock or market. A skilled technical trader will attempt to use this map to his advantage to profit in the future.

Strategies

Here are some key words of advice on trading:

- Have a realistic written goal (such as a percentage return on capital per annum)

- Determine what your entry signal will be and stick to it

- Keep your entry signal simple

- Keep each position small: only risk a small percentage of your capital on each individual trade

- Set a target price when you enter a trade

- Set a sell-stop price when you enter a trade

- Stick to your sell stop (do not override it!)

- Only move sell stops in the direction of the trade i.e. upwards if 'going long' (you have bought the share) and downwards if you are selling short.

There are a vast number of sources for ideas on which shares to trade, including subscription newsletters, financial magazines or the financial press, reading annual reports, identifying demographic or social trends (use your brain!), visiting company management (you can buy one share in a company and attend their

AGM) and many more. If your focus has been taken away from your full-time job, you have the luxury of time, and of being able to wait for an outstanding trade to come along. Sometimes, inactivity can be the smartest choice.

My own preferred trading method is to get to know a few stocks inside out and only trade those shares. Individual stocks have their own trends, and I try to learn everything there is to know about a handful of companies. I want to know the dates they release their results, the dates they declare and pay their dividends (and whether the dividends are franked – be aware that if they are, the share price can fall by more than the value of the dividend on the ex-dividend date), the nature of the management and how they are remunerated, the current operating results and future prospects – right down to the tiniest detail. Then, I sit and watch for outstanding trading opportunities.

Others will have a more active approach to trading, and will want to be trading every day, regardless of the market. It all depends on your own plan for wealth creation, your investing personality and your trading style.

My personal trading style is probably best described as one of mental assessment of outcomes and probabilities used to my advantage in order to profit (sometimes known as Bayesian Analysis). I have included examples of trades I have made later in this chapter as a very brief demonstration of some of the thought processes that I go through.

In time, people tend to find a system of trading that suits them, whether it is day trading, swing trading, momentum trading or whatever it may be. We should be careful not to be inappropriately swayed by bias towards the most recent outcomes; that is, assuming that because a trading style has worked for us once or twice, it is therefore indubitably the best option for our future trading.

As with all of my strands of wealth creation, I am always on the lookout for ways to improve my skills. Some time ago, I read a book called *The Naked Trader* by an Englishman named Robbie Burns. In the book, he details a part of his trading method called the *Traffic Light System*, whereby he takes a company stock-exchange release and highlights positive words (such as 'exciting') in green and words with negative connotations (such as 'challenging') in red. At first, I was disparaging, and dismissed the idea as overly simplistic, and yet when I returned to trading, I began to find that there was indeed great merit in the idea.

As someone who used to be employed to write company releases, I should have known that messages are definitely hidden within the language used. I suppose the lesson is that we should always be open to ideas on how to improve our trading.

Choosing which stocks to trade

As noted above, I like to focus on getting to know a few stocks inside out. I tend to look for stocks in industries that I have some understanding of, as this gives me a head start. I also look for stocks that I would like to own for the longer term anyway. While noting that price and value can be very loosely linked, particularly in the case of smaller companies, this can help to give me some comfort on the downside. While I do not recommend letting losses run and reclassifying them as 'long-term investments', it does help to understand what the downside risk of any given trade is (especially if you generally do not go short on stocks).

These are only a few of the ideas that I use. You may decide that you are better suited to trading options, futures or currencies. My own choice to trade stocks is based upon sticking to my core competencies (what I know best), and my belief that the simplest systems for trading and for wealth creation are often also the best. If you have tried trading stocks and it hasn't worked out well for you, then you probably have little hope of being more successful with more complex markets. Remember too that stocks pay dividends. Buying gold bullion or trading the US dollar can make you money if the market moves in your favour, but it will never earn you a dividend.

Money management

The shorter your time horizon for holding shares, the more important your money-management skills become. There is simply no point in making nine profitable trades only to make a howler on the tenth and lose all of your profits. The most common mistake is to let a bad trade turn into a disastrous one by letting it run further downwards. This approach often destroys trading accounts.

As with all forms of share-market involvement, it pays to keep records and to learn from them. Care should be taken to include all costs in any analysis of records, including brokerage costs or commissions.

Leverage and CFDs

Well, they had to be mentioned sometime: contracts for difference (CFDs). CFDs have been the talk of the financial press for quite some time now, but it is surprising how few people, even now, know what they actually are. A while ago, I watched *Hall Pass* at the cinema, and I still don't know what was more bewildering – some of Owen Wilson's crude gags or the adverts for CFDs in the trailers.

CFD advertisements seem to involve various footage of tsunamis, stockbrokers looking pensive, earthquakes, share-price charts and dramatic voiceovers asking, 'Have you got a mind that works like this?' Glancing around at the confused-looking tweens in the audience, I would guess that I was the only person in the cinema who had even heard of CFDs. The ads certainly didn't explain very much.

Contracts for difference are essentially just another form of lending for investment in shares, only the available leverage is higher. The lender may only require you to put down a deposit of 5% or 10% of the total value of the investment, which naturally gives the investor significant exposure on the upside…and on the downside.

So are CFDs a fantastic thing or a dangerous thing? Well, one analogy is that they are like a supercar: powerful in the right hands and will get you to your goal quickly, but very dangerous in the hands of the inexperienced or the unstable.

It should almost go without saying that CFD trading should only take place with funds that you can afford to lose and are prepared to lose. One could expect that regulation of these products is likely to tighten over forthcoming years. In any case, a lender has little motivation to extend credit of $200,000 to an investor who does not have the means to cover a $200,000 loss. It is just not in their interests to do so.

Personally, I do not use these products, although I suppose that I would consider doing so if a trading opportunity came along that I felt was too good to resist. For the most part, I find that margin loans offer ample leverage (though you will find that for speculative stocks, margin loans will not be offered at all – which may be a blessing, as there are often seemingly exciting trading opportunities in this end of the market!). Moreover, trading shares for income is only a part of my wealth-creation strategy, and I see no need to jeopardise my strategy with reckless trading. Basically, I don't trade CFDs because I don't really need to.

Short selling

Short selling is effectively betting on a share price to go down in value. The concept is not always an easy one for beginners to grasp, as it involves selling something you do not yet own and then buying it back again at a future point in time. Thus, if the share price you are shorting falls in value during this period then you will have made a profit. Conversely, if the share price rises, then you will have made a loss. In essence it is the reverse of buying a share to sell it at a future point in time while hoping for the price to rise in the intervening period.

Personally, I don't go short on shares, at least not directly. There are a number of reasons for this. I am a strong believer in favouring simple systems over more complex ones, as there is less that can go wrong. Short selling is a slightly more complex business than going long. This is not a very trendy viewpoint, as traders all seem to want to talk about short selling these days.

A second reason I do not go short on shares is explained by a long-term chart of any stock market, which indicates that the long-term trend of stock markets is clearly an upwards one. More than this, stock-market crashes can be very severe and sharp, so the market is effectively moving upwards for far more of the time than it is trending downwards ('slowly up the stairs but quickly out the window' as they say). This long-term upward trend is partly explained by inflation, and partly by the selective nature of the index-measurement criteria. A typical stock-market cycle sees share prices moving up for a longer period of time than it sees them moving down (we are all familiar with the phrase 'stock-market crash'). We should remember that when going short, there is technically an unlimited downside to any trade.

Although it is not very likely that a company will be taken over while you hold a short position in it, we should certainly acknowledge this as a possibility. You would do well to remember this simple equation: leveraged short position + takeover = trading account disaster.

Here is an example: one of the stocks I held in July 2011, Eastern Star Gas (ESG), was the subject of a takeover scrip offer by Santos (STO), and I was delighted that the share price of ESG increased by 42% in the first few minutes of trading on 18 July, 2011. The very reason why many of us as shareholders were trading the company was the prospect of a takeover, and Santos had clearly been stalking ESG for a long time and held an existing stake.

Short sellers had been plaguing the stock for a long period of time, so out of interest I took a quick look at the ASX short-sell reports on the day of the takeover announcement and noted that 25% of all sales in the previous week were made by short sellers. These short sellers were quite possibly trading leveraged contracts for difference on a stock that subsequently jumped in price by 42% in a matter of minutes. Ouch. Also remember that if you are short selling, you will not benefit from any dividend payments, which is not the case for a 'normal' share trader who goes long.

One final reason I do not trade on the short side is that it simply does not feel right to me to bet on failure, whether it is punting at Royal Randwick on the TAB, laying odds on *Betfair* or short selling on the stock market. I have realised over time that whether I am dealing in shares or property, I like to try to find a success story or back a winner. Unlike some, I don't go so far as to say that short selling is unethical (contrarian shorters can play a valuable role in controlling asset price bubbles), but it just does not feel right for me.

If you do decide to trade using short-selling techniques, it is important to remember that many of the basic rules that apply to trading on the long side still apply. Money-management techniques are still of vital importance, and if you are using sell stops (which is advisable), they should still only be moved in the direction of the trade, which is downwards.

One final point on short selling, and that is regarding spread betting on shares overseas. I have read in various UK publications of how spread betting can be used, particularly when going short or when trading currencies. I like the idea in principal, for the straightforward reason that a spread bet is classified as a bet (not an investment), and any profits will therefore attract no tax. However, I do not spread bet, and therefore am not well placed to comment. Of course, if you do decide to go down this route, it is highly advisable to do your due diligence. I have heard stories of spread-betting providers closing out positions that their clients wanted to leave open. As they say on the Internet forums, 'DYOR!' (do your own research!).

Temperament

It pays to recognise our temperament. For me, I always need to be wary of my reckless streak. I don't like boring trades with limited upside – like many people, I like exciting trades that can make big bucks. This is in line with my personality. I am very much an optimist, but also can be prone to having a reckless side, though far less so as I move into my mid-thirties. Try to remember that the best traders do not get overly excited, whooping and hollering about their good trades, and breaking down in tears at the bad. Instead, they are cold and calculating, accepting a carefully calculated risk for the opportunity to make a reasonable profit. They are rational decision makers.

Professional share trader and author Dr Alexander Elder introduces the interesting concept of comparing making a loss with taking a businessman's risk[4]. Sometimes, he argues, we should accept that we have followed a good process and made quality and level-headed decisions in alignment with our trading plan, and yet the trade has not cooperated. This can always happen, and we should accept this fact. Sometimes, we will make losing trades, and should accept this as being the case: we have taken a businessman's risk.

After practicing psychiatry for many years, another concept that Elder alerts us to is that of self-sabotage[5]. This quote is absolutely vital, not just to trading but to all wealth creation and our overall attitude to money and finance. Elder believes that if we can first recognise this, we can then go on to rectify our self-sabotage mentality:

'...most failures in life are due to self-sabotage. We fail... not because of stupidity or incompetence, but to fulfil an unconscious wish to fail...we cling to our self-defeating patterns even though they can be treated - failure is a curable disease[6].'

Example trades

I am hesitant to cite too many examples of my own trades for want of sounding like a pretentious twit. I have, however, written about a few example trades below to demonstrate some of my thought processes when trading shares.

Disclaimer: I do not operate as a licensed financial advisor and in no way do any of the stocks I discuss constitute advice to invest in or trade these companies.

Example trade 1 – Wotif.com (WTF) – market overreaction

Figure 12.2 – WTF monthly line chart

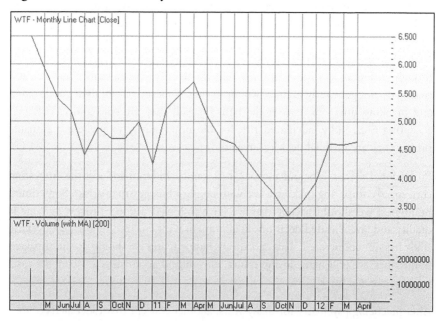

Source: www.asx.com.au

Wotif is a stock that I previously invested in after my other half recommended it to me. Above is a line chart of its historic share price. However, when it hit a share price of $8 and had a PE ratio of around 50, it was simply too expensive, and we both bowed out of trading shares in the company. Following a slightly disappointing profit guidance in April 2010, the share price dipped sharply, and I became interested in trading the company again, buying a small parcel of stock.

The final share price for 2010 was $4.99[7]. In early January 2011, Fox News reported that Queensland was being affected by devastating floods, and the WTF share price dropped by 10% from around $5.00 to $4.60 as a result[8]. Clearly, investors could see that the business was going to be impacted to some extent by the events in the state.

On 12 January 2011, the news continued to report the floods, although as far as I could tell the news was not telling us much that was new, merely providing a status update of the flooding. I was visiting the UK at the time, but I stayed up to watch the share market and saw the price drop even further to $4.21, despite the lack of new developments[9]. Because there was nothing new in the press that I could ascertain, to me this had the hallmarks of a share-price *capitulation*. Capitulations happen from time to time in small and mid-cap stocks, and are often exacerbated by CFD traders being closed out of positions and short sellers relentlessly forcing down the share price.

This was a time for a cool head. My thought processes were these: the initial 10% drop seemed to be a relatively rational response to a natural disaster facing the company that would affect operations. The further 10% drop seemed to represent panic selling and leveraged investors being closed out of their positions.

I rationalised that Wotif generated around 85% of its revenue in Australia and New Zealand. A significant portion of this revenue would come from Queensland, and the company was at risk of losing some of this revenue for half of one holiday season. To me, a share price drop of more than 20% did not represent a rational market movement (particularly in a company I liked the fundamentals of). In other words, the company was not worth 20% less overnight because of temporary flooding in one state.

I built a position of $62,500 with a view to being out of the stock again before the company released any full-year profit guidance (in the previous year, 2010, Wotif released their profit guidance in April). I figured that the company was unlikely to make a significant improvement on its 2010 earnings for the full year, as it had ramped up its advertising expenditure, and the cyclones in New South Wales and floods in Queensland were certainly likely to have some impact on the full-year results.

When the company released its half-year results on 23 February 2011, it issued this statement in the accompanying release:

> 'While it is still too early to extrapolate, we have seen forward booking levels (not check-ins) on Wotif.com over the last 10 days return to double-digit growth. We have seen similar trends on our lastminute.com site[10].'

This is where the traffic-light system can play its role. At first glance, the company release seems to be positive, stressing the improvement in sales. The market certainly read the release this way, and the share price surged upwards, way past $5.00. Yet take a closer look at the language used.

Firstly, the Group Chief Executive says it is still too early to extrapolate, so while he is trying to calm the downward market reaction, he is also telling us to place no reliance on extrapolation. *Red light.* He also bases his figure on only ten days of trading, which looks very much like he may be cherry-picking dates. *Big red light.* There are other references in the same release to consumers 'tightening their purse strings' and room nights sold being down on the prior year. *More red lights.* So while the market reaction was overwhelmingly positive, I was getting ready to sell.

By 28 February 2011, the market reacted by sending the price surging to $5.23[11]. The company was indicating that it would not match its prior-year net-profit figure and yet it was trading at a ratio of more than 23 times earnings. To me, this indicated that a sharp drop in the share price was likely before the company announced its full-year results in August 2011, so I took my money out by closing out of the position. Sure enough, after the full-year results were announced, the share price retraced to around $4.00, and then fell well below that level when market sentiment took a downturn in the middle of 2011.

This is just one straightforward example of getting to know a stock very well, patiently waiting for a trading opportunity and capitalising on a market overreaction.

Example trade 2 – BlueScope Steel (BSL) – range trading

Figure 12.3 – BSL monthly candlestick chart

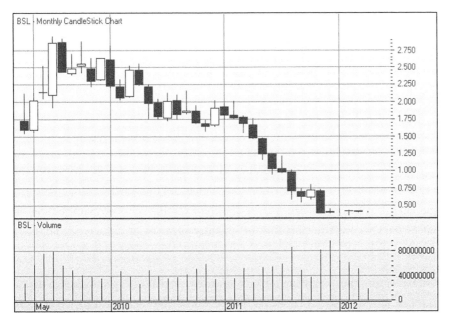

BlueScope Steel is a company I traded based mainly upon technical analysis, and this is a candlestick chart of its share price. BlueScope is (or at least, was) one of Australia's larger companies that was hit phenomenally hard by the global financial crisis, taking its share price down from a high point of well above $12.00 in the middle of 2008 (and a market capitalisation in the billions) to around $2.00[12], where the price continued to hover for some time. The graph shows that the company developed a point of resistance at around $2.50 and a point of support at around $2.00.

On the face of it, the PE ratio appeared very high, and in certain financial periods the company reported a net loss after tax – this is where an understanding of how PE ratios work is important. A company that has fallen substantially during times of economic difficulty can trade at very high PE ratios if it is commonly believed that the company can return to its former glory. This is particularly the case where the company has operating results that are close to breaking even, whereby a small net profit can make the PE ratio seem outrageously high.

It seems crazy to say it now in light of subsequent events, but at the time I felt that the long-term fundamentals of the company in 2009 were sound enough to trade the stock (I wasn't the only one – Martin Roth's book *Top Stocks 2009* included BlueScope in its selections when it was trading at $9.67), and so between July 2010 and April 2011, I traded in and out of BSL six times, netting profits of between 10% and 20% for each trade.

As the economic environment for exporters became very tough, I stopped trading the stock. To pile pain upon pain, the Gillard Government then proposed a carbon tax that BlueScope vehemently opposed due to its potential impact on the steel industry. I stopped trading the stock due to the uncertainty and my own lack of understanding as to how such a tax would affect the industry (as I write, I'm not convinced that anyone really knows how the carbon tax will impact us). This is another example of a company falling on hard times, at least in part due to inability to meet its debt repayments by diluting its stock.

On top of this, the Australian dollar continued its stellar run against the US dollar, running up from just 65 cents in 2008 to a nose-bleed level of 110 US cents in early 2011. With the struggling company announcing a capital raising to improve its balance sheet position, the BSL share price plummeted to below 40 cents[13] by November 2011, and the company announced thousands of redundancies from its Port Kembla plant in the Illawarra region, so I was very glad to be no longer trading the stock on the long side. As I write, the market is waiting to see what will transpire with the carbon tax and the strength of the Aussie dollar. Meanwhile, BSL, a company with significant assets, looks to be a possible takeover target at such a low price.

Example trade 3 – Hillgrove Resources (HGO) – explorer to producer re-rating

I don't normally like to invest in companies with no consistent record of making profits and paying dividends (though Eastern Star Gas was an exception), as there are simply too many good companies to invest in with excellent track records. Speculative stocks such as small mining explorers and early producers carry a higher risk, but also the potential for huge percentage returns, providing you pick the right one.

Figure 12.4 – Hillgrove Resources Limited (HGO) monthly line chart

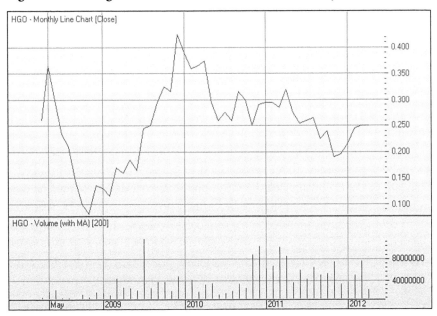

Source: www.asx.com.au

This is a line chart of Hillgrove Resources Limited (HGO). Hillgrove is a company I know a fair bit about, as some years ago I used to work for them. I first got into the stock at 14.5 cents in the aftermath of the 2008 crash (at one stage it stooped as low as 8 cents – a market cap of just $30 million). There was good *arbitrage* at this price, as Hillgrove had an investment in a listed associate company that was worth more than its own market capitalisation at the time. I exercised some options that I had been granted and took a further position in the stock. The share price then moved upwards to a reasonably steady 30 cents, reflecting very strong copper and gold prices and a keen anticipation of first production in late 2011.

The company has copper/gold exploration assets in both Sumba and West Papua (Indonesia) that may or may not prove to be exciting (the market was valuing these at $0, but they offered *blue sky* upside potential, with a number of the mining majors expressing interest in undertaking a joint venture in West Papua), but its main asset is a previously mined copper resource in the Adelaide Hills of South Australia. The company fundamentals looked solid – the copper and in particular the gold price close to or at all-time highs, the company expanding its defined resource and the potential lifespan of its mine, and the overall stock market recovering from its enormous crash during the global financial crisis.

However, the market tends to be very wary of miners at this stage of moving from explorer to producer. There is a risk that the construction and commissioning stages do not pan out according to plan (budget and time overruns being common) or that the commodity prices or stock market may plummet. The market tends to discount the share price fairly heavily until the mine is proven to be operating profitably, at which time the price can be re-rated.

Between May and September 2011, the stock market experienced tremendous volatility, which was predominantly caused by the US running its debt all the way up to its ceiling of $14.3 trillion, followed by the European debt crisis. While US politicians bickered about raising the debt ceiling, the credit ratings agency Standard & Poors downgraded the US rating from AAA to AA for the first time in history. While I believed there to be virtually no chance of the US defaulting on its debts, the stock markets took a very defensive view of the likely impact of the tremendously high debt levels of the global economy. Copper prices tumbled very sharply as the world anticipated a slowdown in China and further debt crises in Greece, Portugal, Italy, Spain and other Eurozone countries.

With the market down more than 20% and Hillgrove's shares falling back to just 17.5 cents (from a high of over 50 cents), I built a position of 400,000 shares. When you believe the odds are strongly in your favour, place a big bet. At below 20 cents, a market capitalisation of only $150 million, I believed that the company was trading at significantly below its intrinsic value. Of course, there is a conflict here between the behaviours noted in Figure 12.1, whereby successful traders limit position sizes, and the concept of the Kelly Optimization Model (place big bets on likely outcomes).

The most important thing to remember is that risk management and preservation of capital are vital. My targeted exit price for the trade is 50 cents (valuing my holding at $200,000) when the mine is operating profitably (hopefully generating free cash flow of between $60 million and $80 million per annum). The company is also able to further explore its mining leases in the Adelaide Hills to discover just how much resource they might have there.

Valuing a resources company where reserves are finite involves a slightly different approach to valuing a company such as, say, Coca-Cola, where the cash flows can be projected forward well into the future. With a mine life of around a decade, I ascertained that when copper prices are near the top of their cycle a discounted cash flow calculation might value HGO at around $400 million when adjusted for risk (or 50 cents per share).

How did this trade turn out? As I write, I don't know yet. Hopefully, if the company can continue to produce copper at a good rate in South Australia through 2012 and continue to drill its potentially lucrative Indonesian areas of interest, the share price will get somewhere close to my 50-cent target price. Companies that are heavily exposed to one commodity tend to have share prices that move in cycles, so a lot depends on the growth of China and the demand for copper. In the short term, an awful lot will depend on the outcome of the debt crises in Europe.

This trade has a lot in common with fundamental investing, as my basis for the trade was a belief that the share price was undervaluing the company. However, the relatively short-term nature of the trade, the speculative nature of the stock and its focus on share-price action determines that in reality, I am trading the company.

Disclaimer: I do not operate as a licensed financial advisor and in no way do any of the stocks I discuss constitute advice to invest in or trade these companies.

Loss-making trades

I make loss-making trades too, for the simple reason that every trader loses some of the time – even the most successful trader makes wrong calls. What separates winners from losers is largely how they deal with trades that do not work out the way they intended. A loser will allow the share price to fall and fall and convince himself or herself that the trade is now a 'long-term investment'. Their justification is normally that by not crystallising a loss, it is not realised and therefore not real. In reality, it only takes a small number of such trades to completely destroy the profits made on the rest of your trading account.

A winning trader acts in precisely the opposite manner. They will not snatch at profits, and they will relentlessly close out losing shares at a low percentage loss to reinvest capital in a better opportunity. If they use automated sell stops, they will only move them in the direction of the trade.

I was planning to write a paragraph here noting in a smug manner how I have not made any trades that have lost more than 10% for some time due to my smart use of sell stops. Oh, how the market treats such arrogance. Not too long ago, I bought a small parcel of shares in a company called Select Harvests (ASX Code: SHV) and due to the small size of the parcel I did not place a sell stop. While I was out doing volunteer work on the Cyclone Yasi disaster relief in Queensland I did not have access to a computer all day as I was out chainsawing fallen trees, building fences, and the like. You can guess where this story is heading.

A little background. I had previously invested in Select Harvests and made a nicely profitable trade. They are a company I liked the idea of, as I like almonds, I try to be a vegan both for health and for moral reasons, and as my wife's family are farmers, I take some interest in agricultural companies. The company had been a golden child in its earlier years, trading above $10, but had fallen sharply over time and then further during the global financial crisis in 2008. I sold my original investment for $4.50 per share, making a nice 30% profit.

The company had some difficulties with a material bad debtor, and its results were hampered by the extremely strong Australian dollar. I ended up buying back in at an average cost of $3.21. You will have heard the phrases 'trend is your friend' and 'never catch a falling knife'. As you have probably guessed (despite the stock being featured as a selection in Martin Roth's *Top Stocks 2011*), I was roundly punished for failing to place a sell stop, and returned from a day of chainsawing to discover that Select had lost a key contract and combined the announcement with a lower profit guidance. The share price fell in value by nearly 20% at the close of trade, then thereafter quickly plummeted to just below $2.00. Ouch. Happily, I do not normally allow this to happen, because I use sell stops.

I also held the stock too long. A simple lesson is this: would I have bought the stock at $2.50? No, because the stock was in a clear downward trend. Therefore, I should simply have sold it at that price, and not deluded myself that the fall in price was a temporary blip that would be corrected over time.

A large number of share traders, myself included, become transfixed at times with the price paid for a share rather than its prospects going forward. There is a time when it is best to swallow your ego and get out of a bad trade. Admit it was a wrong selection and move on, instead of turning it into a stock you hold for a decade on the off-chance that it might 'come back'. Remember, a stock that falls in value by 50% must then double to return to break-even point.

Fortunately for me, this trade only involved a small parcel of shares, so it was not significantly threatening to my trading account. However, this transaction and my related thought processes are a good example of exactly how not to trade. If you act like this, sooner or later you will make a trade that goes bad and wipes out some or all of your hard-earned profits.

Trading seminars

A brief note on trading seminars, though by now you should probably already know what I will say: be healthily sceptical! Seminars cost money to host, so if you go to a free seminar you can expect that you will be invited to buy something.

The quality and integrity of such events and their promoters vary wildly. Always look for a verifiable and successful track record in the organisation or individual presenting. Ask yourself all of the questions that a healthily sceptical investor or trader should ask, especially before you part with any of your valuable capital.

Some seminars will sell three-day training courses that cost thousands of dollars and purport that you will be a successful trader upon completion of the course. Try to remember that you cannot learn to be a successful trader in only a few days, and you can only learn all of the skills of a trader through making mistakes and good trades in the market yourself.

Be wary of video testimonials from traders who claim to have taken a course and now make tens of thousands of dollars per month. They will not be providing you with audited accounts or disclosing any details of the trades they have made. Also be wary of signing up for monthly trading tips. The results of these are likely to be haphazard at best. Finally, think to yourself: if a trader is truly successful, he should not need to charge you too much for his seminars or products, if he's making as much from his trading as he claims!

Summing it up

There are a thousand different ways to trade the market. Hopefully, the above narrative has demonstrated some of my thought processes when trading. Each person will have a different trading style, and therefore it is important to be self-aware and to develop a style that works in harmony with your personality.

I do not trade shares to build wealth, only to supplement my income. My main focus is on building massive wealth over time through investing in and holding properties, shares in fundamentally sound companies and index funds – investments that I am far better attuned to. However, it is certainly true that by committing to continually developing your skills, you can begin to generate useful income from share trading.

Practical Action Points

- Read any books you can find by the authors I have referenced in this chapter, such as Dr Alexander Elder, William J. O'Neill and Van K. Tharp. Note one of the common themes throughout most books on trading: fail to plan and you plan to fail.

- Set up a brokerage account to trade online. Low brokerage fees are very important if you are going to be trading and transacting frequently.

- Research *technical analysis* to ascertain whether there are tools, signals and indicators that can work for you. Most successful traders like to have a system that they can fall back on when they are under pressure.

- Practice by 'paper trading' before risking real capital in the markets, either by using a spreadsheet to record theoretical trades or by participating in a trading competition (the ASX runs these on its website www.asx.com.au).

- Construct a written trading plan for yourself. If you are unsure of what needs to be included in a trading plan, go back and re-read this chapter.

13

MAXIMISE YOUR SUPERANNUATION RETURNS…

Safely

13

Is better possible?

It is no secret that superannuation funds have had a rough ride over the last few years. It seemed that the equity markets were due to continue their recovery in 2011, and yet as debt crises in the US and Europe raised investors' fears, the markets ended with another losing year. Pension funds tend to have a broad exposure to stocks, and as a result they finished another reporting period with mediocre returns.

It is amazing to think how little consideration the average person gives to their superannuation until late in their working lives. Contrary to popular belief, we are not compelled to invest with any particular fund, to pay expensive management fees or even to invest in a managed fund at all. Australians have more money invested per capita in managed funds than any other country. Unsurprisingly, towards the end of 2011 more Australians than ever before began to consider setting up a self-managed superannuation fund (SMSF) in a bid to improve their floundering returns.

Please note that the title of this chapter is not *Sack your Super Fund Manager Now!* nor is it *Super-Gear and Super-Size!* Superannuation – your pension fund – should be an integral part of a retirement plan, and as such it needs to be treated with due respect and common sense. Self-management is not for everyone.

The key question to ask oneself is this: will I be able to improve my superannuation returns *safely* through self-managing my fund? In order to answer this question, it is first necessary to understand a little about how the existing system works and what returns you are likely to receive from a managed fund.

Why fund managers don't beat the index

Take a look at your annual superannuation fund statements, going as far back as you can. Has the fund significantly outperformed the stock market over that period of time, or indeed in any given year? It never seems to, does it?

Often, the headline gains figure can look reasonable enough, but by the time insurance, taxes and fund management fees are deducted, the net return can be anywhere from not much to a nasty loss. Research in the US has shown that the majority of managed funds do not even match the returns of the stock-market index[1]. It is important for us to consider why this is the case in order to understand how we can maximise our returns.

This has been the topic of many a financial text, but briefly, these are the main reasons why the majority of managed funds do not outperform the market:

- Transaction costs from high turnover of portfolios

- Capital gains taxes within the fund on stocks sold

- Market impact

- The bid/ask spread

- The commissions siphoned off by the fund managers themselves.

Each time a fund manager elects to focus on short-term performance targets and turns over the stocks held in your portfolio, there are commissions and potentially capital gains taxes to be paid. Then, when a fund makes a purchase or sale of stock, the transaction itself can impact the market price of the share (due to the parcels of shares traded by funds being far larger than those of the average investor). The fund manager is also battling the bid/ask spread – the gap between the price at which shares can be bought (the lowest offer or ask price) and that at which they can be sold (the highest bid price). The spread on more liquid stocks may appear to be insignificant, but over time the slippage caused by these small percentages that are lost can and do add up.

Over time, the funds industry has developed into a nonsensical and predominantly useless sector. Sometimes you may hear the industry being referred to as *myopic*. Funds are assessed quarterly in the financial press, which makes no sense for what are supposed to be long-term investment products, while investors see a fund that is on top of the returns charts and lurch towards it like lemmings off a cliff. The short-termist method of rating funds leads to short-termist fund management strategies. Managers turn over stocks at an alarming rate in a desperate bid to chase the latest returns, generating transaction costs and tax liabilities.

Fund managers tell clients to 'buy and hold' and 'stay the course', but rarely do they practice what they preach – instead, most fund managers turn over their holdings at a very high rate.

Funds are also measured against the stock market on an annual basis. Woe betide a fund that gives a return that is significantly lower than the stock-market index, as clients may 'pull the pin' and leave the fund. Consequently, funds deliver results that rarely diverge far from the index return itself. Managers are so fearful of significantly underperforming the stock-market index through not holding a hot stock that they end up holding huge numbers of stocks. It does not take a genius to work out that a portfolio of 50, 100 or even 200 stocks is not going to outperform the index by much, if at all.

The great paradox for many fund managers then becomes the fact that they face more risk from the stocks they *do not own* than those that they do. By holding stakes in all the major stocks, it becomes more a case of whether they are overweight or underweight in any particular company. Any stock in which they are underweight, they are effectively short selling. You can start to see the insanity of the system that has been created.

These issues raise an important question for the investor. If it is possible to match or even outperform most managed funds simply by buying an index fund, would you be better served by self-managing your superannuation?

Health warning

Despite all of the points raised above, self-management is definitely not for everyone. If you have never invested in a share, a bond or an investment property before, it may be better to start small and gain experience outside your super fund first. Your superannuation is your nest egg (or at least an important part of it), and therefore ideally you should aim to have a track record of successful investment experience behind you before you take on management of your super.

As is often the case, whether you choose to invest in shares, property or fixed interest investments, the risk does not lie with the investment; it lies with the *investor*.

The role of tax in superannuation

During your working life and the accumulation phase, superannuation is taxed in the following ways:

Figure 13.1 – Superannuation taxation

Contributions	15%
Income in the fund	15%
Capital gains in the fund (> 1 year)	10%

It seems odd that the government introduced compulsory contributions and then decided to tax the contributions. It would have seemed more logical to make the contributions tax free and the contribution percentage lower (companies would make compensating higher taxable profits). Still, this is how the system is set up, and we must work within it.

Although income and gains are taxed at lower rates than they might be outside of your superannuation fund, taxes still have a significant impact on the ability to grow wealth in a fund. Therefore, what is needed is an investment strategy that minimises taxes and transaction costs within the fund. As we have seen, you will not get this strategy from the average fund manager.

Why would you choose to self-manage?

There could be any number of reasons for setting up an SMSF, but essentially, they all fall under one of two broad categories: cost and control.

Cost

Although it may seem illogical, the fees charged to you by a fund manager increase as the balance of your superannuation increases. Therefore, at a certain point in time, you may feel that the cost of fund management outweighs the benefit that the manager is providing.

On average, fund managers charge annual fees of 1–2% of the superannuation balance being managed. It is possible to find funds with lower fees, and this may be a very good starting point if you are aiming to maximise your returns (though funds are prone to charging entry and exit fees, so moving between funds can also be inefficient). Do not be misled into believing that investing in a fund with a higher management fee necessarily means that you will receive a better service, for there is no compelling evidence that this is the case.

As already noted, fund managers can generate significant transaction costs and capital gains taxes within the fund. This should also therefore be taken into account when you are considering the potential benefits of switching to self-management. A superannuation fund is a long-term investment, and this affords you the luxury of being able to take a longer-term view of any self-managed investments therein. In my opinion, it should be straightforward to implement an investment strategy that is more efficient than that of the majority of fund managers. Heck, even buying a low-cost index fund (see Chapter 9) would wipe the floor with the majority of managed funds, so it can definitely be done.

The alternative to self-management is simply to look for lower-cost and better-performing funds. Lower-cost funds are easy enough to find, and some very reasonable funds charge annual management fees of 0.5% of your balance per annum. Picking a higher-performing managed fund can be a more difficult proposition, as the past performance of a fund is no guarantee of its future results. Indeed, 'hot' funds often perform poorly in the years following their great successes *after* investors have swarmed to them.

Control

The other reason for setting up an SMSF is to control your own destiny. It is a simple fact that a fund manager cannot deliberately design and manage a fund that is perfectly in alignment with your aims. By definition, nobody can know more about your own plans, goals and needs than you do yourself. It pays to remember that you can only ever be one small part of a managed fund.

The balance of your portfolio should ideally change as you move closer to retirement. One traditional formula suggested that you should take the figure 100 and subtract your age in order to calculate the percentage of your portfolio that should be held in stocks, with the balance to be held in bonds.

Figure 13.2 – Traditional portfolio balancing

Age	% in shares	% in bonds
20	80	20
25	75	25
30	70	30
35	65	35
40	60	40
45	55	45
50	50	50
55	45	55
60	40	60
65	35	65

While I don't necessarily suggest that you have to follow this formula, the table demonstrates an important point. As you move closer to retirement, it may be preferable to have a lower percentage of your portfolio in volatile assets such as shares. One of the saddest things I experienced in my job in 2008 and 2009 was talking to fellow employees who had planned to retire soon, only to see that their superannuation balances had haemorrhaged by 20% or 30% following the effects of the sub-prime crisis on the world's stock markets.

This risk can be mitigated to some extent by choosing a less aggressive fund as you move closer to the retirement age. Some funds even exist with a specific retirement date in mind. However, you should always keep in mind that you will still only ever be one small part of a larger fund.

Fund managers are not motivated by the same goals as you are. A fund generates its own profits from the fees siphoned from the funds under management. Logically, therefore, the fund's target is to build its assets under management to the highest level it can. You can't really blame the fund management industry, for it simply operates within the system that has been created. Besides, allocating blame will not lead you to a more comfortable retirement – but taking decisive action will.

You must always remember that when you see expensive adverts for your fund, shiny brochure mail-outs, fund sales reps driving expensive new fleet cars and the management company's flash offices in the city, these are all paid for by the management fees deducted from your retirement fund. Above all else, you must not believe the propaganda that there is some mystery to the art of managing your money that the average individual cannot comprehend. The figures prove that there is not. The fund management industry often does not even beat the returns of the stock market, nor does it provide you with adequate insurance in the case of a stock-market crash. Thus, it is definitely possible for an individual to achieve superior returns through adhering to a sensible investment strategy.

Weighing up the costs of an SMSF

Perhaps the greatest flaw in the super system is that fund managers charge their fees based upon a percentage of the balance managed. Consequently, as your super balance grows, you pay ever more in fees.

Figure 13.3 – Fund management – example of annual fees ($)

Balance of fund	Fees at 1%	Fees at 2%
50,000	500	1,000
100,000	1,000	2,000
150,000	1,500	3,000
200,000	2,000	4,000
250,000	2,500	5,000
300,000	3,000	6,000
500,000	5,000	10,000
1,000,000	10,000	20,000

When you look at your superannuation statement for the financial year, you will notice that charges are generally deducted for insurance, taxes and management fees. There has been a shift in the industry towards greater transparency in fee disclosure, which is one positive move.

What is less obvious – particularly to the uninitiated – is the compounding effect of the management fees on your returns, and consequently the quality of your retirement. If you stop to consider what an expected annual stock-market return might be in these days of moderate inflation (8% might be a reasonable suggestion) and the effect of a 2% per annum management fee thereon, you might start to see the problem. In this example, 2% equates to one quarter of your expected annual return. Certain authors have suggested that the compounding effect of management fees can rob you of 60% of your final retirement balance[2].

This is not an easy concept to grasp, but if you run some numbers through a model it becomes apparent that over time, the effect of losing 25% of your expected returns makes a monumental difference to your ability to grow an adequate super balance for retirement. It is the opportunity cost of the fees siphoned off – the compound growth that is *not* allowed to flourish – that makes for the great difference in outcome.

The table below shows the effect of a 6% compounding return and an 8% compounding return on a base figure of $100,000 over 45 years. For the sake of clarity, no additional contributions have been made to the initial $100,000.

Figure 13.4 – Effects of a 2% management fee on likely returns ($)

Year	6% compounding return	8% compounding return
0	100,000	100,000
10	179,084	215,892
20	320,713	466,095
30	574,349	1,006,266
40	1,028,572	2,172,452
45	**1,376,461**	**3,192,045**

It is quite clear that while the effects of a 2% management fee only appear to make a marginal difference in the early years of building a retirement lump sum, over a working lifetime the potential difference is absolutely staggering.

The costs of an SMSF

There is one often-overlooked hidden cost to setting up an SMSF, and that is the exit fees that certain funds charge you to remove your money from their management. I was fortunate in that the funds I had been in only charged administrative fees upon exit, but that was purely through luck rather than judgement. I can tell you, I certainly did not research the entry and exit fees when I signed up for the funds years ago and, let's face it, they aren't exactly disclosed in bold letters on the first page of the brochure (fees that a fund charges are disclosed in the *Product Disclosure Statement* – what used to be known as the *Prospectus*).

Almost unbelievably, some funds charge as much as 5% of your super balance as an entry fee, another 5% as an exit fee and 2% of your balance per annum through the duration of the management period. Other funds more sensibly only charge an administrative exit fee. It certainly pays to read what you are signing up for when you are selecting a superannuation fund, rather than simply signing whatever piece of paper is put in front of you.

There are two further types of costs in running your own SMSF. One is the dollar cost of setting up the fund, and the other is the ongoing cost of administration and compliance.

You might also want to add to this the cost of your time. For all of the bad press the fund management industry receives, and however much we may dislike it, it's the only system we have, and it does serve a very real purpose for millions of people. A significant percentage of the population have never bought a share, never invested in a property and never built anything even approximating an investment portfolio. Others, rightly or wrongly, simply do not believe they have the time or the inclination to manage their own money. A vast number of people believe that they are not responsible for their own wellbeing in retirement, instead believing that the government should take care of them, which is a prime reason why the number of Australians now drawing the age pension is counted in *millions*.

The cost of setting up an SMSF varies depending on which advisors you use, the structure you choose for your fund (a corporate trustee structure may cost a little more than an individual trustee structure, for example) and a number of other factors. The total cost may come to a few thousand dollars, but could be significantly less.

Similarly, the ongoing costs of accounting, audit, tax advice and compliance (an SMSF must submit a tax return every year – remember that if taxes are due, you must have a balance available in your fund to pay them) and administration will vary depending on the complexity of your fund and the fees of the professionals hired to ensure your compliance. Again, the fees could be as low as a thousand dollars per annum, but might come to several times this figure. If you keep good records and can do some basic bookkeeping, this may help to keep the fees under control. Fees incurred will be paid by the SMSF and are tax deductible within the fund.

The bookkeeping requirements are not onerous; all that is needed is a simple record of contributions made to the fund, expenses paid from the fund and details of profits and losses made from investments.

At what point does an SMSF become viable?

The answer to this question will vary depending upon who you ask. Some (particularly those with a vested interest) might say that you would need a super balance of around $200,000 before setting up your own fund becomes cost-effective and worthwhile. When my balance passed $100,000, I felt that I could no longer justify paying fund management fees, and I switched to self-managing. My super funds (I had two) had returned almost nothing over six years, so the decision was made somewhat easier for me. What I found particularly galling were the fees that were charged in the loss-making years – not only had I received no benefit at all over six years, I had been charged handsomely for the privilege.

I feel that if you are looking to invest in equities, you would need a balance of more than $50,000, and if you are aiming to invest in property, a balance of at least $75,000 to $100,000 would be recommended.

Pooling funds

One action you can take to make a self-managed fund viable sooner is to pool your funds with your spouse. In fact, you can pool funds with others too, but it should go without saying that if you are going to follow this path, you should choose your fellow investors very carefully.

Pooling of funds is definitely something worth considering. For example, you may not feel that an SMSF is viable if you have a balance of $50,000, but if your spouse or partner also has a balance of $50,000, then you may feel that you are in a better position to self-manage jointly.

Using an SMSF to buy property

The great advantage of an SMSF is that you can now elect to gear and buy investment property.

Until relatively recently, it was not possible to gear in this manner via an SMSF. Even among senior finance professionals, it seems that there is no widespread awareness of the rules with regard to gearing in self-managed funds.

As I write this, there are SMSF loan products available that permit a loan-to-value ratio of 72% – that is, they require a deposit of 28% of the purchase price of an investment property. If you have a significant super balance with net assets of more than $300,000, then you may find that 'super-gear' products become available that allow a loan-to-value ratio of 80% on residential investment property. However, what is certainly the case is that by the time this book goes to print, lending sentiments and lending products will have changed, for that is the nature of the industry. The key message, therefore, is to *check out what is available*, either via a mortgage broker or through Internet research.

Although we have already considered the benefits of leverage and compound growth earlier in the book, I want to do so again here to demonstrate a very important point. Let's take a look at what a super balance of $110,000 might be able to do.

Figure 13.5 – Using an SMSF to buy a $300,000 property ($)

Super balance	110,000
Set up SMSF and trust structure	(4,000)
28% deposit on $300,000 property	(84,000)
Stamp duty and mortgage transfer fees	(10,000)
Legal fees	(2,000)
Balance to cover future costs	10,000

Figure 13.6 – Returns on $300,000 property at 6% growth ($)

Value of property	6% growth
300,000	18,000 in Year 1

How does this compare with the returns you might get on equities from an equivalent super fund balance of $110,000? If we suppose that you could attain an 8% return on shares including dividends being reinvested (which might seem generous after the poor returns over the last five years), you would be looking at fund growth of $8,800 in the first year. I have assumed no set-up costs for a super fund that invests in equities here, though in reality there would be some administrative costs, and you may need to engage a qualified financial planner to assist with a written investment strategy.

Let's take the property example a little further. You have purchased an investment property for $300,000 using a 28% deposit and an interest-only loan. We have already looked at the returns that you might target for investment property using the strategies of investing with the property cycle, buying properties in high demand such as prime-location investment units and adding value through cosmetic renovation. Let's use a reasonably conservative growth rate of 6% per annum, which is broadly in line with the current growth of household incomes.

Figure 13.7 – Compound growth on investment property at 6% capital growth per annum ($)

Year	Property value at 6% growth	Mortgage	Equity
0	300,000	216,000	84,000
1	318,000	216,000	102,000
2	337,080	216,000	121,080
3	357,305	216,000	141,305
4	378,743	216,000	162,743
5	401,468	216,000	185,468
6	425,556	216,000	209,556
7	451,809	216,000	235,089
8	478,154	216,000	262,159
9	506,844	216,000	290,854
10	537,254	216,000	**321,254**

As an interest-only loan has been used, the mortgage balance remains unchanged, while the property's value continues to grow and compound. Of course, as we have already seen, growth is unlikely to occur in this linear fashion – instead, values plateau, fall and boom in cycles. Over the long term, however, it is likely that property values will continue to increase as household income increases.

In the above example, even though no additional contributions have been made to the fund, and a growth rate of 6% has been used, equity of $321,254 has been created over a decade. Think back to the point I made in Chapter 1 about average super fund balances at retirement. Even this very simple strategy has easily outperformed the average super balance at retirement in just one decade. Why? Because the value of the asset has been allowed to grow unencumbered by capital gains taxes, fund management fees and recurring transaction costs.

It is worth noting, however, that because the property requires a 28% deposit, the great advantage of leverage that property has over shares as an asset class is less pronounced than it would be outside of the fund. Note that while it is possible for an SMSF to use leverage to invest in equities, derivatives, CFDs and options, the inherent volatility of these asset classes make them less suitable for a self-managed fund. I would not suggest going down this route unless you are a sophisticated investor with a very significant superannuation balance. The stamp duty and initial transaction costs also reduce the effectiveness of the property strategy to some extent, and it will not be possible to refinance the property in the conventional manner, for properties within a super fund cannot be used as collateral for other investments.

Let's check out what returns might be possible in an SMSF from investing in equities without leverage using an assumed 8% return per annum.

Figure 13.8 – SMSF invested in equities at 8% growth per annum ($)

Year	Balance
0	110,000
1	118,800
2	128,304
3	138,568
4	149,654
5	161,626
6	174,556
7	188,521
8	203,602
9	219,891
10	**237,482**

Again, for the purposes of a simple comparison, I have assumed that no further contributions are made to the fund and have ignored the effects of audit and administration fees. We can see that investing in shares has the notable advantage of not incurring stamp duty on acquisitions in Australia. If we were to choose the equities route, we would, of course, need to be careful not to generate excessive transaction costs (and capital gains taxes) through hyperactive trading.

What the tables above show is that while property might show a 'better' return than shares, the difference is not as marked as it might be outside a superannuation fund, because the effects of leverage are diminished. Property has the advantage that you do not have to actively manage a portfolio of shares; shares have the advantage of lower initial transaction costs (and shares do not incur a negative cash flow, as an investment property might).

I draw the conclusion that investing in either property or shares can produce superior returns to simply leaving your super with a fund manager. My suggestion would therefore be to consider your superannuation in the context of how it fits into your overall investment portfolio. If you are already overweight in investment property (or you have no investments outside of owning your own home), this might be an ideal opportunity to develop your share-investment skills. The reverse also applies.

Cash flow on properties in an SMSF

One of the great benefits of investment property that has made it such a popular asset class for investments is negative gearing. Investing in property via your super fund is different. There are still tax benefits within an SMSF – for example, rental income is only taxed at 15% – but they are less alluring.

The cash flow on an investment property in your SMSF does not have to be significantly negative. As lenders are likely to insist on a more substantial deposit, the lower loan-to-value ratio (LVR) is likely to result in a stronger cash flow.

With interest rates falling at the end of 2011, it became possible to secure three-year fixed rates at below 6%. Below is an example of how the cash-flow profile of a property might look on a $300,000 investment unit with a 28% deposit having been paid. A good rental yield of 5.5% and a mortgage rate of 6% are assumed.

Figure 13.9 – Example of annual cash flow on an SMSF investment property ($)

Rental income at 5.5% yield on $300,000 property	16,500
Interest on $216,000 mortgage at 6%	(12,960)
Strata Fees – 4 quarters * $400	(1,600)
Property management fees at 5% of rent	(825)
Repairs/other	(500)
Net cash flow per annum	615

In the above example, the combination of a reasonably strong rental yield, the substantial 28% deposit and the favourable 6% mortgage rate have resulted in a positive cash flow for the year. Of course, interest rates can and will increase again in the future, but as ever, rental income will also increase over time with inflation. The purpose of the above example is merely to show that with a deposit of around 30%, the annual cash flow on an investment property need not be a significant drain on your funds.

Using an SMSF to invest in equities

If you are going to invest in equities through your SMSF, similar principles apply as for share investing outside of a fund. You will need to consider whether your strategy is to be that of a buy-and-hold value/focus investor (placing meaningful slices of your fund balance into a few outstanding stocks when they represent great value) or whether you will attempt to time your entries to and exits from the market through recognising cycles and allocating your funds accordingly. These strategies have been covered in detail in Chapters 10 and 11.

As I have already mentioned, you should always have a written investment strategy, for if you do not have a recorded investment plan, how do you know if you are meeting your goals? However, it is doubly important that you have a written strategy for your SMSF, because if you don't, your fund will not be compliant. It is also imperative that having prepared a written investment strategy, the strategy is not subsequently violated, for this could also result in the non-compliance of your fund.

You must also consider diversification. Having read Chapters 10 and 11, I'm sure you were going to do so anyway, of course, but in fact consideration of diversification is a requirement of an SMSF as stated by the Australian Taxation Office[3]. The ATO also requires that you consider investment risk. What you definitely cannot do is plunge your entire superannuation balance into a speculative coal seam gas exploration company – but then, if you were going to do that, frankly you should be leaving the entire management process to a professional anyway.

In terms of the returns you should be targeting from equities, I would suggest that your benchmark should be the returns of the XJO (the ASX top 200 stocks). If you can outperform the returns of the stock market, then your self-management will have been more than worthwhile, for you will be building a better retirement balance, you will not have to pay a fund manager 1–2% of your balance each year and you will be learning invaluable investment skills as you go. You will also have direct control over the generation of capital gains taxes and transaction costs.

That said, don't become too obsessive in your benchmarking comparison to the returns of the stock market in each financial year. As Warren Buffett sagely pointed out, stock prices pay no heed to how many times the earth has orbited the sun. Superannuation is a long-term game. In some years you may dip behind, and in other years you may forge ahead, but if you have developed a strategy of investing in outstanding stocks for the longer term, you should outperform the fund managers who are frantically turning over their portfolios in order to chase results for the next quarter.

Compliance and practicalities of setting up an SMSF

This is not the forum for a long and tedious list of every step in the process required to set up an SMSF. You can find these very easily on the Internet. I suggest that if you are at all uncertain about what you are doing, speak to a qualified financial planner, and when it comes to superannuation, *always do your due diligence.* Some financial planners are better than others, so choose wisely. It can definitely be worth spending some time with a financial planner up front to ensure that you get your strategy right. There are other strategies available that I have not covered here. For example, it can be advantageous to salary sacrifice into an SMSF and to pay for life insurance through the fund, where it can attract a tax deduction (not the case for an individual).

There is simply no point in getting involved in an SMSF if you then fail to comply with the regulations. Pensions are always heavily regulated for obvious reasons. In Australia, superannuation is regulated by the *SIS Act* (1993), the *Financial Services Reform Act* (2002) and a number of other bodies including APRA, ASIC, ASFA, the SCT and the ATO. Penalties can be harsh, in the form of fines, and if your fund fails to comply, it may be that you lose the concessional tax rate advantages too. Thus, if there is a chance that you will not comply for any reason, you would be better served spending your time seeking out a low-cost managed fund and persevering with that.

The very first thing to do if you are considering self-managing is to ensure that your employer will be happy to pay contributions into an SMSF. Provided you don't have a workplace agreement that dictates otherwise, they will probably be happy enough to do so, but it is certainly best to check this before spending money setting up an SMSF.

If you decide that an SMSF is for you, then you will need to start the process of setting up the correct structure (use an experienced accountant for this) by creating an SMSF trust deed, registering for a Tax File Number (TFN) and Australian Business Number (ABN), and electing for the fund to be regulated by the Australian Taxation Office (ATO). While this may sound like a lot of work, I cannot stress strongly enough that you must *never* allow a small amount of paperwork to stand in the way of taking responsibility for your financial future. The administration time involved is minimal when you consider that the alternative might be measured in many years of additional time in the workforce.

The next step is the rolling over of your balances from your existing fund into a separate bank account specifically named (in the names of the trustees or the company) and designated for your SMSF. What you absolutely must never do is draw funds out of your SMSF account to use for other purposes, not even for half a day. Naturally, fund managers are never in a hurry to release any of their assets under management, so the rollover process may take a month or two to play out. This is the perfect time to get your written investment strategy completed.

Practical Action Points

- Pull out your superannuation fund annual statements and determine what returns have been generated for you by your fund manager.

- Find out what fund management fees you are paying as a percentage of your super balance.

- Consider what you expect the future returns from your fund manager might be, and whether you could outperform these returns through self-management. Remember that the majority of fund managers do not outperform the stock-market index.

- Calculate whether you believe an SMSF could be viable for you. If the costs seem prohibitive, consider (carefully) whether pooling funds with your spouse or perhaps another family member or friend might make self-management a viable proposition.

- If you decide that an SMSF is the route for you to take, engage the appropriate advisors to guide you through the process of setting up a fund. Do your due diligence and seek referrals where possible.

- Consider your overall investment portfolio and how your superannuation will fit in with it.

- Devise a written investment strategy for your SMSF and get ready to outperform!

14
SUMMARY:
A PLAN
For Achieving Financial Freedom

14

Financial plans

Every person is different, and therefore no one plan can be right for everybody. Below, I present the plan for wealth that worked for me. It can be adapted to suit your preferences. For example, if you are more inclined towards shares than property, you might decide to move a significant proportion of your wealth into a portfolio of shares in outstanding companies. The possible variations are infinite, but the plan outlined below will provide a guideline that can be tailored to your needs.

It should be clear by now that I believe the traditional route of taking the highest-paying job you can get, buying a big house and placing a heavy reliance on a highly taxed salary for your financial future is a potentially dangerous plan.

I also believe that the average investor will find it more difficult to achieve financial freedom using a plan that relies upon timing investments precisely. Instead, I propose a plan that involves accumulating quality appreciating assets and holding them for the long term.

A plan for achieving financial freedom

The plan I suggest is to generate a portfolio of appreciating assets made up of index funds, shares and residential property. The value of the assets will vary upon your retirement goals. My own target was a multi-million-dollar property portfolio, supported by a portfolio of shares, index funds and a reasonable buffer of cash.

1. Reduce your commitments

Start *today* by living within your means. Pay off credit cards and bad debt (i.e. non-investment debt) as quickly as possible. Credit card debts and loans for depreciating goods ensure that the power of compounding is working against you rather than for you. Reduce expenditure on unnecessary items and consider budgeting and tracking your expenditures. If you are not willing to reduce your expenditure, then this is an indication that you are not committed to a goal of financial freedom, and you will need to reflect on your motivation.

One option that can really help reduce your monthly expenditure is to rent your place of residence. This can free up more capital for you to invest in assets such as shares and investment property. Remember that interest on a mortgage for a principal place of residence is not tax deductible, but loan interest on mortgages for investment properties does attract a deduction.

Most importantly, *do not* take on new bad debt for depreciating luxuries and other items. This path only leads to compound interest working against you. To achieve financial freedom, you need compound growth to work *for* you.

2. Earn and add value

Add more value at your place of work. Do not expect pay rises for tenure; instead, aim to add so much value that your employer is compelled to give you a rise or a bonus. Make yourself invaluable. Remember, Napoleon Hill's advice: if you can't think of ways in which you can add more value, think harder. Consider how you can make your passion your job too.

We know that salaries in Australia are taxed heavily, so it is important to structure your tax affairs intelligently. This is discussed in more detail in Chapter 15.

3. Pay yourself first: automated investing

Invest 10% (or more if you can) of your net salary in a low-cost index fund or a low-cost managed fund if you prefer. By paying in an amount each month, or *averaging*, you will reduce your risk, provided that you are aiming to follow this plan for the long term. If you feel so inclined, you may decide to pick your own stocks, but investing in an index fund may cause you less stress.

4. Build your wealth through the equity markets

Take another 10% or more of your net salary and write a detailed plan to grow your capital through the share markets. Remember to consider all of the points I made on share trading and investing. There are many ways to make money in the markets, but they generally work on the same principles – receiving and reinvesting dividends, and buying low and selling high. If you are trading shares over the shorter or medium term, be sure to limit your losses and let your profits run.

Alternatively, you may prefer an approach of value investing, picking a portfolio of outstanding companies to invest in for the long term. Whichever approach you decide to take, remember to use tax-favourable strategies, and make a commitment to yourself to never stop learning.

5. Buy investment property (and consider renting yourself)

Whenever you can afford to do so, and the bank will lend to you, buy investment property. Remember to invest in harmony with the market cycle, aiming to invest counter-cyclically. I have a preference for units and apartments in the inner or middle-ring suburbs of capital cities, particularly those that are going to see the greatest population growth over the next 30 years, though you may of course consider other areas. Look for cities or areas where a significant period of time has passed since they last experienced a boom period.

Look for lifestyle suburbs with excellent transport links to the CBD and with limited land available for development. Investment units with views or that are close to the ocean are often highly sought after. Whether you decide to invest in houses or units, ensure that you are choosing properties that will consistently be in high demand in the future. Look out for properties that you can add value to through cosmetic renovations.

One huge step that you can take towards achieving your financial freedom is relieving yourself of the pressure of taking on a huge mortgage on your principal place of residence. One of the reasons I was able to quit my full-time job at 33 is that I did not have a mortgage for a principal place of residence. Of course, I had many mortgages on investment properties, but these were being paid for by tenants.

6. Improve your property

Manufacture capital growth and higher rental yield by improving your investment property. Start with smaller and more manageable cosmetic renovations. When you become more experienced and more confident, you may look at more complex or larger-scale renovations, or at replacing a house with a block of units. Always remember to be reasonably risk averse, and to limit your downside risk. There is no point in making your millions only to overstretch yourself and lose it all on a risky development.

7. Refinance and repeat

Each time you have an investment property that has grown significantly in value (perhaps by 50%), consider refinancing the property up to an LVR of around 80% (if the banks will lend you this much) and using the new funds to buy further investment properties. This is the snowballing effect of property investment at work. Again, be mindful of your use of debt and ensure that you can comfortably manage your debt repayments. Allow reasonable headroom for unexpected repairs or strata levies, and make a contingency for any periods of vacancy.

If you decide to follow this path, it is important to continue to invest in harmony with the property cycle. If you have investment properties in one state that have increased sharply in value, it may be wise to consider investing in a different state that has not experienced a recent boom. While this may involve researching new cities and suburbs, this approach does add some diversification to your portfolio (and in the case of large portfolios, it may help to reduce or eliminate land tax, which is levied at the state level).

8. Strategies for finishing full-time work

When you have built yourself a substantial amount of equity, you have many options in terms of retiring or finishing full-time work. One option is to sell some of your investment properties to extinguish related debt, pay any associated capital gains tax and generate a residual lump sum of capital. The lump sum can then be used to pay down some of the debt on your other property investments or to move into income investments.

My preferred option would be to take out a line of credit against some of the properties that have appreciated. Remember that a line of credit is classified as borrowing rather than income, and therefore is not taxed – *some* of the line of credit can then be used for living expenses (note that interest on a loan taken out for the purpose of living expenses is *not* tax deductible). This approach allows you to hold on to your property investments for the future. It should almost go without saying, however, that this is a strategy that must be used conservatively. Your circumstances can change and property prices may flatline or even fall for years, therefore do not over-stretch yourself, and live well within your means.

9. Supplementary income

There is a huge number of ways to generate supplementary income to aid your break from the rat race. I have already mentioned the option of working part-time or as a contractor. Alternatively, you could set up a part-time business or a home business, or work in network marketing or in a freelance business.

Another good plan could be to move more of your capital into income stocks, that is, blue-chip shares that pay you substantial dividend income (for example, one of the big insurance companies or one of the banks). The options are infinite. You will need to consider what suits you best, and then tailor a plan to meet your needs.

10. Never stop learning

While the principles of wealth creation remain constant, the details of how wealth is created do change. The wealthy and the successful commit to continuing to learn about investment. Commit to building friendships with like-minded and positive people, and consider how you can add to your financial education every day.

Summary

This is my suggested blueprint for achieving financial freedom. I have deliberately kept it simple and not included too many details here. A key message is that the simplest wealth-creation strategies are often the most effective. By focussing on continuing to acquire appreciating assets such as index funds, shares in outstanding companies and prime-location investment property – and holding for the long term – the power of compound growth can build you very significant wealth. The assets you acquire can build you more and more growth, while the salaried worker with his linear income must work harder and harder in an attempt to keep up.

15
TAX
MATTERS

15

Tax in Australia

The tax rates in Australia in the 2012 financial year for individuals are:

Figure 15.1 – 2012 financial year tax rates

Income bracket ($)	Rate
0 – 6,000	0%
6,001 – 37,000	15%
37,001 – 80,000	30%
80,001 – 180,000	37%
180,000+	45%

Source: Australian Taxation Office[1]

On top of this, the government charges a 1.5% Medicare levy, and may at various times impose other levies, such as the flood levy in 2011. With compulsory superannuation rates at 9%, and likely to soon rise to 12%, it is not hard to see why it is difficult to get rich from your salary. If you start to earn a high salary, the government takes around half of it before you even see it. Let's take another look in more detail at what Kerry Packer said to the Senate about tax in this country:

'I pay what I'm required to pay, not a penny more,
not a penny less. If anybody in this country doesn't minimise
their tax, they want their heads read because, as a government,
I can tell you you're not spending it that well that we
should be donating extra[2].'

I believe we can infer several things from this quote:

1. The rules are there to be followed

2. It is not immoral to minimise your tax

3. The government wastes a *vast* amount of taxpayers' money

4. If you don't minimise your tax, you are foolish.

1. Rules are to be followed

Packer is absolutely right. The government makes the tax law, and it is policed by the Australian Taxation Office. As Australian citizens, we are compelled to follow the tax law. While I suggest that we should all aim to minimise our tax liabilities (a staggering number of people do not, which frankly astonishes me), we should never, ever fiddle our tax returns. It is simply not worth it. It is too easy to reduce your tax legally, so why bother taking short cuts?

2. Paying low tax is not immoral

You may hear people air the opinion that paying low taxes is immoral. It is a charge that has been levelled at me in the past, since my income tax rate is currently 0%. It is, in my view, nonsense to say that this is immoral. The tax office introduces tax deductions for a reason – negative gearing benefits are available to property investors because the government simply cannot afford to house the entire population of Australia. Therefore, the government needs landlords to take up their slack. Don't forget that as a property investor, I pay my fair share of taxes in the form of stamp duty every time I buy a property. Not to mention the duties that we all pay on fuel and other commodities.

Please remember that tax avoidance (legal) and tax evasion (illegal) are two very different things. Enough said.

3. Government waste

As a forensic investigative accountant, I have been involved in looking at cases of fraud and mismanagement, and even to my healthily sceptical eye the amount of taxpayers' hard-earned cash that is wasted by some government agencies is simply *phenomenal*. Why should we as individuals want to contribute excessively to such a hugely inefficient enterprise?

If you think that the law forces large companies to pay their fair share of the tax bill, think again. Although the company tax rate is theoretically 30% of profits, many big companies have not been paying such a high rate for years. Companies have many legal loopholes, such as moving entities offshore, or using clever group structures, to ensure that tax is minimised. This is not something that is specific to Australia; it happens overseas too. For example, General Electric has long been accused of not paying its way in the USA. Barclays Bank paid just £113 million in UK corporation tax in 2009, a year in which the bank reported profits of £11.6 billion[3], causing furious protesters to occupy the Tottenham Court Road branch in Central London[4].

4. Not minimising your tax is foolish

Based on the evidence above, it should be obvious that minimising personal tax should be a priority for all of us. We are fortunate in Australia in that the system is relatively flexible. The following section looks at some of the ways in which we can minimise tax legally.

Minimising your tax

I am not going to go into a vast amount of detail in this section. Instead, I will touch briefly on some of the methods by which it is possible to reduce your tax. Above all else, my number one tax tip is to find yourself a good accountant and talk through the possible ways in which you can legally reduce your tax. Here are a few considerations.

Property

The tax benefits of investing in property are currently very generous. I strongly suggest you use an accountant with experience in property investment, rather than the cheapest local accountant you can find, otherwise you may miss out on significant deductions.

The first and most important way to avoid incurring unnecessary tax is simply by not selling your properties and incurring the ensuing capital gains tax. It sounds so obvious, but it is what undoes so many investors, who believe that they must sell a property in order to access the gains from capital growth. As previously discussed, it is possible to access the unrealised capital gains via a line of credit. By not selling property, capital gains tax is deferred.

The rental income from property is taxable, but certain costs associated with the property purchase and costs associated with letting the property are deductible. At the time of writing, these include, but are not limited to:

- Property management fees, letting fees/advertising costs, postage, etc.
- Repairs and maintenance (not capital items)
- Borrowing expenses (i.e. the interest on the mortgage)
- Strata fees and body corporate costs
- Cleaning, gardening/lawn mowing, security patrol fees
- Water rates and charges
- Insurance

- Electricity and gas (where not covered by the tenant)

- Certain administration expenses (such as telephone calls for property management)

- Capital allowances/depreciation.

I have mentioned before that it is very important to pay a surveyor to prepare a depreciation schedule for you. The cost will be relatively minimal – around $500 – and is tax deductible, and they will save you plenty more than this in tax.

Remember that tax law can change at any time, so it would be very wise to check the current law before making assumptions.

Shares

Just as with property, the simplest way to avoid tax on shares is to avoid selling them, instead planning to hold them for the long term. Warren Buffett has built vast wealth in this manner by buying shares and holding them for as long as he can: hopefully forever. Buffett refers to unrealised capital gains as an 'interest-free loan from the Treasury'[5].

Another very smart way to defer tax is by paying into index funds for the long term. Instead of a fund manager frantically churning your stocks, generating unnecessary capital gains tax and brokerage costs, you can simply hold for the long term safe in the knowledge that over the longer term, the trend of the index is an upwards one.

At the time of writing, I am pleased to say, there is no stamp duty payable when we purchase shares in Australia. This is not the case in some countries, and we should be glad that we do not have this burden. Some of the costs of share investment are also tax deductible. At the time of writing, these include brokerage costs and interest on margin loans. Again, remember that tax law can change at any time, so it would be very wise to check this before making assumptions.

Other

There are many other expenses that may be deductible. Charitable donations are one very obvious example. Another often-overlooked area is that of home office expenses. Refer to the Australian Taxation Office website for the current rules. Here are some other areas where you may have expenditure that may be deductible:

- Work-related expenses

- Self-education expenses

- Car expenses

- Gifts

- Clothing expenses for certain occupations.

Again, I strongly recommend that you research this via the Australian Taxation Office website and by speaking to your accountant.

The effect of paying 0% tax

Still need any convincing of why minimising your tax is worth your while? In my last full-time role, I was paid a decent salary per annum plus a bonus: a good package, for sure, but not one that was going to make me a millionaire too quickly, through my salary at least. Now, I only aim to work occasionally for extra income to cover living expenses.

Suppose I take a consultancy contract at $100 per hour. Consider the scenario outlined below.

Figure 15.2 – Contractor with negative gearing benefits at 0% tax rate vs. full-time executive

	Contractor 0% tax	Executive – full tax
Hours per week	45	50–70+
Pay	$100 per hour	$250,000 per annum
Tax rate	0%	Up to 45%

Figure 15.3 – Net pay contractor at 0% tax rate vs. full-time executive

	Contractor	Executive – full tax
Hours per month	189	210–294+
Gross pay per month	$18,900	$20,833
Tax	–	$(7,170)
Net pay per month	$18,900	$13,663
Net pay per hour worked	$100	$45–$63

Source: www.taxcalc.com.au

Note: in the 2012 tax year a flood levy and the Medicare levy were payable: these have been ignored for the purposes of this calculation.

A full-time executive would likely receive a bonus and possibly share options too. As contractors, we can and do negotiate other benefits, such as paid accommodation, travel and relocation expenses and per diem expenses when working in remote locations (often the case for mining and resources contracts). If you can do this, then **100%** of your earnings may flow into your bank account to be invested in wealth-creating assets such as shares and property. This can really supercharge your financial plan.

My wife and I have both discovered that by combining the strategies of working short-term contracts, paying tax at 0% and not having a mortgage for a principal place of residence, it is possible to build up investment capital very quickly.

I must reiterate that what is important here is the principle rather than the absolute figures. You may earn significantly less or significantly more than the amounts noted above, but that doesn't matter; the point is to maximise your returns and minimise your tax.

Practical Action Points

- Find and review your PAYG Summary for the last financial year. Do you pay a lot of tax?

- Consider if and to what extent tax is impeding your progress towards financial freedom.

- Has your accountant got the requisite skills for preparing your tax return and minimising your tax? For example, if you are going to invest in property, you will need an accountant with property experience.

- Are you missing out on any deductions? Check the website of the Australian Tax Office for confirmation of what is a deductible expense. If in doubt, check with your accountant.

- Consider how your investment plan is going to be tax-efficient. Will this be by buying and holding for the long term? By not selling your investments? Through capitalising on negative gearing rules? Remember that the wealthiest people have built their fortunes in a tax-favoured or tax-deferred manner.

16
LIFE LESSONS, LIFE'S OBSTACLES

16

Life lessons, life's obstacles

Attaining financial freedom is not easy. If it were easy, more people would do it. Investing is an emotional activity, and we, as human beings, respond emotionally. While I am only in the first quarter of the *Game of Money*, I have experienced a fair amount over my life, and here I will try to impart a little of the knowledge I have gained by discussing a few of the life lessons I have learned.

Financial behaviour

It has long been recognised that many people who acquire large sums of money quickly manage to rid themselves of it. Many of us are not comfortable with success. Self-sabotage can stem from a lack of self-belief or a lack of self-worth. If we somehow don't believe that we are worthy of success, then we can subconsciously act in such a way as to sabotage it.

Most people do not have the mindset of the wealthy, as is reflected in the low percentages of people who ever attain and retain wealth in their lives. The best thing we can do is to be aware of the risks of self-sabotage and then do our best to avoid them, while committing to learning to develop the mindset of a wealthy and successful person.

This is one of the reasons why I recommend paying regular amounts into index funds and buying and holding investment properties for the long term. The buy-and-hold approach limits the opportunities you have for making self-sabotaging decisions. Compare this with a share trader who has a high percentage of his net worth in a few speculative stocks, always aiming for the big win that will make him or her rich. Sooner or later, this person will probably make a decision that costs them dearly. This is why Anthony Robbins says that the average person has holes in their financial foundations[1] – they may come into money through speculative activity, but they have no context for *investing* it, so the money eventually slips through their fingers.

More than anything, we must have the courage of our convictions and behave differently to the herd. If you act in the same way as everyone else, you will get the same results as everyone else. Be mindful of your finances and financial behaviour.

Education and career

When I was in my mid-twenties, I used to bemoan my choice of career and whinge that if I had my time again I would learn a trade and become a builder. This was typical of my mindset at the time, as comments such as this achieve nothing and are representative of an excuse mentality.

Now I am older and a little more mature, I am grateful that I trained as a Chartered Accountant and completed other financial diplomas. My career taught me a huge amount about finance, economics, how companies operate, how to write and analyse company releases and annual reports, and much, much more. Being qualified in finance gave me an excellent head start when learning to be an investor. My CA qualification has also allowed me the huge comfort of knowing I could go back to being a full-time accountant if I so wished, as well as the option of working part-time as a contractor to earn additional income.

When it comes to choosing a career, the most important thing of all, I believe, is to choose a career that you are suited to and one for which you have a passion. Even if the initial salary of your chosen career is lower, if you have a passion for that career, you are far more likely to succeed. We have probably all seen countless examples of professionals who are deemed to be high achievers but have no passion for their careers.

Whatever career you choose, do not be misled into believing that a high salary is essential for creating wealth. In *The Millionaire Next Door*, the authors discovered that doctors and other professionals with high salaries are often very poor accumulators of wealth[2]. Conversely, many low-income earners save a high percentage of their income and are in a far better position to invest. Remember, to create wealth it is necessary to live below your means, invest in appreciating assets and reinvest your gains. It is not a prerequisite that you earn a high salary in order to do this.

I have witnessed this among my peers. I know people who earn less than $50,000 but live below their means and are able to invest effectively, and I know others who earn many times this amount and yet are deeply in consumer debt.

Circle of friends and family

I have touched briefly on this subject before. It is undoubtedly the case that friends, family and your spouse may hold you back in your quest to achieve financial freedom. The reasons can vary. Your immediate family may think that you are getting involved in something dangerous by investing, especially if they have limited experience of investing themselves. Alternatively, your spouse or partner may have a different attitude to finances and a different risk profile. It is important to recognise that when you invest, someone will always be there to tell you that you should be doing so differently. Therefore, it is important to invest in your own education, and to have the courage of your convictions.

Your peers may become distinctively uncomfortable with your investing, and even be uncomfortable discussing investment as a subject. Note that successful people tend to associate with other successful people. Of course, this does not mean that you should shun your existing friends and family, but you should be aware of when people are trying to hold you back or drag you down to their level. If you need moral support in your investing endeavours, consider joining an investing club, or even a chat forum. Remember that pessimistic people are very rarely successful people.

Divorce and separation

It is an unfortunate fact that around one in three marriages in Australia end in divorce. If, like me, you have parents who have separated, you will be only too aware of the financial impacts of a divorce. The only thing I will note here is that we need to be prepared and have a plan for these outcomes should they occur. Divorce destroys so many financial plans, and not just because of the splitting of assets. On the other hand, a relationship can be a very powerful force if it operates effectively towards a common goal.

How can you protect against the risks? Every relationship is different of course, but endeavour to discuss investment openly with your spouse. Confirm the investment boundaries with your partner, and encourage them to share your journey.

Addictions and hedonistic behaviour

An addiction may be defined as continued involvement with a substance or activity despite the negative consequences associated with it. More complex definitions refer to problems associated with brain reward and motivations. Addictions come in many forms – sex, pornography, food, gambling, drugs, alcohol – and are worth mentioning here because addicts very often have poor financial habits. People with addictions frequently have a problem with lying. They lie to and delude themselves, and they lie to others. Liars tend to make poor financial decisions.

Gambling is a massive problem in Australia, and is an obvious example of an addiction that can destroy finances. The government appears reluctant to tackle the gambling issue, presumably because the industry generates massive revenues.

In my opinion, this is unethical. Casinos operate in the full knowledge that a very significant proportion of their profits are generated from problem gamblers, and yet rather than tackling the problem, our laws seem to make it extremely easy for punters to blow their cash. The gambling industry continues to literally destroy the lives of thousands and thousands of people each year.

Some people may simply be addicted to spending or credit cards, sometimes known as 'retail therapy'. Again, the financial effects of an addiction to spending are fairly obvious. What is perhaps less obvious is that hidden addictions to alcohol and other substances can also cause personal finances to be severely impacted. Indeed, being constantly in debt and in financial turmoil can sometimes be an indicator of substance abuse or addiction. In *The Millionaire Next Door*, the authors noted that smokers and alcoholics are poor accumulators of wealth, with seemingly small ongoing purchases adding up to a phenomenal expenditure over the long term[3].

If you have an addiction, it is vital to take steps towards overcoming it. Addictions control you and your behaviours. To be financially and spiritually free, you must not be controlled by an addiction.

Health, fitness and diet

When I first saw references to health and fitness in investment books I thought it seemed a little incongruous. You buy finance books to learn about finances, right? I have since learned that health, fitness and nutrition have a definite role to play in being a successful investor.

A successful investor needs to have a clear head, to be free from stress and anxiety and to feel fit, alert and in control. Author and share trader Stuart McPhee notes how going for a run helps him in his trading endeavours[4], and it is well documented how exercising for around 30 minutes each day can have huge benefits for our physical and mental health. Exercise releases endorphins to the brain, which helps us to be happier people.

Part of being *wealthy* is about feeling great and looking forward to springing out of bed each morning to get on with living life. Modern-day dietary habits are generally very poor, and consist of a lot of junk food, a normal day commencing with a high-sugar or high-cholesterol breakfast washed down with half a gallon of caffeine. This is a poor way to start the day. Caffeine is not required to get you started in the morning!

If you want to feel energised, there is no better way to kick off your day than with a freshly made fruit juice with some vegetables blended in: both nutritious and delicious. So much modern-day food is poor in its nutritional content, and often unnatural. Don't even get me started on aspartame and chemical sweeteners; these are truly evil inventions, and may be carcinogenic. Nature has given us, in fruit and vegetables, delicious food naturally, and food that is perfectly designed for your body to process.

I've been a vegetarian for some time now, and although it is sometimes extremely difficult, I try to live by vegan principles as far as I can. As a former meat-eater, I would never pretend to preach on the subject, but I would urge people to at least consider the benefits of a vegetarian lifestyle. Excessive consumption of meat is dreadfully unhealthy for you personally, being a major cause of heart disease and cancer, and the animal industry is also destroying the planet. The breeding and slaughter of tens of billions of animals each year, quite apart from being inhumane, is also the cause of a shocking amount of needless carbon pollution and water shortages. Millions are starving every year because of our misuse of resources.

Consider committing to exercising for at least 30 minutes each day. Exercise does wonders for your mental health, and the old cliché is true: health body, healthy mind.

Your code of conduct

Anthony Robbins recommends that you draw up a code of conduct for yourself, and try to stick to it impeccably at all times[5]. His logic is sound. Part of being a wealthy, happy and successful person is living by a code of conduct that you have set for yourself. Consider what principles you believe in, and list them in a code of conduct that you plan to live by.

17
WHAT NEXT?

17

What next?

I have crammed as much information as I can into this book. There is so much more I would like to include, but space will simply not permit. So, where to next? Firstly, if there any points in this book that you would like me to elaborate on or clarify, please email me (contact details on my blog).

Meanwhile, here are a few more ideas to help you on your way to financial freedom.

1. Check out my blog at http://petewargent.blogspot.com where I regularly post my thoughts and ideas on finance, investment and the markets.

2. You need to believe that you can achieve your financial freedom. How can you believe that something you previously felt was impossible is possible? Start by challenging your fears.

3. Write down your goals; remember to be specific, *think big* and see the big picture.

4. I have tried to squeeze as much as I can into these few chapters but, as I noted, space *is* limited. Resolve to read more books on finance and investment. I have provided a short list in the recommended reading section at the end of this book. If you are enjoying the research, read all of the books referred to in the references as well, and you will then be well on the way to having a commanding knowledge of the different types of investment.

5. Take an interest in finance news and read the business section of the newspaper.

6. Pay off your credit cards! Take immediate steps to reduce any other consumer debt.

7. You can start making a huge difference to your financial health today by keeping a budget of your expenditure and thinking very carefully before buying anything!

8. Think of as many ideas as you can on how you can add as much value as you can to as many people as you can in what you do.

9. Resolve to pay yourself first from every future pay packet, and invest in appreciating assets.

10. Don't delay, ***start today and take action***! If you do the same as you have always done, you can expect the same results.

I hope you have enjoyed reading this book, and have found it both interesting and enlightening. Now it's up to you. Get a financial grip and go for it!

REFERENCES

Chapter 1

1   *Who Took My Money? Why Slow Investors Lose and Fast Money Wins!*, Robert T. Kiyosaki with Sharon L. Lechter (Warner Business Books, New York, 2004)
2   *Building Wealth through Investment Property*, Jan Somers (Somerset Financial Services, Brisbane, 1992)
3   *'Australians can't afford to grow old poor'*, www.dailytelegraph.com.au (2011)
4   *What Were the UK Earnings and Prices Then?*, Lawrence H. Officer (MeasuringWorth, 2011)
5   www.taxcalc.com.au
6   www.domain.com.au
7   *The Winning Investments of Warren Buffett and George Soros*, Mark Tier (St. Martins Griffin, Hong Kong, 2006)
8   ibid.
9   www.kerrypacker.com
10   www.johntreed.com
11   ibid.

Chapter 2

1   *A History of Modern Britain*, Andrew Marr (Macmillan, London, 2007)
2   ibid.
3   *'Pension Black Hole Doubles'*, www.bbc.co.uk, (2003)
4   www.parkhillflats.co.uk, website by Sarah-Jayne Davis

Chapter 3

1   *CASHFLOW Quadrant: Rich Dad's Guide to Financial Freedom*, Robert T. Kiyosaki with Sharon Lechter (Warner Books, New York, 2000)
2   ibid.
3   *The Winning Investments of Warren Buffett and George Soros*, Mark Tier (St. Martins Griffin, Hong Kong, 2006)
4   *Let's Get Real About Money*, Eric Tyson (Pearson Education, New Jersey, 2008)
5   www.hollows.org.au
6   ibid.
7   *A History of Modern Britain*, Andrew Marr (Macmillan, London, 2007)
8   Australian Taxation Office, www.ato.gov.au

Chapter 4

1   *7 Seconds to Success in Selling*, Willie Gayle (Prentice Hall, New York, 1963)
2   *Unlimited Power*, Anthony Robbins (Ballantine Books, New York, 1987)
3   *Change your Life in 7 Days*, Paul McKenna (Transworld, London, 2004)
4   *Unlimited Power*, Anthony Robbins (Ballantine Books, New York, 1987)
5   *Accidental Millionaire*, Steve Fagan (New Holland, Sydney, 2006)
6   ibid.
7   ibid.
8   ibid.
9   *Unlimited Power*, Anthony Robbins (Ballantine Books, New York, 1987)
10   ibid.

11   *Think and Grow Rich*, Napoleon Hill (Random House, New York, 1960)
12   *Thriving not just Surviving in Changing Times*, Michael Yardney (Wilkinson, Melbourne, 2009)
13   *Awaken the Giant Within*, Anthony Robbins, (Simon & Schuster, New York, 1991)
14   ibid.
15   ibid.
16   ibid.
17   *The Millionaire Next Door: Surprising Secrets of America's Wealthy*, Thomas J. Stanley and William D. Danko (Simon & Schuster, New York, 1996)
18   ibid.

Chapter 5
1   *Unlimited Power*, Anthony Robbins (Ballantine Books, New York, 1987)
2   www.bwts.com.au , *'Building Wealth through Shares'*, website by Colin Nicholson
3   ibid.
4   ibid.
5   ibid.
6   *Let's Get Real About Money*, Eric Tyson (Pearson Education, New Jersey, 2008)
7   *The Gone Fishin' Portfolio: Get Wise, Get Wealthy…and Get on with your Life*, Alexander Green (John Wiley & Sons, New Jersey, 2008)
8   ibid.
9   *'A New Interpretation of Information Rate'*, J. L. Kelly Jr., *Bell System Technical Journal*
10   *Berkshire Hathaway Annual Report*, (1991)

Chapter 6
1   *'Top 10 Richest Men Of All Time'*, www.askmen.com
2   Real Estate Institute of Australia, www.reia.com.au
3   ibid.
4   *How to Be the Next Property Millionaire: Take the Challenge*, Toney Fitzgerald and Dave Dorian (Property Millionaire, 2008)
5   *Go for Your Life*, Chris Gray and Lowell Tarling (Go for Your Life, Sydney, 2005)
6   ibid.
7   ibid.
8   *The Effortless Empire*, Chris Gray and Lowell Tarling (Go for Your Life, Sydney, 2008)
9   ibid.
10   *Go for Your Life*, Chris Gray (Go for Your Life, Sydney, 2005)
11   ibid.
12   *Building Wealth through Investment Property*, Jan Somers (Somerset Financial Services, Brisbane, 1992)
13   ibid.
14   *'Japan's Elderly Population Rises to Record, Government Says'*, www.bloomberg.com

Chapter 7
1   *Real Estate Riches: How to become Rich using your Banker's Money*, Dolf De Roos (John Wiley & Sons, USA, 2004)
2   *The Seven Habits of Highly Effectively People*, Steven R. Covey (Simon & Schuster, New York, 1989)
3   *From 0–260+ Properties in 7 Years*, Steve McKnight, (Wrightbooks, 2006)
4   www.propertyinvesting.com , website by Steve McKnight
5   *How to Maximise Your Property Portfolio*, Margaret Lomas (Wrightbooks, Milton, Qld, 2003)
6   ibid.
7   *How to Invest in Managed Funds*, Margaret Lomas (Wrightbooks, Milton, Qld, 2002)

8   Australian Taxation Office, www.ato.gov.au
9   *Your Money Your Call*, Sky News Business (2010)
10   Australian Bureau of Statistics, www.abs.gov.au
11   ibid.
12   *Evening Standard* newspaper, London, (1937)
13   www.taxcalc.com.au
14   *Property. Prosper. Retire*, Kevin Young (Goko, 2008)

Chapter 10

1   *The Snowball: Warren Buffett and the Business of Life*, Alice Schroeder (Bantam Dell, New York, 2008)
2   *The Warren Buffett Way: Investment Strategies of the World's Greatest Investor*, Robert G. Hagstrom (John Wiley & Sons, USA, 1994)
3   ibid.
4   *Berkshire Hathaway Annual Report*, (1991)
5   *Berkshire Hathaway Annual Report*, (1998)
6   ibid.
7   *The Warren Buffett Portfolio: Unleashing the Power of the Focus Strategy*, Robert G. Hagstrom (John Wiley & Sons, USA, 1999)
8   ibid.
9   ibid.
10   *Berkshire Hathaway Annual Report*, (1991)
11   'The Behavior of Stock Market Prices', Journal of Business 38: 34–105, Eugene Fama
12   *The Warren Buffett Way: Investment Strategies of the World's Greatest Investor*, Robert G. Hagstrom (John Wiley & Sons, USA, 1994)
13   *The Intelligent Investor: A Book of Practical Counsel*, Benjamin Graham (Harper & Brothers, New York, 1949)
14   ibid.
15   *Online Investing on the Australian Share Market*, Roger Kinsky (John Wiley & Sons, Camberwell, Vic, 2007)
16   *The Intelligent Investor: A Book of Practical Counsel*, Benjamin Graham (Harper & Brothers, New York, 1949)
17   *The Winning Investments of Warren Buffett and George Soros*, Mark Tier (St. Martins Griffin, Hong Kong, 2006)
18   ibid.
19   'Billionaire who Broke the Bank of England', www.telegraph.co.uk, (2002)
20   *The Warren Buffett Portfolio: Unleashing the Power of the Focus Strategy*, Robert G. Hagstrom (John Wiley & Sons, USA, 1999)
21   *The Winning Investments of Warren Buffett and George Soros*, Mark Tier (St. Martins Griffin, Hong Kong, 2006)
22   *The Warren Buffett Portfolio: Unleashing the Power of the Focus Strategy*, Robert G. Hagstrom (John Wiley & Sons, USA, 1999)
23   ibid.
24   ibid.
25   www.coca-cola.co.uk
26   *Rule #1: The Simple Strategy for Successful Investing in Only 15 Minutes a Week!*, Philip B. Town (Three Rivers Press, New York, 2006)
27   *Losing my Virginity: How I've Survived, Had Fun and Made a Fortune Doing Business My Way*, Richard Branson (Three Rivers Press, New York, 1998)
28   *The Warren Buffett Portfolio: Unleashing the Power of the Focus Strategy*, Robert G. Hagstrom (John Wiley & Sons, USA, 1999)

29 ibid.

30 ibid.

31 ibid.

32 ibid.

33 ibid.

34 ibid.

35 *The Intelligent Investor: A Book of Practical Counsel*, Benjamin Graham (Harper & Brothers, New York, 1949)

36 *The Warren Buffett Portfolio: Unleashing the Power of the Focus Strategy*, Robert G. Hagstrom (John Wiley & Sons, USA, 1999)

37 ibid.

38 *The Intelligent Investor: A Book of Practical Counsel*, Benjamin Graham (Harper & Brothers, New York, 1949)

39 ibid.

40 ibid.

41 *The Warren Buffett Portfolio: Unleashing the Power of the Focus Strategy*, Robert G. Hagstrom (John Wiley & Sons, USA, 1999)

42 ibid.

43 ibid.

44 Various *Sydney Morning Herald* articles (2011), Marcus Padley

45 *The Warren Buffett Way: Investment Strategies of the World's Greatest Investor*, Robert G. Hagstrom (John Wiley & Sons, USA, 1994)

Chapter 11

1 *Building Wealth in the Stock Market: A Proven Investment Plan for Finding the Best Stocks and Managing Risk*, Colin Nicholson (John Wiley & Sons, Milton, Qld, 2009)

2 ibid.

3 *The Intelligent Investor: A Book of Practical Counsel*, Benjamin Graham (Harper & Brothers, New York, 1949)

4 ibid.

5 *Security Analysis*, Benjamin Graham and David Dodd (McGraw-Hill, USA, 1934)

6 ibid.

7 ibid.

8 ibid.

9 Australian Securities Exchange, www.asx.com.au

10 *Stock Market Secrets*, Marcus Padley (Slattery Media Group, Melbourne, 2009)

11 *Building Wealth in the Stock Market: A Proven Investment Plan for Finding the Best Stocks and Managing Risk*, Colin Nicholson (John Wiley & Sons, Milton, Qld, 2009)

12 ibid.

13 *Trading for a Living: Psychology, Trading Tactics, Money Management*, Dr Alexander Elder (John Wiley & Sons, USA, 1993)

14 *Trading in a Nutshell*, Stuart McPhee (John Wiley & Sons, Richmond Vic, 2001)

15 ibid.

Chapter 12

1 *Trading for a Living: Psychology, Trading Tactics, Money Management*, Dr Alexander Elder (John Wiley & Sons, USA, 1993)

2 *How to Make Money in Stock: A Winning System in Good Times or Bad*, William J. O'Neill (McGraw-Hill, USA, 1998)

3 *Trade Your Way to Financial Freedom*, Van K. Tharp (McGraw-Hill, New York, 1999)

4   *Trading for a Living: Psychology, Trading Tactics, Money Management*, Dr Alexander Elder (John Wiley & Sons, USA, 1993)
5   ibid.
6   ibid.
7   www.tradingroom.com.au
8   ibid.
9   ibid.
10   Australian Securities Exchange, www.asx.com.au
11   www.tradingroom.com.au
12   ibid.
13   ibid.

Chapter 13

1   *Payback Time: Eight steps to outsmarting the system that failed you to getting your investments back on track*, Philip B. Town, (Random House, New York, 2010)
2   ibid.
3   Australian Taxation Office – www.ato.gov.au

Chapter 15

1   Australian Taxation Office, www. ato.gov.au
2   www.kerrypacker.com
3   'Barclays reports profits up to 11.6 billion', www.independent.co.uk, (2010)
4   'Fury at Barclays Tax', www.news.com.au, (2011)
5   *The Warren Buffett Portfolio: Unleashing the Power of the Focus Strategy*, Robert G. Hagstrom (John Wiley & Sons, USA, 1999)

Chapter 16

1   *Awaken the Giant Within*, Anthony Robbins, (Simon & Schuster, New York, 1991)
2   *The Millionaire Next Door: Surprising Secrets of America's Wealthy*, Thomas J. Stanley and William D. Danko (Simon & Schuster, New York, 1996)
3   ibid.
4   *Trading in a Nutshell*, Stuart McPhee (John Wiley & Sons, Richmond, Victoria, 2001)
5   *Awaken the Giant Within*, Anthony Robbins, (Simon & Schuster, New York, 1991)

GLOSSARY OF TERMS

Algorithm – a step-by-step problem-solving procedure. May be used in relation to share trading to refer to a system designed to always beat the market.

Appreciating – increasing in value.

Arbitrage – buying shares or securities on one market for immediate resale on another market in order to profit from a price discrepancy.

A-REITS – Australian Real Estate Investment Trusts. A security that sells a stock on the securities exchange, thus allowing investors to invest in property without owning any property directly.

ASX – Australian Securities Exchange.

Balance sheet – a financial statement that summarises assets and liabilities.

Bears or bearish – expectant of falling prices.

Beta – the measurement of the volatility in a company, also known as the systemic risk.

Bid/ask spread – the difference between the highest bid price (the price an investor is prepared to buy a particular company's share at) and the lowest ask or offer price (the price an investor is prepared to sell a particular company's share for).

Blue-chip stocks – shares in what is perceived to be an established and financially sound company.

Bond – a debt investment whereby an investor loans money to an entity (a company or a government) that borrows the funds for a defined period of time at an agreed fixed interest rate.

Brokerage – fees charged by a stock-market broker for each trade you make.

Bulls or bullish – expectant of rising prices.

Commercial property – types of commercial property include not only office space and industrial units, but also shopping centres, medical centres and more.

Compounding or compound growth – the ability of an asset to generate returns that are then reinvested, thus creating higher returns.

Contract for Difference (CFD) – a trading product that offers significant leverage. An agreement is made to exchange the difference between the entry price and exit price of an underlying asset.

Conveyancing – the branch of law concerned with the preparation of documents for the transfer of property.

Consumer Price Index (CPI) – a measure of changes in the purchasing power of the currency and inflation.

Debt to equity ratio – the level of debt held by a company compared with its shareholders funds. The ratio is one measure of how much money a company should safely be able to borrow over time.

Deflation – a decline in general price levels, sometimes caused by a reduction in the supply of money or credit.

Depreciation – a decline in economic value. In property, an allowance can be claimed on the tax return for the decline in value of certain items. In respect of a company, a non-cash depreciation charge can impact the company's profit figure – a book-entry is made to reflect the decline in value of certain assets (such as plant and equipment or fixtures and fittings).

Discounted cash flow calculation – a method of ascertaining the attractiveness of a company (or project) using the time value of money. All future cash flows of the company or project are projected and are then discounted to today's value to give a net present value.

Discount rate – a term for the annual growth rate of an investment, which is used when a future value is assumed and you are calculating the required net present value.

Diversification – a portfolio strategy that aims to reduce the exposure to risk by combining a variety of different investments.

Earnings – the amount of profit a company produces during a specific period of time (e.g. a quarter, a half-year or a year).

Earnings per Share (EPS) – the net profit after tax of a company divided by the number of ordinary shares the company has on issue.

Emerging markets – those economies with a low to medium per capita income.

Entry price – the price at which you 'enter' a trade, or buy a share.

Exchange Traded Funds (ETFs) – managed funds that can be purchased via the securities exchange.

Exit price – the price at which you 'exit' a trade, or sell a share.

Focus investing – a strategy of concentrating a portfolio on a few quality stocks.

Foreign exchange risk – the risk of the value of an investment changing due to movements in currency exchange rates.

Franked dividends – see *franking credit*.

Franking credit – where a company pays a dividend from profits that it has already paid tax on, the investor may receive a tax credit to the extent that the company has already paid tax. This system is known as *dividend imputation*.

Free cash flow – operating cash flow minus capital expenditure; this represents the cash flow that a company can retain after expending the cash it needs to expand its asset base.

Financial Times Stock Exchange (FTSE) – the stock market in London.

Fundamental analysis – a method of evaluating a company through attempting to measure its intrinsic value (normally by looking at its future cash flows).

GFC – global financial crisis, used in reference to economic events of 2007–2010.

Hawks or hawkish – used especially in reference to inflation to describe those who have a preference for hard-line or tightening policies.

Income statement – the profit and loss account, a financial statement showing the income and expenditure of an entity or person.

Index Fund – a passively managed fund that is designed to mirror the returns of a specific market or index.

Inflation – an increase in the general prices of goods and services, effectively making each dollar of currency worth less. Hyperinflation is where a currency is rapidly becoming worthless, either due to a sharp increase in the currency in circulation or because people do not want the currency (if they view it as lacking in worth).

Interest cover – a ratio that measures how easily a company can service its debt repayments in relation to its earnings.

Interest-only loan – a loan in which the borrower only pays the interest on the principal balance. The principal balance remains unchanged until the end of the loan period, when the principal is repaid.

Intrinsic value – the true value of a company (or other asset) based upon underlying assumptions.

Investment grade – usually refers to a bond that is considered sufficiently likely to meet payment obligations that major banks are allowed to invest in it.

Large cap – large-capitalisation companies, being the largest companies by market capitalisation (generally with a market capitalisation running into the billions of dollars). Also known as 'Big-cap' companies.

Leverage – the use of debt or other financial instruments (usually with the goal of magnifying returns).

Liability – a debt or financial obligation.

Line of credit (LOC) – similar to a big credit card, this is a facility whereby the bank extends a specified amount of credit to the borrower, who does not repay the principal until the end of the life of the facility.

Listed Investment Company (LIC) – an investment company that has a fixed number of shares on issue and is itself listed on the stock market. The company will invest in the shares of other companies and other assets.

Liquidity – the degree to which an asset or security can be bought or sold in the market without affecting the asset's price. An illiquid share is more likely to have few willing buyers or sellers close to the price of the last trade.

Loan-to-value ratio (LVR) – the ratio of the size of the loan in relation to the value of the asset for which the loan was taken out.

Loss aversion – the tendency in humans to prefer avoiding financial losses to acquiring financial gains.

Margin loan – a loan taken out to invest in managed funds or shares. The security consists of the portfolio of managed funds or shares itself.

Margin of safety – the difference between the intrinsic value of a share and its quoted market price.

Market capitalisation – the value of a company, calculated by multiplying the number of ordinary shares on issue by the last traded share price, i.e. the total dollar value of all the outstanding shares.

Median price – often used in reference to property values, this is a mathematical result whereby half of the results are higher and half are lower, thereby resulting in the value of the 'middle' property.

Mid-cap or mid-capitalisation stocks – there is no official definition, but this may refer to companies of around $1 billion to $5 billion in value, perhaps less for Australia.

Modern portfolio theory – an investment theory that strives to achieve maximum growth for a given level of portfolio risk.

Negative gearing – financial leverage whereby the income from the asset does not cover the costs of holding the asset.

Net profit margin – the ratio of the net profit to revenue – that is, net income divided by total sales.

Net realisable assets – the selling price of assets less the expenses incurred in the selling thereof.

Open-high-low-close (OHLC) chart – a securities chart that shows the opening and closing shares prices, and the day's highest and lowest prices.

Paper trading – simulated trading where the trader mimics and records theoretical purchases and sales without actioning them.

Pareto's law – also known as the '80/20 rule', a theory that supposes that 80% of outputs are derived from 20% of the inputs. For example, 20% of the population may earn 80% of the income of a country.

Passive income – income that flows to you without you having to work for it.

PAYG – pay as you go taxation, the tax that is deducted from salaries at source by employers.

Position size – the dollar value invested in a particular security.

Positive-cash-flow properties – properties that generate a cash-flow profit after the effects of depreciation and tax rebates are taken into account.

Positively geared properties – properties that generate a profit immediately through having rental income that exceeds all expenses, including the mortgage repayments.

Price-to-earnings (PE) ratio – the most common measure of how expensive a company is to invest in, calculated as the current share price (per share) divided by the earnings per share.

Principal-and-interest loan – a loan where the borrower repays the interest charge and a portion of the principal during each repayment period.

Recession – a period of general economic decline, often defined by commentators as a decline in GDP for two or more consecutive quarters.

Reserve Bank of Australia (RBA) – its powers are used to aid the stability of the currency, full employment and economic prosperity. The RBA is responsible for controlling inflation through its monetary policy and setting of interest rates.

Risk-free rate – the theoretical rate of return of an investment with zero risk. Often, the yield of a 10-year government bond is used to represent the return of a 'risk-free' investment, though some now question whether even a government bond is risk-free.

Scrip – paper assets given in lieu of currency (sometimes in the form of shares).

Sell stop – an instruction to sell at the best available price after certain conditions are met (such as the share price falling below a certain level).

Shorting or short selling – essentially a bet that the value of a share or other asset will decline, whereby the investor borrows and sells now and buys back at a future point in time.

Small-caps or small capitalisation stocks – there is no official definition, but perhaps this could be taken to refer to stocks of companies with a market capitalisation of up to $1 billion (or perhaps slightly less for Australia).

SMSF – self-managed superannuation fund.

Sovereign risk – the risk that a foreign central bank amends its foreign exchange regulations, thus reducing or nulling the value of foreign exchange contracts.

Speculative stocks or shares – shares in a company with a high risk of not producing a positive return.

Strata fees – fees charged to the owners of a strata-titled property each quarter. Can cover building insurance, common electricity and water usage, pest control, cleaning, maintenance and repairs of common areas, common garden maintenance and management fees to the strata company.

Survivorship bias – the tendency for failed companies to be excluded from performance studies. This can skew quoted average growth rates of indices, for example.

Technical analysis – various techniques used for evaluating shares by analysing statistics generated by market activity.

Tick – one movement in the share price. For example, a movement in a share price from 20 cents to 20.5 cents may be referred to as one up-tick.

Tracker fund – a passively managed fund designed to track the movements of an index or market.

Tracking error – the rate of divergence between the price behaviour of a portfolio and the price behaviour of an individual share or index of shares.

Value investing – the strategy of investing in shares that are trading at less than their intrinsic value.

Vendor financing – see *Wraps*.

Volatility – the relative rate at which the prices of securities or other assets move up and down.

Wraps – in property, a form of vendor financing. The loan may take many different forms and may involve the vendor lending the purchaser the difference between the existing loan and the purchase price.

XAO – Australian All Ordinaries Share Index, comprising all companies listed on the ASX.

XJO – Australian ASX 200 Share Index, generally comprising the largest and most liquid 200 listed companies in Australia, weighted by market capitalisation.

Yield – the income return on an investment, normally measured in percentage terms on the capital invested. For property, yield refers to rent. For shares, yield often refers to dividends paid.

RECOMMENDED FURTHER READING

It is amazing how many books regurgitate the ideas of others and do not list a bibliography. I have tried to include reference notes where I can throughout the text. However, I must acknowledge that if I listed all of the material I read and every source of information I considered in producing this book, the list would be nearly as long as the book itself. Here, I have simply listed six key books, which is a realistic target for a motivated reader.

In my opinion, these are the best six books for Australian readers to focus on. Notably, only two of these books are written by Australian authors. Regardless of where the authors hail from, read these texts and I can assure you that your financial future will be a better one than if you had not read them.

Mindset and motivation

Awaken the Giant Within, Anthony Robbins, (Simon & Schuster, New York, 1991)

All of Robbins' books are worth a read, especially this one. He crams a huge amount of information into his books, and some of it is almost certain to be useful to you.

Wealth creation and financial profiles

Rich Dad Poor Dad, Robert T. Kiyosaki with Sharon L. Lechter (Warner Books, New York, 2000)

At times, he is accused of being slippery and boastful, but Kiyosaki is still an entertaining read. This book was a huge best-seller that explains financial profiles in simple, easy-to-understand terminology. Kiyosaki does not offer much in the way of specific advice, but rather he encourages readers to invest in their own financial education.

Residential investment property

How to Grow a Multi-Million Dollar Property Portfolio: in your Spare Time, Michael Yardney (Wilkinson, Melbourne, 2006)

Yardney has decades of experience in property behind him and this is the best property book written for Australian investors in recent years. Much of the terminology and many of the ideas can be traced back to Jan Somers' *Building Wealth through Investment Property*, which is also an outstanding read, though perhaps now a little dated in terms of its quoted figures.

Value investing in shares

The Warren Buffett Way: Investment Strategies of the World's Greatest Investor, Robert G. Hagstrom (John Wiley & Sons, USA, 1994)

This book and its sequel, *The Warren Buffett Portfolio*, tackle some relatively complex concepts and present them in a very lucid manner. A must-read for the value investor.

Shares – timing the market

Building Wealth in the Stock Market: A Proven Investment Plan for Finding the Best Stocks and Managing Risk, Colin Nicholson (John Wiley & Sons, Milton, Qld, 2009)

An excellent book that describes how to time your trading in the Australian stock market through understanding Dow Theory and a combination of fundamental and technical analysis. Also, this book details Nicholson's own personal investment plan, which might be a very handy starting point for budding investors.

Trading shares for income

Trading for a Living: Psychology, Trading Tactics, Money Management, Dr Alexander Elder (John Wiley & Sons, USA, 1993)

This book and its sequel *Come Into My Trading Room* are strongly recommended for any would-be traders. Elder is a doyen of share-trading literature.

'Do the thing we fear, and the death of fear is certain.'
– Ralph Waldo Emerson

Disclaimer

This book is written to provide competent and reliable information on the subject matter covered. However, I do not operate as a licensed financial advisor.

This book is written on the understanding that the author disclaims any liability from the use or application of the contents of this book. The reader should always consult a financial advisor before making any investment decisions.

Pete Wargent
Sydney, 2012

ABOUT THE AUTHOR

Pete Wargent has a strong financial background having worked for a number of professional finance organisations in Australia and the UK. He holds several top financial qualifications being a Chartered Accountant, Chartered Secretary and having a Financial Planning Diploma.

Having worked in the professional environment for the past decade he understands the mindset of today's workforce, and what financial and investment advice is needed to achieve financial freedom. He's not just a theorist, having achieved financial freedom and the ability to live the life he chooses at the age of 33, using the financial plan detailed in his book. Pete now manages his investment portfolio and travels regularly. He works as a consultant in the finance industry from time to time and is passionate about living an enjoyable, ethical and sustainable life.

Pete is a keen blogger and regularly posts his thoughts on finance and investment at http://petewargent.blogspot.com.